Behavior modification of the mentally retarded

Behavior modification of the mentally retarded

EDITED BY
TRAVIS THOMPSON
Professor
Departments of Psychiatry and Psychology
University of Minnesota

JOHN GRABOWSKI
Post-doctoral Research Trainee
Department of Psychiatry
University of Minnesota

New York
Oxford University Press
London 1972 Toronto

RC
570
T46

Second printing, 1974

Copyright © 1972 by Oxford University Press, Inc.
Library of Congress Catalogue Card Number: 72-179360
Printed in the United States of America

To the residents
of Faribault State Hospital
in the hope that their lives
have been made a little better

Preface

In November of 1968, I paid my first visit to Faribault State Hospital. Dr. Roger Johnson, the Medical Director, had asked me to consult with his staff on the development of training programs for their adult retarded residents. Having worked with educable retarded children in the past, I thought that visiting an institution for the mentally retarded should present no surprises. It did. On entering Dakota Building, a typical institutional structure for the retarded, constructed in 1913, I was confronted with sights, sounds, and smells which I had never before experienced and hoped that I would never witness again. Seated in the middle of a large ward area shackled to a chair was a young man in his twenties with all of his skin abraded from his knees and blood running down his shins. Along the seventy-foot wall of the ward were seated approximately fifteen men, huddled in fetal positions, with their heads between their knees. Most of them sat totally still, a few rocked from side to side, a few rocked forward and backward. Beneath half of the chairs were puddles of urine. The room reeked of urine and feces, and feces were smeared over the floor, over the arms and legs, and on the trousers and shirts of numerous residents. Approximately half of the men were partially or totally unclad. Another twenty or so residents were walking, running, or twirling about the room. Some were rapidly twiddling their fingers in front of their faces, others were gnawing at their hands and forearms. Most residents were scarred or exhibited recent wounds such as scratches, abrasions, or scabs. The noise level was unbelievable. The ward echoed with hoots, shrieks, and wails resembling those from the worst class-B horror movie. The two psychiatric technicians who were on duty were continually mopping urine or attending to fights between residents and treating the wounds and abrasions; one patient bit another so forcefully that the wound required medical attention.

One hoped somehow that Dakota Building was a nightmare, a unique phenomenon which occurred nowhere else. But unfortunately it wasn't. During the Christmas season in 1965, Blatt and Kaplan visited five institutions for the retarded in four different states and observed basically the same kinds of events which I witnessed in Dakota Building. They collected a series of photographs published under the title *Christmas in Purgatory*. In the introduction to their book, they said "There is a Hell. It is on Earth. In America we have our own special inferno." They were referring to many of the institutions for the retarded.

Dakota Building housed only sixty-seven residents, but it is estimated that there are in excess of 92,000 people in the United States living in a comparable condition. In addition, there are another six million residents who are in a less unfortunate condition. It is impossible to pay a visit to this "special inferno" without feeling that something must be done to help the retarded. The present volume grew out of efforts to do something about the unfortunate plight of the mentally retarded in one institution, and will hopefully be instructive to others sharing our concern. The several programs described in this volume illustrate that the mentally retarded need not live in a state in which one would not keep farm animals, but that they can live constructive lives. They deserve the maximum human dignity which can be afforded them. This volume describes one way in which this can be achieved.

Minneapolis   Travis Thompson
May 1971

Acknowledgments

The title of this book, *Behavior Modification of the Mentally Retarded,* is a misnomer in a sense. The book might more aptly be called "The Faribault Story," for it describes the transition of Faribault State Hospital from a largely custodial institution to an educational-therapeutic environment. The words and graphs contained in these pages do not begin to tell the human side of this story. The phenomenal changes in the lives of many of the residents, and the deep satisfaction of those of us who have worked to assist our fellow men, are difficult to convey in simple quantitative terms. In a real sense, this book is the story of the 450 retarded people and the staff working with them, over a two-year period of major social change. While some of the residents involved in this program remain obscure, many are people whom we have come to know individually. They have become very special to us.

    No one person nor a few people can be identified as accomplishing this change. If a few must be singled out for their contributions they would include Eric Errickson, Roger Johnson, and Heinz Bruhl, the administrators who were responsible for initiating the change. Harold Gillespie and Arnold Madow, their successors, must share equally in making the change a viable reality. Among the many others who must receive special thanks are

Florence Wangsness, Johanna Finstuen, Yvonne Anderson, Grace Crosby, and Winefred Meyers, the Unit Directors who took the administrative steps to actually implement the behavior modification programs at Faribault State Hospital. The building staff, of course, was the backbone of it all. They were the ones who carried out the programs on a day-to-day basis, and were under the greatest pressure during this period of change. While it is not possible to identify all the staff members involved, they, above all, deserve recognition and thanks for their support and effort.

There are some to whom a simple word of thanks hardly seems adequate. Valeria Blomquist, the assistant program director, has served as an invaluable guide, assisting the editors in overcoming their shortcomings where their knowledge and skills were sorely lacking and helping them avoid stubbing their toes when blundering into administrative matters where the ignorant are inclined to tread. Special thanks are due Judy Volinkaty and her staff for their patience and careful work in clerical preparation of the manuscripts.

Minneapolis T. T.
September 1971 J. G.

Contributors

George Bigelow
Department of Psychiatry
Johns Hopkins University
Baltimore, Maryland[*]

Eric Errickson
Special Education
Duke University
Durham, North Carolina[**]

Leonard Fielding
Private Practice
Minneapolis, Minnesota
Consultant, Faribault State Hospital

William Fullmer
Psychiatry Research Unit
University of Minnesota
Consultant, Faribault State Hospital

John Grabowski
Psychiatry Research Unit
University of Minnesota
Consultant, Faribault State Hospital

Roland Griffiths
Psychiatry Research Unit
University of Minnesota
Consultant, Faribault State Hospital

Roger Johnson
San Mateo Mental Health Clinic
San Mateo, California[**]

O. Linda McConahey
Laurelton State Hospital
Laurelton, Pennsylvania[*]

John Raw
Recreation Department
Faribault State Hospital

Travis Thompson
Psychiatry Research Unit
University of Minnesota
Consultant, Faribault State Hospital

Occupational Therapy Department Staff, Faribault State Hospital:
S. Kinsella, C. Berg, K. Smith, P. Scudder, A. Westling, L. Fellner,
B. Nelson, J. Woodman and M. Ahern

[*] Formerly consultant at Faribault State Hospital
[**] Formerly staff member at Faribault State Hospital

Contents

I Background and principles

1. History of treatment and misconceptions concerning the mentally retarded • TRAVIS THOMPSON   3
2. The behavioral approach to retardation • GEORGE BIGELOW   17

II Illustrative programs

3. Initial ward-wide behavior modification programs for retarded children • LEONARD FIELDING   49
4. A behavior modification program for behaviorally retarded institutionalized males • JOHN GRABOWSKI AND TRAVIS THOMPSON   77
5. An intensive teaching unit for severely and profoundly retarded women • GEORGE BIGELOW AND ROLAND GRIFFITHS   99
6. A token system for retarded women: behavior modification, drug therapy, and their combination • O. LINDA MCCONAHEY   139

III Special applications

7. Changing the behavior of the retarded in the special education classroom • WILLIAM H. FULLMER   181
8. Behavior modification in occupational therapy • OCCUPATIONAL DEPARTMENT, FARIBAULT STATE HOSPITAL   213

9. Behavior modification in therapeutic recreation • JOHN RAW AND ERIC ERRICKSON   237

10. Guidance for the parents of retarded children • ROGER JOHNSON   251

IV   Implementing programs

11. Implementing behavior modification programs • JOHN GRABOWSKI AND TRAVIS THOMPSON   269

Index   291

1
Backgound and principles

1
History of treatment and misconceptions concerning the mentally retarded

TRAVIS THOMPSON

Historical background

THE BEGINNINGS: 1800-1900

The attitude of the layman and the educated alike toward the retarded before 1800 can be characterized by the following quotation from Martin Luther: "Eight years ago, there was one at Dessau whom I, Martinus Luther, saw and grappled with. He was twelve years old, had the use of his eyes and all his senses, so that one might think that he was a normal child. But he did nothing but gorge himself as much as four peasants or threshers. He ate, defecated and drooled, and if anyone tackled him, he screamed. If things didn't go well, he wept. So I said to the Prince of Anhalt: 'If I were the Prince, I should take this child to the Moldau River which flows near Dessau and drown him.' But the Prince of Anhalt and the Prince of Saxony, who happened to be present, refused to follow my advice. There upon I said: 'Well, then the Christians shall order the Lord's Prayer to be said in church and pray that the dear Lord take the Devil away'" (Kanner, 1964, p. 7). The mentally deficient have variously been regarded as an object of contempt and fear throughout history and have until recent times received little attention from those interested in education and medicine. It is noteworthy that in the Laehr compilation of writings covering the period 1459-1799, including many thousands of references, the only reference to retardation is found in occasional interest in cretinism toward the end of the Middle Ages (Kanner, 1964). In the early nineteenth century an interest in mental retardation emerged in France and Switzerland, spreading eventually to the rest of Europe and the United States. Itard (1801) had attempted to cure the so-called "wild boy" of Aveyron, and in Switzerland Guggenbühl (1839) had set about curing cretins. Though both investigations were failures in the sense that they did not "cure" their charges, they proved that it was possible to ameliorate some of the behavioral problems of the retarded, leading to the assertion that the mentally retarded were educable in accordance with their degree of deficiency. The first institution created specifically for the mentally retarded was established near Berne, Switzerland, in 1839, under the direction of Guggenbühl.

In the United States there was no institution or private facility for the training, treatment, or care of the retarded until in 1848 Dr. Wilbur took defective children into his home at Barre, Massachusetts, beginning with the seven-year-old son of a distinguished lawyer (Haskell, 1944). In 1848, due largely to the efforts of Dr. Samuel Howe, the State of Massachusetts created "an experimental school," the Perkin's Institution for the teaching and training of ten idiotic children. In 1855 the school was moved to South Boston and renamed the Massachusetts School for Idiotic and Feebleminded Youth. In the forty-year period following the establishment of the experimental school in Massachusetts, fifteen state institutions opened their doors to the mentally retarded. In 1879 Minnesota joined the list by the addition of the School for Idiots, Imbeciles, and the Feebleminded at Faribault, which was later renamed the Minnesota Institute for the Defective. In 1894 one building was added which was classified as a "distinct custodial or asylum building for those children who were unable to profit from school room training" (Curtiss-Wedge, 1910). By 1900 the institution had a core of twenty teachers who conducted a school in which manual and industrial training were predominant features. Girls were taught knitting, basket weaving, sewing, as well as mending and darning, lace making, ironing, domestic work, and gardening. The more competent girls were given the opportunity to work in the mending room, kitchen, dining room, laundry, etc. The boys, on the other hand, received training in mat braiding, sewing, brush making, basketry, and netting. When they became sufficiently competent, they were allowed to work in the mattress and cabinet shops, the barn, laundry, greenhouse, garden, farm, and in the dairy. By 1910 the institution housed some 421 mentally retarded residents, as well as epileptics and physically handicapped patients.

Though the initial intention of state institutions such as Faribault State School and Hospital was to educate and train the retarded, a feeling arose among certain segments of the population that the major function of these institutions was to protect society from the residents. Some asserted that the mentally defective were a menace to civilization, incorrigible at home, burdens to the schools, sexually promiscuous, breeders of feebleminded offspring, and victims and spreaders of poverty, degeneracy, crime, and disease. Instead of functioning to aid in training the mentally retarded, by the early 1930's state institutions became areas of detention for "undesirable elements of society." "The pleas for their maintenance and enlargement carried tunes altogether different from the hymns of hope entoned by the originators of the notion of institutional care and training as constructive, therapeutic enterprises" (Kanner, 1964). Associated with the shift in attitude toward the retarded was a change from a training to a custodial orientation. "For the idiot, unimprovable, nothing is needed beyond the asylum, giving that care and attention found in every well regulated nursery of delicate children, the *sina qua non* being regular hours, simple nourishing foods, frequent baths and tender mothering. As numbers can be cared for here with more efficiency and greater ease than one in the ordinary family, and as the child very often does not recognize the hand that administers to its physical want, the mother herself is soon forced to admit that the asylum is best, not only for the good of the child but also for the welfare of the home" (Barr, 1904).

1900-WORLD WAR II

From the first decade of the twentieth century until World War II there was virtually a total lack of national concern for or awareness of any problem in the area of retardation in the United States. If there was a policy at all, it was one of implicit rejection of the subnormal individual and the assumption that nothing could be done to help him. At best, large institutions similar to Faribault State School and Hospital were created far away from large cities where the subnormal individuals could be segregated "to protect society." This treatment of the retarded was probably due mainly to: (1) the absence of any feeling of public responsibility; and (2) the view that very little could be done to help the behaviorally subnormal individual to adapt to usual community settings (Sarason and Doris, 1969).

During World War II some 716,000 men were rejected from the armed forces on the grounds of mental deficiency. This fact alone brought national attention to the problem of subnormality, though many of those rejected would not be considered severely or profoundly retarded. The realization that cultural, racial, educational, and regional factors contribute to low behavioral functioning helped develop interest in the area of retardation.

POST WORLD WAR II INSTITUTIONALIZATION

Thus, the growth of state institutions for the mentally retarded has been a mixed blessing. While there was an initial emphasis on training the retarded resident, there has been a shift to almost purely custodial care in many institutions. That institutionalization can have a marked detrimental effect is clear (Goldfarb, 1943, 1944, 1947). In comparing children raised in foster homes with those left in institutions, Goldfarb discovered that the institutional children showed immature speech development, more maladjusted behavior, and inferior performance on psychological development tests. Similar findings were reported by Provence and

Lipton (1962) in a study of seventy-two institutional infants compared with a matched group living at home. The deficits ranged from inappropriate postural adjustments when held and inability to control the head to lack of evidence of personal attachment and speech retardation. When older age groups are compared—one group having had earlier institutionalization, the other living at home—there is a significantly higher incidence of mental retardation in the institutionalized group. The evidence suggests that institutionalization can actually *cause* or *promote* the development of retardation. What is it about institutionalization that contributes to retardation? Thormalen (1965) studied the manner in which ward technicians spent their time while on duty. He found that technicians devote 1.9 per cent of their working time to formally training patients in independent skills and 37 per cent of their time promoting dependent behavior, i.e. doing things for the child that he could do for himself. The ward program tended to emphasize physical care, with little opportunity for training. Interestingly, the marked tendency for the staff to promote dependency was in conflict with stated institutional goals.

Does institutionalization necessarily accelerate retardation? Klaber (1969) studied six institutions for the retarded in an effort to compare the degree of effectiveness in helping the retarded help themselves. He found that the degree to which the institutions promoted self-sufficiency varied greatly. Observing the children repeatedly during the day, and recording specific behavioral indices of "happiness" (e.g. smiling and laughing), Klaber found that children in institutions which promoted a high degree of self-sufficiency also seemed to be the happiest. He found that in the typical institution the severely retarded resident spent from 33 to 50 per cent of his time *doing nothing* (not even watching television), and another 15 to 20 per cent engaging in autistic behaviors. Frequently such institutions are clean and the patients' physical well-being is very adequately cared for, but next to nothing is done to improve their behavioral adjustment and development. The *effective* institution, according to Klaber, is one "in which children are happy, self-sufficient, show intellectual growth, manifest minimal stereotypy (such as rocking) and manifest no excessive need for social reinforcement . . ." (Klaber, 1969, p. 165). By this yardstick many, if not most, of our state institutions fall short. In recent years such evidence has begun to affect the way institutional staff treat patients. Programs providing stimulating environments, implementation of remotivation therapy, music therapy, occupational therapy, and recreation therapy have contributed to improving the living conditions for the retarded. Unfortunately, for many who have lived in institutions more than a few years, these methods have come a bit late. Behavior patterns become deeply ingrained and are not easily changed. Autisms (rocking, twiddling fingers), self-abuse (head-banging, biting hands and arms), and virtually total dependency on staff have in many cases been practiced for ten to twenty years. Powerful methods must be used to overcome histories of this sort.

Beginning in 1949 a series of laboratory and clinical investigations were reported demonstrating the applicability of operant conditioning* principles to the treatment of a variety of human behavior problems. Fuller (1949) trained a simple response in an eighteen-year-old "vegetative idiot" by rewarding that response with sugar milk. Also using an operant technique, Ayllon and Haugton (1962) re-trained anorexic chronic psychotic patients to feed themselves, after an extensive history of staff feeding. These general methods were extended on a much broader scale to a variety of behaviors in a ward of forty-eight chronic psychotic patients at Anna State Hospital in Illinois (Ayllon and Azrin, 1965). During the same period, increasing attention was given to treating the retarded by using operant conditioning principles.

---

* The systematic application of conditioning principles to the improvement of human behavior (e.g. elimination of maladaptive behavior and/or strengthening of adaptive behavior) has been called *behavior modification*. Hence, the title of this book: *Behavior Modification of the Mentally Retarded*. It is noteworthy that Itard trained the wild boy of Aveyron to recognize words using the principles of operant conditioning. Correct responses were rewarded with milk (Itard, 1962).

Ellis and Pryer (1958), Barrett and Lindsley (1962), and Lindsley (1964) reported the application of operant methodology to the retarded, and a special program was established for retarded girls at Parson State Hospital in Kansas (Girardeau and Spradlin, 1964). These reports indicated that it was possible to modify longstanding maladaptive behavior patterns and to establish new ways of responding, even in severely retarded and chronically psychotic patients. These early studies suggested that perhaps the powerful tool needed to re-train and modify the behavior of the institutionalized retarded patient was to be found in the principles of operant conditioning. In the following decade pilot projects were developed in parts of wards, cottages, or wings of buildings of large institutions to explore the applicability of these methods to treating larger groups of patients. Some were successful, some went by the wayside. Failures were often due to problems with funding, staff, and administrative support, and sometimes to a lack of understanding of the fundamental principles by those initiating the programs. In the chapters that follow, several programs are described that began with a single ward of severely retarded girls and had extended at the time of writing to seven buildings, housing approximately 420 patients, and to a special school.

Misconceptions regarding retardation

It is clear from the preceding introduction that the retarded have been the subject of myth and confusion throughout history. Many misconceptions remain, making it difficult to initiate change, particularly in large state institutions. Some misconceptions lead to institutionalization of retarded people who do not belong in such a setting and who suffer deleterious effects.

Despite the great variation in gross physical appearance and the obvious variability in performance levels of any population of retarded residents, one still hears the statement, *"All retarded people are basically alike when you get right down to it."* The simple fact is that there are *many* types of retardation, which have been classified three ways (Robinson and Robinson, 1965).

A. *Classification by severity of the symptoms.* The terms "idiot," "imbecile," and "moron" were formerly used to denote I.Q. ranges of 0-30, 30-50, and 50-70 respectively. Subsequently, the American Association for Mental Deficiency introduced a new classification scheme for mental retardation: (1) *Borderline*: 68-83 I.Q.; (2) *Mild*: 52-67 I.Q.; (3) *Moderate*: 36-51 I.Q.; (4) *Severe*: 20-35 I.Q.; and (5) *Profound*: below 20 I.Q. This approach emphasizes the fact that certain aspects of the behavior of mentally retarded people exist on a continuum.

B. *Classification according to cause.* A distinction can be made between retardation resulting from an external cause (exogenous retardation) and retardation resulting from intrinsic genetic make-up (endogenous retardation). Exogenous retardation includes injury or infection to the brain during or after birth, while endogenous retardation is limited to an intrinsic general pattern not resulting in gross neurological abnormalities.

C. *Classification according to clinical symptoms.* Doll (1949) and Kugelmass (1954) have proposed systems of classifying mentally retarded patients according to the composite symptom picture they present. For example, the syndrome of microcephaly, in which the head is small and cone-shaped, can be caused by numerous exogenous factors, yet it involves a single clinical syndrome.

Thus, there is no such thing as *the* retarded patient or "retarded patients in general." Behavioral variations and differences in performance levels are vast.

A second major misconception concerning the mentally retarded is that they are necessarily *better off in an institution for the retarded* (Klaber, 1969). Our earlier discussion indicated some of the problems with institutionalization; however, certain comments made by parents and guardians of the retarded require further attention.

A. It is sometimes felt that institutions have better educational facilities, particularly for the retarded child, than do the special classes in the public schools. "Most states exempt their own, state-operated facilities from the requirements of certification for teachers, remedial specialists, and other professional personnel. Thus, the retarded child is less likely to be instructed by fully qualified (i.e. certified) teachers in the state institution than in his own community" (Cain and Levine, in Klaber, 1969).

B. Some would like to believe that the institution has a staff of medical and behavioral specialists readily available to deal with the special problems of the retarded. Klaber (1969) surveyed six institutions in three eastern states and found a very small percentage of board diplomates among physicians and not a single board diplomate among psychologists. Under such circumstances fully qualified professional personnel may not be available.

C. Some believe that the retarded person is happier among other retarded people. "The argument that certain individuals are happier among 'their own kind' is indeed a specious one and has been used frequently for unsavory ends. In fact, our evidence strongly suggests the opposite . . ." (Klaber, 1969, p. 184).

D. Finally, some have operated in the vain hope that the therapeutic milieu of the institution would accelerate maturation among young retarded residents. As discussed in the preceding section, the data lead us to believe that in general just the opposite happens. The institutionalized retarded resident tends to deteriorate maturationally rather than accelerate.

A third general misconception is that *it is not appropriate and/or not worthwhile to attempt to educate and train the retarded resident*. On inquiring of the staff at large state institutions concerning the seeming absence of training programming, one receives several common replies:

A. *Their I.Q.'s are so low they couldn't profit from training.* Low I.Q. is merely a scapegoat. Even profoundly retarded patients can benefit from intensive training. It is probably correct to say that most profoundly retarded adults cannot greatly benefit from a typical elementary school classroom situation. However, it is equally true that using appropriate training methods, the majority of profoundly retarded residents can learn most of the self-care activities which staff members customarily do for the residents. Our experience with a range of residents—from mildly to profoundly retarded, from young children to geriatric patients—indicates that I.Q. is at best a very rough indicator of functioning level in institutionalized residents, and is more commonly a deterrent to training efforts.

One subset of this category is the "untestable." Frequently the label carries the connotation of retardation of the severest degree. A resident may be untestable due to short attention span, hyperactivity, or a variety of responses incompatible with the usual I.Q. test evaluation.

B. *These patients are brain damaged and can't learn.* Recourse to brain damage is an even more inexcusable "out" which has been used to justify lack of effort on behalf of the mentally retarded. Many people who function within normal ranges are brain damaged to varying degrees, but we do not dismiss educating so-called normal children on the grounds they are imperfect. The fact that the retarded are generally brain damaged to a greater degree does not justify dismissing efforts at education. One of our more dramatic cases was a thirty-one-year-old patient whose I.Q. was 27 and who was described as a "quadraplegic" by the staff physician. He had no use of his arms and limited use of his legs at the beginning of the program. He exhibited gross motor tremors, had difficulty visually fixating, was non-verbal, was unable to clothe or feed himself, and was only partially continent. After one and a half years of daily training, the patient partially clothed, fed, and toileted himself. He had partial use of both arms and was ambulatory. He is currently learning to lace his shoes. There is no question that this patient is severely brain damaged. It is also unquestionable that he was capable of learning many of the self-care activities that had previously been carried out by staff.

C. *They are happy the way they are.* When one-third to one-half of the residents are sitting doing literally nothing, and another 15 to 20 per cent are engaged in autisms and self-abuse, it is difficult to contend that these patients are "happy the way they are." Even geriatric retarded patients, who are often assumed to enjoy sitting and doing nothing but rocking, deserve the freedom to zip up their own fly, make their own bed, knit their own scarf, and, if possible, read their own book. Staff members too often take it upon themselves to assume that the patient enjoys vegetating, partially because the staff fails to understand the reasons for lack of behavior of the resident, and partially because it makes life easier for the staff. After all, having no training in the skills necessary to assist the residents in learning or relearning adaptive behaviors makes the staff's job insurmountable, and hence it is easier to ignore the problem. Data from studies on children's wards make it abundantly clear that children who are trained to be more self-sufficient are happier, which makes sense. Self-sufficiency provides the resident with far greater skills and freedom to interact and deal with both his physical and social environments.

D. *The patients are hyperactive, uncooperative, and have too short an attention span to learn anything.* It is often true that patients in state hospitals move about apparently randomly, pay little or no attention to a task, and fail to follow directions. After all, there is no reason they should sit quietly and attend to a task. In all probability, nothing of consequence will happen if they follow the staff member's directions. Studies in a variety of settings reveal that even highly hyperactive patients with extremely short attention spans can be taught to sit quietly and attend to a task if the consequence of their sitting and attending is meaningful to them. Chapter 2 describes methods used at Faribault State Hospital which have been successful with a large number of such patients. Hyperactivity, lack of cooperation, and short attention span are inversely related to adaptive behavior, painstakingly trained by the staff.

E. *The patients in this ward are too different from one another to use any single method.* The diversity of the mentally retarded was discussed above, and it goes without saying that there will be a range of abilities in any single institution ward. There is also a range of abilities in any classroom of normal children. Certain general educational principles apply in both situations and must be adjusted for varying performance and ability levels in each. Just as modern classroom teachers use materials of graded levels of difficulty, the staff member training the mentally retarded must program activities at several levels of difficulty for sub-groups of patients. We do not suggest that it is easy to devise activities and tasks for a variety of ability levels, but we do contend that it is necessary if patients are to learn.

References

Ayllon, T., and N. H. Azrin. The measurement and reinforcement of behavior with psychotics. *Journal of the Experimental Analysis of Behavior,* 1965, 8, 357-83.

Ayllon, T., and E. Haughton. Control of the behavior of schizophrenics by food. *Journal of the Experimental Analysis of Behavior,* 1962, 5, 343-52.

Barr, M. W. *Mental Defectives, Their History, Treatment and Training.* Philadelphia: P. Blakistar's Son and Co., 1904.

Barrett, B. H., and O. R. Lindsley. Deficits in acquisition of operant discrimination and differentiation shown by institutionalized retarded children. *Amer. J. ment. Defic.* 1962, 67, 424-36.

Bijou, S. W. Theory and research in mental (development) retardation. *Psychological Record,* 1963, 13, 95-110.

Blatt, B., and F. Kaplan. *Christmas in Purgatory.* Boston: Allyn and Bacon, Inc., 1966.

Curtiss-Wedge, F. *History of Rice and Steele Counties, Minnesota.* Chicago: A. C. Cooper Jr. & Co., 1916.

Doll, E. A. Mental deficiency. In V. C. Branham and S. B. Kutash (Eds.), *Encyclopedia of Criminology.* New York: Philosophical Library, 1949. Pp. 228-31.

Ellis, N. R., and M. Pryer. Primary versus secondary reinforcement in simple discrimination learning of mental defectives. *Psychological Reports,* 1958, 4, 67-70.

Fuller, P. Operant conditioning of a vegetative human organism. *Amer. J. Psychol.,* 1949, 62, 587-90.

Girardeau, F., and J. Spradlin. Token rewards in a cottage program. *Mental Retardation,* 1964, 2, 245-51.

Goldfarb, W. Infant rearing and problem behavior. *Amer. J. Orthopsychiat.,* 1943, 13, 245-65.

────── The effects of early institutional care on adolescent personality. *Amer. J. Orthopsychiat.*, 1944, *14*, 441-47.
────── Variations in adolescent adjustment of institutionally-reared children. *Amer. J. Orthopsychiat.*, 1947, *17*, 449-57.
Haskell, R. H. Mental deficiency over a hundred years. *Amer. J. Psychiatry*, 1944, *100*, 107-18.
Itard, J. *The Wild Boy of Aveyron*. G. and M. Humphrey (Trans.). N.Y.: Appleton-Century-Crofts, 1962.
Kanner, L. *A History of the Care and Study of the Mentally Retarded*. Springfield, Ill.: Charles C. Thomas, Publ., 1964.
Klaber, M. M. The retarded and institutions for the retarded—a preliminary report. Ch. 9 in S. B. Sarason, and J. Doris, *Psychological Problems in Mental Deficiency*. N.Y.: Harper and Row, 1969.
Kugelmass, I. N. *The Management of Mental Deficiency in Children*. N.Y.: Grune & Stratton, 1954.
Lindsley, O. R. Direct measurement and prothesis of retarded behavior. *Journal of Education*, 1964, *147*, 60-81.
Provence, S., and R. C. Lipton. *Infants in Institutions*. N.Y.: International Universities Press, 1962.
Robinson, H. B., and N. M. Robinson. *The Mentally Retarded Child*. N.Y.: McGraw-Hill, 1965.
Sarason, S. B., and J. Doris. *Psychological Problems of Mental Deficiency* (4th ed.). N.Y.: Harper and Row, 1969.
Thormalen, P. W. A study of on-the-ward training of trainable mentally retarded children in a state institution. *California Mental Health Research Monograph*, No. 4, 1965.
Tredgold, A. F. *A Textbook of Mental Deficiency* (7th ed.). London: Bailliere, Tindall and Cox, 1949.
Wollen, J. E. Training of the severely retarded, viewed in historical perspective. *J. gen. Psychol.*, 1966, *74*, 107-27.

2
The behavioral approach to retardation

GEORGE BIGELOW

Retarded individuals have many different labels—mentally retarded, mentally deficient, learning disabled, developmentally retarded, etc. These labels refer to a condition in which the retarded individual has failed to acquire the range of behaviors which other "normal" persons his age have mastered or has lost behaviors once learned. That is, the actual characteristic which distinguishes the retarded is the fact that they lack various behaviors. They have failed to learn things that their peers have learned. The specific behaviors which are lacking will be different from one individual to the next. Some individuals may not have learned to use the toilet; others may not have learned to speak; others may not have learned to read and write when their classmates did. Behavior modification focuses upon the specific behavioral deficiencies which each individual has and attempts to correct them.

Positive approach. Behavior modification, then, is a *teaching* procedure; it does not attempt to explain retardation. The aim is the positive one of producing improvement, rather than the passive one of observing and explaining. A case of retardation is not considered "hopeless." The retarded *can* learn. Behavior modification attempts to teach individuals the specific skills they have failed to learn earlier—skills which will help them to function more effectively, enjoy wider experiences, and put them in a position to continue learning other valuable skills.

The focus is always upon improvement. No limit is set on what an individual can learn, other than the limits of his own rate of progress. Some individuals may progress quickly, others more slowly, but all are capable of learning. This positive approach of focusing upon teaching *specific* skills can drastically alter one's view of retardation. Frustration and pessimism is minimized once we see the residents learning. The requirements for this learning to occur are: (1) an effective teaching technique, which is provided by behavior modification; and (2) deciding what we should teach, which should be guided by considerations of practicality and relevance.

Practicality. Teaching goals must always be limited to what seems practical at the time. Though long-term goals might be quite ambitious, immediate goals must be more modest. For example, a hyperactive resident may pace actively about the ward all day. From his personal history it may appear that he could learn to read, but, obviously, to include him in a reading class in his hyperactive state would be completely impractical. An initial, practical goal should be to teach the resident to sit quietly in a chair for a few minutes.

Often decisions about the practicality of a particular teaching goal will be based upon such natural hierarchies. There are certain behavioral prerequisites which have to be taught first. To teach a resident to name colors, he must first be taught to look at the colors. To teach a resident to assemble a puzzle, he must first be taught to work at a simple task for more than a few seconds. Thus, one always starts with the basics and gradually builds up to the more elaborate tasks. By starting with the things that are easiest or most essential to accomplish, other higher-level tasks will become possible.

Relevance. Relevant behaviors are those that will be useful to the resident in his normal environment, or which will be regularly rewarded in that environment. There is no point spending time teaching the resident skills that he could just as well do without.

Generally, the most relevant behaviors are those which concern self-care—toileting, dressing, eating, washing, etc. So long as the resident remains in a teaching environment, skills which will facilitate further education are relevant. For many residents it may be desirable to aim toward preparation for work in special sheltered jobs. For those who are likely to remain permanently within an institution it is important to develop behaviors which allow the resident to occupy his time—recreational activities.

Whatever the particular behavior which is selected to be taught on the basis of these considerations, it must be specified clearly and precisely. If what is to be achieved is not specified, we can except to achieve nothing. Having a precise behavioral goal is an essential first step for any successful treatment program.

Behavioral methods

At Faribault State Hospital the methods of behavior modification have been taught to the ward staff, and it has generally been they who have actually applied the principles and produced the improvements described. In teaching behavioral principles to the ward staff emphasis has been placed on two facts: (1) *Behavior is caused.* It is important that staff realize that there are causes for any behavior. Behavior is not a fixed characteristic of an individual. It can be changed—if the causes can be found. This means there is hope of improvement if the staff has the patience to hunt for and try to alter the causes of behavior. (2) *The main cause of current behavior is its past consequences.* This directs attention to a specific and major cause of behavior which can be changed in order to accomplish therapeutic gains.

CONSEQUENCES OF BEHAVIOR

The success of behavior modification rests upon careful attention to and arrangement of the consequences of behavior for behavior occurs mainly because of the effects which it produces. Learning (or any change in behavior) is most easily produced by careful arrangement of the consequences of behavior. It is on this simple fact that behavior modification is established.

Recognition that the most immediate cause of behavior is some characteristic of the situation rather than some characteristic inside the individual opens up the hope of substantial behavioral improvement for the mentally retarded. The situation can be arranged so that it teaches.

The relation between a behavior and its consequence is called a *contingency*—a specification of what leads to what. Another name often given to behavior modification is *contingency management*. Thus, it is mainly through the arrangement of proper contingencies that behavioral changes are accomplished.

The simplest statement of what is involved in contingency management (or behavior modification) is that *one should reward desirable behavior and not reward undesirable behavior*. Behavior which is rewarded (or *reinforced*) tends to be repeated, while behavior which is not reinforced tends not to be repeated. This is how behavior modification teaches: by guaranteeing that desirable behavior has reinforcing effects, and that undesirable behavior does not.

There are two types of goals which may be sought in the application of behavior modification. The first is *teaching*—the development of some new behavior in the individual. The second type of goal is the *elimination* of some undesirable behavior which the individual already displays. For example, in one situation the goal may be to teach a resident to take a bath without staff assistance, while in another the goal may be to eliminate the behavior of banging loudly on furniture. For both teaching and eliminating behavior, the procedures depend upon the scheduling of appropriate consequences to behavior.

TEACHING PROCEDURES

When behavior modification programming is first introduced into an institution, the implicit suggestion is usually made that the roles of the ward staff should be drastically changed. Behavior modification is not simply providing a better technique for the staff to do their old job. The staff's role must be changed from caretaker to teacher.

Often the main job of institutional ward staff has been to clean up after the residents and to try to help them—help them in the paternalistic way of doing things *for* them. Under such circumstances the residents learn little, if any, desirable behavior. In fact, the behavioral deterioration which so often results from chronic institutionalization is well known (Chapter 1). Many of the worst behavior problems in institutions develop *after* the individual arrives in the institution.

The custodial role of ward staff should be changed to a teaching role. Only through establishment of such a teaching relation can hope of improvement be offered. Generally any improvement in the lot of the residents means a comparable improvement in working conditions for the staff. Thus, a thorough behavior modification program can result in a wide-ranging change in the nature of an institution.

The basic procedures in teaching desirable behavior evolve from two principles: (1) *reinforcement*—the reinforcing consequences of a behavior are the main determinants of its occurrence; (2) *small steps*—in teaching a task, small, graduated steps must be used.

Reinforcement

When a behavior is reinforced, it will tend to be repeated. Any effective teacher uses reinforcement to help students learn, although the teacher may not realize that he is using this principle.

Regardless of the task being taught, if residents are reinforced for each bit of progress toward the final goal, their learning will be speeded up.

The major tenet in using reinforcement is that it must be given *only* for desirable behavior. If undesirable behavior is reinforced, it too will increase. It is not simply the act of providing reinforcers which improves behavior. The crucial aspect is the *contingency*—the relationship between a behavior and the events following it. If those events are reinforcing, then the behavior is strengthened. The characteristics of the behavior make no difference. If the contingencies are wrong, the wrong behavior will be strengthened.

Contingencies exist whether they are carefully planned or left to chance. If they are left to chance, many of them will be arranged improperly and undesirable behavior will be strengthened. Therapeutic behavioral improvements are best achieved when contingencies are planned rather than left to chance.

REINFORCE DESIRABLE BEHAVIOR

As the staff's orientation changes from caretaker to teacher, they will attend more to desirable behavior on the part of the residents. Initially, some staff may have an unfortunate "don't-bother-him-while-he's-being-good" attitude, which is directly incompatible with effective teaching. It is precisely when an individual is behaving properly that staff should interact with him and reinforce him. If staff members fail to reinforce the residents when they are behaving well, then the residents will probably get most of their reinforcement for misbehavior. This is how serious behavior problems arise.

Generally residents can guarantee that they receive a certain amount of reinforcement—in the form of staff attention. They develop a variety of behaviors which essentially force the staff to interact with them. Tactics such as following staff around and pestering them will often work. However, there are many more unpleasant methods which are also effective—smearing feces, attacking other residents, self-mutilation, screaming, breaking objects, etc. When residents must resort to such misbehavior to gain desired staff attention, their behavior will deteriorate dramatically.

When staff members act in the role of caretakers, they tend to react to problem behaviors or misbehaviors (things that need "caring for"), and the residents actually suffer in the long run. When staff members act in the role of teachers, however, they react to desirable behavior and to each sign of improvement by the residents.

PRINCIPLES OF REINFORCEMENT

Much of the effectiveness of teaching depends on adequately breaking the task into small teaching steps, as will be discussed later. Once a desirable behavior has been selected and attempts are made to reinforce it, there are several rules to be followed for it to be maximally effective. Reinforcement must be provided immediately and frequently.

Immediacy. For any behavioral consequence to be effective, it must be immediate. *Consequences exert their effects on the immediately preceding behavior.* Thus, when using reinforcement, staff must be certain that the reinforcer is presented *immediately* following the behavior to be strengthened. Delays between behavior and reinforcement greatly weaken the power of the reinforcer. Delays also introduce the risk that some inappropriate behavior will occur during the delay and be accidentally reinforced.

This need for immediacy of reinforcement has introduced some limitations on the types of reinforcers that are commonly used. Often candy is used since it can be easily carried and quickly handed to residents at the proper time.

In general, it is not effective to reinforce residents at the end of the day, or even at the end of a teaching period, for having behaved well. The reinforcement should immediately follow specific instances of proper behavior. Thus, if a resident helps to clean up the ward room in the morning, it will not be a very effective reward to give him an extra dessert at the noon meal. An immediate reinforcer, even though smaller, will be more effective. It is the immediacy of a reinforcer which tells the individual what he did was good.

Effective teachers learn to interrupt what they are doing in order to reinforce immediately when good behavior occurs. The ability to do this is especially important when a generally ill-behaved resident finally does something appropriate. For instance, if a resident who has been sitting on the floor rocking gets up and starts to play constructively with a toy, he should be reinforced immediately. The best teachers will do this even if it means abruptly walking away from a conversation with the hospital director—and the director *should* be pleased.

Frequency. When a task is first being taught, reinforcement should be given frequently. During this initial teaching phase, it is best to reinforce the resident *every time* he performs the new task. Or, if the final task is complex and the teaching involves a series of steps designed to lead to the final task, reinforcement should be given frequently for bits of progress before the task is completed. It is not possible to say exactly how often a resident should be reinforced. The aim should be to maintain the resident's attention to the teaching task and gradually to develop more and more appropriate behavior. Enough reinforcement is being given when the behavior being taught steadily improves without signs of the resident becoming frustrated or losing interest. Some residents, of course, will require more reinforcement than others.

After some learning has occurred the need for frequent reinforcement is no longer so urgent. Once a resident has learned to tie his own shoes, he no longer needs to be reinforced every time he does it. However, some reinforcement is still necessary to maintain the newly learned skill. *Reinforcement is not just a teaching tool; it must be used to keep behavior occurring even after learning.* The great practical utility of reinforcement lies in the fact that only occasional reinforcements are needed to maintain what has been taught.

The transition from reinforcing a behavior always to reinforcing it occasionally must be handled very gradually. Abrupt changes in the frequency of reinforcement may interrupt or set back progress already made. If a resident is being taught to name colors, one might begin by reinforcing each correct name, then proceed to skip reinforcements occasionally. Soon the resident may be averaging three correct answers for one reinforcement. It is important that reinforcements are not reduced so rapidly that the resident becomes frustrated and begins to make errors. If correct performance continues, the number of correct answers per reinforcement can gradually be increased.

When reinforcement is given intermittently, it is best that a fixed pattern of reinforcement is not adopted (e.g. every fifth correct answer). The resident's attention will be maintained better and he will be more cooperative if reinforcements are unpredictable. If on the *average* every fifth correct answer were reinforced, reinforcement would actually come, for example, sometimes after the second, sometimes the ninth, sometimes the fourth answer, and so on.

For other types of behavior the goal may not be to teach the resident to make the response more often, but to keep at the task for a longer period each time. If the goal is to teach a hyperactive resident to sit still and play with a toy, for example, at first he must be reinforced after only a few seconds with the toy. Gradually, however, reinforcement would only be presented after longer and longer periods of playing. Again, it will be most effective if the actual intervals between reinforcements are unpredictable.

REINFORCERS

Reinforcers are the most important tool of the effective teacher. They are basically rewards. They can be anything that the individual likes. Most people are reinforced by a wide variety of things—eating, playing, socializing, money, etc. The things which are reinforcing to the retarded are basically of these same types.

There is a tendency to think that profoundly retarded individuals, who sit and do nothing all day, everyday, lack effective reinforcers. Personnel who have worked with the resident for years may say there is nothing the individual likes. Actually, only rarely is difficulty encountered in finding reinforcers for any individual. Even for the most behaviorally debilitated residents, effective reinforcers can usually be found.

Edibles. Among the most universally effective reinforcers are edibles—candies, crackers, nuts, cookies, etc. When used in small bits, these treats can serve as effective reinforcers throughout the day. They are especially important as reinforcers for individuals who have not developed adequate social responsiveness.

The use of edible reinforcers can be instrumental in establishing increased social responsiveness. Initially, some residents may withdraw even when staff members reach out to hand them a piece of candy. However, since social interaction is the medium through which the edible treats are received, soon social interaction itself will become more rewarding to the resident. Ultimately, these same residents can be reinforced much of the time by being spoken to and patted by the staff.

Attention. Social interaction or attention is probably the next most powerful reinforcer available. For most residents physical contact or simply talking with staff members will be reinforcing.

It is essential that all staff members come to realize that their attention is reinforcing to residents. This is especially necessary since attention is involved to some extent in *all* interactions with residents—even those interactions which most of us would not expect to be reinforcing. Some residents even appear to be reinforced by scoldings, by being handled roughly, or even by a scuffle before being placed in seclusion. Since reinforcers can strengthen *any* preceding behavior, it is quite important that attention not be given for inappropriate behavior. Unfortunately, when institutions are understaffed and when staff members are forced to serve as caretakers, much staff attention is consequent upon misbehavior—aggression, disruptiveness, soiling, etc. Under such conditions the behavior of residents can deteriorate drastically.

Most institutions have several residents who have developed bizarre and disruptive behaviors to receive attention. A common example is yelling. Variations and improvisations around this attention-getting theme include flooding the bathroom, knocking over furniture, head-banging, and hitting others. Often the consequence of these behaviors (which is apparently reinforcing) is simply that of being told "shut up" or "calm down." Residents whose misbehavior is maintained by attention can often be recognized because they tend to follow staff around or to look at staff members when they misbehave. However, many residents who may appear quite disinterested in staff are, nonetheless, very reinforced by staff attention.

The fact that these behavior problems can develop is adequate proof of the power of attention as a reinforcer. Much more dramatic proof results when one of these behavior problems is eliminated by altering staff social reinforcement—by ignoring misbehavior and by interacting with and praising residents for proper behavior.

Idiosyncratic reinforcers. In addition to these two nearly universal reinforcers, an infinite variety of unusual and unexpected reinforcers is available. Idiosyncratic reinforcers are effective only for particular individuals. For some residents sounds may be reinforcing—music, even buzzes, clicks, and rattles. For others a magazine or a Sears catalogue, a favorite dress or toy, or a doll or piece of jewelry may be reinforcing.

In treatment programs involving a group of residents who are all worked with simultaneously, the use of such idiosyncratic reinforcers can be cumbersome and impractical. However, they may be necessary if other reinforcers are ineffective. Idiosyncratic reinforcers may also be useful in individualized one-to-one treatment programs.

Activities. The opportunity to engage in certain activities may serve as a reinforcer. Sitting in a special chair, going for a ride or a walk, playing games, going to a movie or a dance may all be reinforcers for some residents. As a rule it can be said that activities in which a resident engages with greater frequency can serve as reinforcers for other less frequent activities. Thus, for one resident who would spend most of her day rocking in a rocking chair if it were available, giving her access to a rocking chair served to reinforce her participation in other activities. Likewise, for one severely withdrawn girl who insisted on spending her day in a room alone, access to the isolation room was used as a reinforcer to develop participation in group teaching activities.

Tokens. Often, in more advanced treatment programs, tokens are used as reinforcers. The tokens can be any arbitrary object chosen to serve as "money" within the treatment program. The tokens, of course, have no intrinsic value of their own, but the residents learn to value them because tokens can be exchanged (just like money) for other reinforcers. The process of teaching residents to value tokens is described in Chapters 3, 5, and 6.

Tokens have a number of benefits. They avoid any disruption of the teaching process which would be caused by consumption or use of the reinforcer. With tokens the reinforcement of desirable behavior is immediate, but the use of the reinforcer is delayed until some more appropriate time. It is not clear that all residents can tolerate even this delay, so tokens may be ill-advised for some of the most profoundly retarded residents.

Tokens make the therapeutic program more similar to the conditions in the larger community—i.e. outside the institution. They eliminate the problem of becoming tired of a single type of reinforcer (satiation) by allowing residents to choose from a variety of alternatives. This makes it possible to use many reinforcers which would not be practical for use throughout the daily routine. Both idiosyncratic reinforcers and reinforcing activities can be used which could not conveniently be delivered immediately during teaching. The token provides a tangible reminder to help carry the resident through the necessary delay period.

SMALL STEPS

Proceeding in small steps is a principle used in virtually every theory or technology of teaching. A main purpose of teaching a task via a series of small steps is to minimize the number of errors made by the resident. Errors slow down the learning process. They increase the likelihood of more errors.

In some cases learning will occur when a task is broken into a series of easy steps even though the individual would *never* learn if he were simply given prolonged training on the final task. For example, consider the task of teaching a resident to name colors. If the task is approached by trying to teach the resident several colors at the same time, progress may be very slow. Presenting red, yellow, green, blue, and black to the student in a single teaching period can be quite confusing, and some residents might never master the task when taught in this way. However, if the task is broken into small steps, with one color being taught at a time and additional colors being included as the resident improves, then learning will be easier, and more residents will master the task.

A sequence of steps (or teaching program) provides the staff with an outline of how to proceed with the teaching job. Learning will be fastest if all staff members teach the activity in exactly the same way. By recording how many of the small steps the resident has already mastered, each staff member will be able to start teaching at that precise point in the task where the resident most needs instruction. Thus, the use of a sequence of small teaching steps also makes it easier for several different teachers to teach the same task without having to worry about working at cross-purposes.

In behavior modification there are three basic techniques by which tasks are broken into small steps for teaching: (1) shaping; (2) chaining; (3) fading. In practice these techniques are often combined within a single program.

SHAPING

Shaping involves gradually changing the definition of what constitutes adequate behavior. The behavior which is reinforced is gradually changed to require more and more from the resident. This method is sometimes called *successive approximation*.

When shaping behavior, one begins with the behavior which already exists, that is, one begins at the beginning. An aspect of existing behavior which has something in common with the final desired behavior is selected and reinforced. This reinforcement will cause the selected aspect of behavior and variations of it to occur more frequently. From these variations the staff can then select some aspect to reinforce which is even closer to the final desired behavior. As behavior is gradually changed in this way, and as the staff gradually changes the requirement for reinforcement, the resident's behavior will begin to resemble more closely the behavior desired.

Talking. Many of the residents at Faribault State Hospital either do not speak or have very rudimentary verbal behavior. A typical shaping program to establish speech might be as follows:

1. Looks at staff
2. Imitates mouth movements
3. Makes sounds
4. Echoes sounds made by staff
5. Echoes single-syllable words
6. Echoes two-syllable words

The first step in this task is to look at the staff doing the teaching. This is accomplished by instructions, prompting, and reinforcement of looking. When the resident is looking at the staff, the task becomes one of getting the resident to move his mouth. This is done by instructions, demonstration, and reinforcement of movements. When mouth movements start to occur, reinforcement is no longer delivered for just looking at the staff. This change in the criterion for reinforcement must be gradual. If mouth movements are rare, then some reinforcement must be given for looking in order to maintain the resident's cooperation. Transitions between steps must always be gradual in this respect.

The importance of the first step—"Looks at staff"—should be emphasized. For some readers it may not make sense to start at this point. But paying attention to the teacher or relevant materials is a prerequisite for mastering any activity. Therefore, if necessary, paying attention must be taught via reinforcement at the beginning of the task.

CHAINING

Chaining techniques are used to teach behaviors which normally occur in a fixed order or sequence. The distinguishing characteristic of chained activities is that the task is taught *backwards*. That is, the last step of the task or the last step of the sequence is taught *first*. In essence, the residents are taught to *finish the task*. Initially, this requires doing very little—just the final step—and then they are reinforced. But, as training proceeds, more and more is required to finish the task. Never is much new behavior before the resident finds himself at a stage over which he has already demonstrated him mastery.

Chaining procedures are very important to understand. They are appropriate to teaching large numbers of activities which go on throughout the day in most institutions—washing, toileting, dressing, making beds, assembling puzzles, etc. The method of teaching these activities by chaining is quite different from that which common sense might suggest. The popular notion to "begin at the beginning" does *not* apply to chained activities. When an activity is to be taught by chaining one must *"begin at the end."* It is this divergence from common practice which necessitates thorough training of staff in chaining procedures. Staff efforts to teach in the "common sense" (forward) direction may be met with considerable difficulty. The use of chaining procedures can greatly facilitate teaching of a wide variety of activities.

Hand washing. As already mentioned, chaining procedures are appropriate for many self-care skills. As an example, consider a program for teaching residents to wash their hands under a running tap (as opposed to a filled wash basin). The reader will probably recognize that this is an activity which he himself normally performs in a fairly ritualized sequence. Writing a program for such an activity simply requires that we list the steps in that sequence. Since the activity will be taught backwards (last step first), the steps are numbered in the same backwards order:

10. Approaches sink	5. Rinses
9. Turns water on	4. Turns water off
8. Picks up soap	3. Takes paper towel
7. Washes	2. Dries
6. Returns soap	1. Throws out towel

As this program has been used, reinforcement has always been delivered following the completion of the final step ("Throws out towel"). Staff members always assured that the residents completed all the steps—by guiding their hands if necessary. The consequence of skipping a step was that a staff member would intervene and start the resident over at that step and insist that it be completed. The score the resident received on this activity was the number of consecutive steps at the end of the sequence that were completed without staff assistance. Mastery of each new step would get the resident to the final step and to reinforcement sooner.

Puzzles. Assembling puzzles is another activity ideally suited to be taught by a chaining procedure. It is also used as an example because the staff is generally inclined to teach this in a forward direction. If a resident is given even a very simple wooden puzzle (i.e. one with a frame into which pieces are placed) with all the pieces disassembled and asked to assemble them, the task may be too great for him to master. Initially it might seem satisfactory if the resident were able to put in one piece properly. Yet if the task is taught from the beginning, putting in one piece still does not make the puzzle picture look like anything familiar to the resident. There is no intrinsic reward for the resident. If the task were chained, the whole puzzle would be assembled except for the last piece, which would be placed just adjacent to its proper place. Then, only a very small effort is required for the resident to complete the task and see the final product. Extrinsic reinforcement is also delivered as a consequence of finishing the task. As the resident masters more of the task, the staff performs fewer and fewer of the initial steps. First, the resident must move only the last piece a short distance. Later, he must move it a greater distance and turn it to fit it into place. Still later, two pieces must be assembled, and so on. Ultimately, the resident completes the entire task alone.

FADING

A third useful procedure in breaking a task into small steps for teaching is called stimulus fading, or just *fading*. This involves gradual changes in the situation (stimulus condition) in which a behavior occurs. Fading does not involve changes in the nature of the task itself, only in the conditions under which the behavior occurs. This technique is used when a desired behavior occurs under some condition and the goal is to get it to occur under other conditions.

For example, a resident may be quite disruptive when in the dining hall with other residents but will behave properly during meals when he is fed alone in a separate room. The procedure in such a case is gradually to change the eating location. Steps might involve having the resident eat alone in several different rooms, then eat alone in a hallway, then alone in the dining room. Once he is eating in the dining room, additional residents would be introduced to his eating situation, so that ultimately the resident eats in the dining room with all the other residents.

Naming. Teaching residents to name objects after they have learned to echo words can be accomplished by a fading procedure. Initially, the object or a picture of the object is shown to the resident as the staff says the word and the resident repeats it. If the verbal prompt by the staff is gradually reduced, the resident will come to respond just to the object or its picture by repeating the name.

Coloring. Residents can be taught to color within lines by using fading. Initially residents are taught to color inside a heavy raised outline (a cardboard template, or yarn glued to the paper). Later the height of the outline is reduced, and still later replaced by a heavy drawn outline (magic marker), and ultimately by just the usual printed outline.

Stimulus control. Involved in the process of fading is the concept of stimulus control, which should be more fully explained. Thus far we have emphasized that behavior is mainly controlled by the stimulus events which follow it, e.g. reinforcement. However, the situation preceding a particular behavior can also determine whether or not it occurs. This is called stimulus control. For example, in the above-described instance of teaching an echoic individual to name objects, we are bringing the resident's verbal comments under the stimulus control of the object, rather than under the stimulus control of the teacher's own words. Thus, fading is a technique for changing stimulus control.

Stimulus control, however, is relevant in situations other than fading. Virtually all normal behaviors of any practical significance are under some form of stimulus control. Therefore, at some point in a teaching task attention must be devoted to establishing proper stimulus control. For example, in teaching residents to talk we do not want to train individuals to simply echo the words that they hear, but we must at some point bring their talking under the stimulus control of the appropriate objects and situations.

Establishing proper stimulus control does not require any other procedures than the use of properly placed reinforcement. As a basic rule, it can be stated that a *behavior will tend to occur in situations in which it has been reinforced in the past*. To teach that a behavior should occur in one situation and not in others, one has to reinforce the behavior in the desirable situation and not reinforce it in the undesirable situation.

Occasionally, this fact that behavior will occur most frequently in the situations where it is reinforced can be useful diagnostically. For example, if a particular resident misbehaves only during one staff member's work shift, then we might suspect that that staff person is accidentally reinforcing the misbehavior. Likewise, if a resident is more cooperative and can do more for himself during one staff member's shift, then we might suspect that that staff member is more effectively reinforcing the desirable behaviors. Whenever the likelihood of particular behaviors differs from one situation to another, it is a good bet that the frequency of reinforcement for those behaviors differs in the situations accordingly.

Whenever some form of misbehavior has come under strong stimulus control, there is a special consideration when attempting to extinguish that misbehavior. Extinction will occur most rapidly if the individual is placed in a different situation for the extinction period. For example, if a resident is a severe head-banger, who is under the stimulus control of a particular building or set of staff members, then it might be dangerous to attempt extinction in the same building with the same staff. Extinction would be faster and safer if the individual were moved into a novel situation during the therapy period.

Thus, when one is faced with a misbehavior which is under strong stimulus control, the therapy program calls for weakening the misbehavior by drastically altering the stimulus situation. Whereas, if one is faced with a desirable behavior which is under inappropriate stimulus control, then the therapy program calls for use of a fading procedure, which maintains the desirable behavior while gradually altering the stimulus situation under which it occurs.

Behavior elimination procedures

One of the first tasks which faces institutional staff is the problem of eliminating bizarre or disruptive behaviors which the residents already exhibit. It is an unfortunate fact that in most institutions the custodial atmosphere has allowed residents' behavior to deteriorate so badly that when "improvements" are contemplated, highest priority is given, not to teaching new behaviors, but to eliminating certain existing behaviors.

One should, as much as possible, orient any treatment program in a *positive* direction, toward *teaching desirable behaviors*. At times, however, it will be necessary to focus on some undesirable behavior, and then it will be important that procedures are available to bring the offending behavior under control.

It is important to realize here that the goal is to bring the behavior under control and reduce its rate of occurrence—not to produce a merely temporary cessation. This goal is emphasized because it is so easily forgotten in the very situations where it is most important that it be remembered. To keep this goal in mind in practice requires considerable fortitude and self-control in the staff.

When an instance of misbehavior occurs, the most natural tendency for most staff present is to make the behavior stop as soon as possible. Keeping in mind the long-range goal, staff may have to make some sacrifices in the pleasantness of their own immediate situation. But these sacrifices will be well rewarded in the long run, as the undesirable behavior ultimately declines in frequency.

With undesirable behavior, just as with desirable behavior, the overwhelming determinant of the behavior's occurrence is its consequence. Reinforcing consequences will also cause undesirable behavior to occur more frequently, and non-reinforcing consequences will cause it to occur less frequently. This refers to *future* occurrence of the behavior. The *immediate* effects of these consequences may be the reverse. Thus, the immediate effect of a reinforcing consequence may be that the behavior stops; likewise, the immediate consequence of a non-reinforcing consequence may be that the behavior continues and becomes more intense. Staff must learn to ignore these short-term, immediate effects and concentrate upon the long-term goals.

Consider a case where a resident sits and bangs his head against the wall. Staff may discover that if they sit with the individual and hold his hand he will stop banging his head, though the attention of sitting with the offender and holding his hand is a reinforcer. Under such circumstances, the over-all frequency of the behavior will increase. This kind of behavioral accident occurs quite frequently in institutions. Residents have been known to develop an amazing array of bizarre and disruptive behaviors which are maintained in frequency by the accidental reinforcement provided by the staff.

Extinction. Since most bizarre and disruptive behaviors are maintained by the reinforcement they receive, the most crucial requirement for eliminating such behaviors is to eliminate their reinforcement. This is called *extinction*.

When a behavior is being extinguished, it should receive *no* reinforcement. The most common type of reinforcement provided accidentally is *staff attention*. Staff must learn to *ignore undesirable behavior*. This is a difficult job, and one which requires practice. It means: act as though the resident were not there. Do not *touch* the resident, *talk to* the resident, or even *look at* the resident. If possible walk away—even out of the room.

As a rule, only desirable behavior should receive staff attention. This means that staff should not talk to residents about their misbehavior. Even a scolding or reprimanding may act as a reinforcer. If staff members attempt to reprimand an individual repeatedly and try to remind him not to misbehave again, the resident may discover that an instance of misbehavior sets the occasion for an unending stream of reinforcing staff conversations throughout the day.

In applying extinction procedures, it is important that staff keep in mind that the immediate effects of behavioral consequences may be the reverse of their long-term effects. If the rate or intensity of undesirable behavior increases when extinction is begun, staff should not think that this indicates failure. Actually, it suggests that the procedure *is beginning to work*. This reaction of frustration indicates that the offender does perceive the altered consequences of his behavior. Just as we will shake a vending machine when it fails to deliver its goods, so the head-banger who does not get the attention he wants may bang his head a bit harder.

In some behavioral situations total extinction of the undesirable behavior may be either impractical or insufficient. When it is impractical, and some attention must be given to the undesirable behavior (i.e. to protect residents or staff), that attention should be held to a minimum. It is essential that residents be able to receive more reinforcement for good behavior than for bad behavior. The use of additional procedures may be necessary to eliminate some undesirable behaviors.

INCOMPATIBLE BEHAVIOR

The most useful method of eliminating an undesirable behavior is to extinguish that behavior and concurrently to reinforce some incompatible behavior. That is, we attack the problem on two fronts simultaneously. This double approach will increase the speed of the treatment program.

On the one hand, extinction procedures will cause the undesirable behavior to occur less frequently. On the other hand, reinforcement of some incompatible desirable behavior reduces the opportunities for engaging in the undesirable behavior. This technique of strengthening some positive alternative behavior is a very powerful therapeutic tool.

The reinforcement of incompatible behavior sounds easy, but there are some difficulties in achieving its implementation. It simply fails to fit in well with the medical model of reacting to the symptoms of a disorder. It may be difficult to convince some that with behavior a pathological symptom may disappear if it is ignored and that therapeutic efforts will best succeed if they focus on characteristics of the individual other than his presenting symptoms.

Whenever someone suggests some behavior to be eliminated, it is always reasonable and valuable to ask the question, "What would you prefer that the resident do?" The answer to this question tells us what positive, desirable behavior we should reinforce to help eliminate the undesirable behavior. In some cases the answer will be obvious; in others we will have to create some new alternate behavior. In general, it is a good idea to provide access to the same reinforcer which maintained the misbehavior, but not as a consequence of the desirable alternative behavior.

Virtually any desirable behavior to be reinforced will be in some way incompatible with misbehavior. Some will be incompatible in a rather indirect way by occupying the individual's time. Others will be more directly incompatible, in the sense of its being physically impossible for an individual to perform both behaviors.

For example, in one situation an elderly male resident had developed the habit of urinating on other residents' beds or in their dressers during the day. The obviously desired alternative was that he should urinate in the toilet. The therapeutic program involved periodically taking the resident into the bathroom and reinforcing him for properly using the toilet. In conjunction with this reinforcement of incompatible desirable behavior, it was also necessary to ensure that the resident received no reinforcing staff attention as a consequence of his misbehavior.

In other situations a desirable alternative behavior is less obvious. One profoundly retarded woman held her hand several inches in front of her face and stared at her palm when staff attempted to work with her. The frequency of staring at her hand declined when staff worked with her on a visual-motor coordination task requiring that she keep her hands occupied in order to finish it and be reinforced. Thus, picking some arbitrary behavior which required that the resident use her hands succeeded in reducing her aberrant staring.

Similarly, in the case of a resident who bangs his head against the wall, there is no obviously desirable behavior to substitute for the offending behavior (except the "non-behavior" of sitting quietly and doing nothing). In this case systematic reinforcement and development of just about any behavior may serve to reduce the head-banging. Extinction of the misbehavior itself, combined with reinforcement for participation in a variety of group teaching activities, is often successful in eliminating self-abuse or self-stimulation.

The fact that deviant behavior may tend to develop as an attention-getting technique in situations where little reinforcement is available (e.g. an overcrowded, understaffed ward) explains why it is both impractical and impossible to expect residents to sit quietly all day. If reinforcement is not provided for desirable behavior, the residents will improvise some form of undesirable behavior to gain staff attention. Certain types of deviant behavior are almost certain to require staff attention, despite any ongoing attempt at extinction of the offending behavior (e.g. aggression). In such cases, where the complete extinction of the undesirable behavior is impossible, the reinforcement of some alternative behavior is a crucial element in the therapeutic approach. Here the essential factor is that the residents receive more reinforcement for desirable behavior than for undesirable behavior. Thus, even when complete extinction of the undesirable behavior is not feasible, reinforcement of incompatible behavior may bring success.

Though reinforcement of incompatible behavior and extinction are powerful techniques for eliminating undesirable behavior, occasionally the need is felt for more stringent procedures. As already mentioned, the tendency for most staff is a desire to do something *when the offending behavior occurs.* The two procedures discussed next are for use at this time—when the offense occurs. It is important that they be used consistently, and immediately contingent upon an offense.

TIME OUT

One effective way of dealing with an instance of undesirable behavior is to introduce a period of *time out from reinforcement.* This means more than extinction. It involves a direct attempt to *eliminate reinforcement from any source for any reason for a short period of time.* Thus, the consequence of misbehavior is the loss of any opportunity to gain reinforcement. Generally, this involves some form of social isolation for the duration of the time out. This can be accomplished in a number of ways, depending upon the situation.

Sometimes the offender can, as in extinction, be completely ignored—not looked at, talked to, or touched. Even more effective is to walk away abruptly. Either of these approaches might be used if working with a resident on a one-to-one basis when the undesirable behavior occurs. For example, if one is talking with a resident and suddenly the resident starts pounding on a table or yelling, one should turn and leave just as suddenly.

In some situations, social isolation of an offender may require his removal from a particular area. For example, if a resident were to start banging on a table or yelling in a group teaching room, one might remove the resident from the teaching table and seat him in a corner facing the wall for five minutes. Such a procedure is often effective with the less disruptive residents. Of course, the disruption experienced by the other residents present must always be minimized, while at the same time minimizing the reinforcement which they provide to the offender. So, if taking the offender away from the table is ineffective, expelling him from the room might work. It is necessary, in this case, that the resident normally receive reinforcement in the group teaching room. The purpose of time out is to remove the chance for reinforcement immediately following misbehavior. Time out will only be effective if the offenders go *from* a place of reinforcement *to* a place of non-reinforcement. Thus, for most people it would not be an effective time out procedure to expel them from a dentist's chair for being noncooperative.

Similar to expulsion from an area in which reinforcement can be earned is expulsion from the entire environment—or temporary isolation. This is often accomplished by means of a "time out room," which usually is a small room where an individual can be confined for a short period with minimal but humane furnishings. The qualification "short period" must be emphasized. The duration of a time out should be only about five to ten minutes.

Expulsion from an area and the use of a time out room will both require some staff interaction with the resident. It is important that this interaction be handled so as to minimize its reinforcing aspects. Staff should try to avoid looking at or talking to the resident in the process of expelling him or taking him to the time out room. The time out room should be nearby, or going to it will require too long an interaction. There should be little or no delay between the misbehavior and the beginning of time out. The resident should be told simply why he is being put in the time out room, and that after he has quieted down, he may return.

Once an individual is in time out staff must be certain not to provide any reinforcement. A one-way viewing screen should be available for checking on the occupant of the time out room so as not to provide excessive attention. There should be no talking to the resident inside. At the end of the short fixed period the resident should be released, provided his misbehavior has stopped. If misbehavior continues inside the time out room (e.g. banging, yelling), release should be delayed until this stops. The rationale here, of course, is to be certain that misbehavior inside the time out room is not reinforced by release from the room. Aside from this consideration, increasing the duration of time out will not appreciably increase its effectiveness. Indeed, extended periods of social isolation or seclusion (as non-therapeutic isolation is called in institutions) often make the patient's behavior worse.

When an individual is released from time out, it is essential that no grudges be held by the staff. They should attempt to act as though the episode never occurred. Reinforcement for proper behavior must be readily available to the returning offender. The whole purpose of a time out procedure is to limit reinforcement loss to a brief period immediately following some misbehavior. Normal reinforcement must be available immediately upon return to the normal situation. The reinforcement which is made available, however, must be for desirable behavior only. Staff must continue not to discuss the misbehavior with the resident or scold or reprimand him. Otherwise the risk is run that the misbehavior may be reinforced and occur more frequently in the future. While reinforcement must be readily available to residents as soon as their time out period is over, that reinforcement must be only for adaptive behavior and must not be related in any way to their misbehavior.

The general technique of time out has been shown by experience and by research to be a very valuable tool for the elimination of undesirable behavior. When the procedure is properly used, it raises no ethical objections. Any risk of misuse of a time out room can be minimized by setting proper rules and requiring that records be kept of time out room use. Rules should specify the duration of time out (five to ten minutes), the contingencies for release, and should clearly indicate which misbehaviors warrant time out (e.g. physical attacks, breaking objects, continual disruptive screaming). Records should indicate the times the resident enters and leaves the room, a description of his offense, and an identification of the staff responsible.

PUNISHMENT

Punishment is the delivery of an unpleasant (usually painful) consequence following a behavior in order to make it less likely that the behavior will be repeated. This definition makes punishment sound like the ideal technique for eliminating behavior. However, for ethical, humane, and practical reasons, the use of punishment is discouraged. The risks of its misuse are too great, and, generally, milder techniques seem more appropriate for handling problems of misbehavior. In addition, except in the most carefully planned and supervised situations, punishment may be used improperly or may produce unwanted side effects, e.g. increased hostility.

Officially the use of punishment in institutions is rare. Unofficially, however, its use may be frequent in some institutions. This unofficial use of punishment is sometimes called patient abuse. Its elimination can be one of the beneficial results of making effective behavior change procedures available to staff via the introduction of behavior modification programming.

On rare occasions punishment has been found to be the therapeutic technique of choice with certain types of behavior disorders. For individuals with severe self-destructive behavior, e.g. some autistic children, punishment may eliminate self-mutilation when other techniques would be unsuccessful. It may not be safe to try to extinguish this type of misbehavior. Recall that when extinction of a behavior is begun its rate and intensity may *increase* for a while—seemingly a frustration effect. When the behavior is self-mutilation, there is the real risk that the individual may injure or kill himself as a result. Thus, other behavior elimination techniques are necessary. However, it is only after all other techniques have failed, and the maladaptive behavior is seriously damaging to the patient or others around him, that punishment should be considered.

The rules for application of corporal punishment are basically the same as those for reinforcement. The punishment must be delivered consistently, and immediately contingent upon the misbehavior. A further rule concerning punishment is that it should be intense. If the punishment is too weak, it will not be effective. If the intensity is gradually increased, the patient may adapt to it. Therefore, start intensely. Clinical investigators have thus far generally used a brief, harmless, but quite intense electric shock.

Because of the ethical problems involved, no one should ever initiate a procedure involving punishment without thorough administrative clearance. Programs will best focus on the development of desirable behavior through reinforcement, combined with use of the milder elimination procedures when necessary.

It may be misleading to the reader to have so much space devoted to a discussion of behavior elimination procedures, when in fact the overwhelming emphasis of programs should always be on the teaching of desirable behaviors. The justification can only be that elimination problems, when they arise, may threaten serious injury to the patient, and will be very important and sometimes irritating to the staff. It is necessary that adequate procedures be available and that staff know how to handle these problems.

Bibliography

The following selected sources can provide further information on the therapeutic application of behavior modification principles:

Ayllon, T., and N. Azrin. *The Token Economy: A Motivational System for Therapy and Rehabilitation.* New York: Appleton-Century-Crofts, 1968.

Bensberg, G. (Ed.). *Teaching the Mentally Retarded: A Handbook for Ward Personnel.* Atlanta: Southern Regional Education Board, 1965.

Journal of Applied Behavior Analysis. Published quarterly by the Society for the Experimental Analysis of Behavior, Ann Arbor, Michigan, 1968ff.

Larsen, L. A., and W. A. Bricker. A manual for parents and teachers of severely and moderately retarded children. *IMRID Papers and Reports,* 1968, 5 (22), J. F. Kennedy Center for Research on Education and Human Development, Nashville, Tennessee.

Meacham, Merle L., and Allen E. Wiesen. *Changing Classroom Behavior: A Manual for Precision Teaching.* Scranton, Penn.: International Textbook Company, 1969.

Ulrich, R., T. Stachnik, and J. Mabry. *Control of Human Behavior: From Cure to Prevention.* Glenview, Ill.: Scott, Foresman and Company, 1970.

Watson, L. Application of operant conditioning techniques to institutionalized severely and profoundly retarded children. *Mental Retardation Abstracts,* 1967, *4,* 1-18.

II
Illustrative programs

3
Initial ward-wide behavior modification programs for retarded children

LEONARD FIELDING

Behavior modification based on consumable reinforcers

From a historical vantage point, early work with the retarded at Faribault State Hospital evolved because of the concomitance of several factors which, at the time each appeared, were seemingly unrelated.

The existence of a "bad press" had been a reality for at least two decades. During the legislative sessions in the 1966-67 biennium, the Minnesota Association for Retarded Children exerted pressure for the creation of a separate Division of Mental Retardation within the State Department of Public Welfare. Although this was not accomplished, the pressure created priority conditions in mental retardation programs. Secondly, the unfortunate poor start in the use of operant techniques, resultant publicity, and subsequent development of Minnesota Guidelines for Operant Conditioning (Lucero, Vail, and Scherber, 1968) established treatment rules which would prevent, were they followed in program design, later in-process interference and interruption. The appointment of a young, psychiatrically unsophisticated Medical Director, whose background was basically pragmatic, led to a favorable attitude at the medical-administration level. At the same time, an Institutional Program Coordinator was appointed whose abilities as an expediter and implementer were well known and whose detailed follow-up reduced to a minimum the administrative and logistic problems usually encountered in dramatic program changes. The appointment of a new Hospital Administrator, highly experienced in the development of effective communication systems and administrative activities within government institutions, was essential for the changes in staff attitudes needed to carry out these programs.

The presence of funded federal projects, including an Education Title I Grant, provided the necessary personnel with which it would be possible, given administrative support, to develop a specific demonstration program which would point up the value of using behavior modification techniques.

A number of factors were considered prior to implementation of a specific demonstration program:

1. The project to be undertaken would have to flow smoothly without necessitating intensive training and educating of line staff or middle-management staff* in behavior modification theory, terminology, and techniques.

2. The project would have to be one which would not usurp large amounts of the line staff's time.

3. The project design would have to be such that all of the residents in the ward population were involved as rapidly as possible. This led to the development of "administrative application" techniques using a staff ratio of one line staff to five residents. For the duration of the demonstration portion of the program, individual application programs were removed from consideration.

4. The project design would have to operate so that at the terminal end the condition necessary for training behaviors on an individual basis could continue, using the number of personnel available for treatment.

5. Finally, the project selected would have to clearly show a

---

* Line staff includes psychiatric technicians; middle-management staff includes supervisory nurses, unit directors, and others responsible for supervising line staff.

marked change in the residents' behavior in the area where the demonstration took place. This would have to be demonstrable not only in a statistical manner, but also obvious to the average person walking through the building.

Local expectations of the program can best be described by the Green Acres Unit Program Director, Mrs. Florence Wangsness, R.N., who at the Regional American Association of Mental Deficiency Convention, Sioux Falls, South Dakota, October 13, 1969, reported:

> What can we do with these residents; where do we start on programming?—it always ended with being glad to get off the ward . . . to me it was just mass confusion with twenty residents milling around and three-fourths of them trying to touch anyone that came on the ward. It just seemed a hopeless situation. . . . In March of 1968, we knew Project Teach* would be starting in Maple [Building]. . . . In April, though we did have a ratio of one staff to about five residents, we still had no program. . . . In October of 1968, we had no idea of where to begin programming for these residents.
>
> Initially a time study was undertaken to determine what was happening with the residents and the ward staff. It was found that much of a technician's time was spent in dressing and *redressing* the residents, dealing with aggressive and inappropriate behavior, and mopping up. There was no time left for programming. Residents who sat quietly on the ward and did not cause any major problems were "appreciated," but ignored. This situation was conducive to neither teaching nor training; the residents did not benefit, and from the staff's point of view, it was not a rewarding place to work. The next step called for a plan of "staff-action." Specific behaviors to be extinguished, or strengthened, were pinpointed for adequate description and then manipulation for treatment purposes. To develop teaching programs, it would be necessary to train the residents to follow simple directions such as "come," "follow me," and "wait quietly." It was at this point that the Building Blocks were begun. Aside from having the residents follow these simple commands another short-term goal was to break the undesirable habit of "clinging"; but at even the outset, the long-term goal was to have each resident become more socially independent.

These factors resulted in a simple stimulus control project, arbi-

* Project Teach was an Educational Title I Program.

Table 3-1

		Maple building	Cedar building
1968			
October	South I:	Block I Block II	
November	South I: North I	Block III Food grabbing extinction program Blocks I and II	* *
December	South II: North II:	Blocks I and II Blocks I and II	
1969			
January	Special program: Charles North I: Block III (started recording results)		Blocks I and II First Time study before saturation staffing and structured programming Food grabbing extinction program
February	South II: Block III North II: Block III Toothbrushing program		
March	first alteration in Block III (a.m. and p.m. check)		
April	Bathing program		"Clothes-on" program
May			Second time study
June			
July			
August	Individual records for Block III		Scheduled toilet training program
September			Face washing program (23 steps)
October	Second alteration in Block III		
November			
December	South II: Block IV token economy		

** Birch Building — extinction of SIB, November 1968.

trarily called Building Blocks I and II. Each Block had as its goal the establishment of progressively greater stimulus control over large samples of productive behavior. They were based on the need for residents to learn to act effectively as a group in congregating at appropriate times, moving from one activity area to another, and developing some degree of patience until staff had time to deal with a resident's individual needs. The Building Blocks had the goal of training the resident to: (a) line up when called by the staff; (b) wait for the remaining residents; (c) move with the designated staff to another area in or out of the building, (d) wait at a predetermined site; and (e) follow the designated staff back into the ward areas. This had to be accomplished without the residents wandering, engaging in self-injurious or aggressive behavior, or disrupting the environment.

Building Blocks I and II were instituted initially in Maple and Cedar Buildings. In Maple there were eighty profoundly and severely retarded hyperactive male residents between the ages of eleven and twenty-one, functioning at a very low level. They resided in two upstairs wards and two downstairs wards, twenty patients in each. Cedar Building housed female residents of comparable description in two wards, thirty in each ward.

LINING UP

Building Block I developed "line up to follow me" behavior. The program was written for a ward housing approximately twenty residents, with one staff member for each group of five to seven residents, plus a "staff leader." The behavior to be taught to the residents was "lining up" in preparation for an event (such as meals, medications, toileting, or activities) and waiting quietly until the signal was given to "follow me." Teaching this behavior required that it be *shaped* when its occurrence was *not* necessary. For instance, "lining up" behavior could be shaped only when it was *not* necessary for the residents to line up to go anywhere. This was because if the residents *had* to be taken to a specific place, the staff got them there by using all the traditional resident "transport" movement techniques.

The equipment used in the program included a whistle to signal "line up"; four or five colored floor markers ten feet long (two feet per resident); consumable reinforcers (e.g. cookies, candy, Pizza Spins); a stop watch; a counter; and one "goodie bag" for each staff member. A whistle was used to gain resident attention since it had minimal similarity to other sounds on the ward such as shouts, name calling, or other efforts to be heard over the din.

The first step of the shaping procedure was to expose each resident to the consumable reinforcer fifteen minutes before the first training period. Depending upon the reinforcer (M & M's, sugar pops, Sudden Action mouth spray, etc.), the amount of initial exposure varied. For each training session one staff member was positioned at the head of each line. The staff leader then blew the whistle and the staff members went to the residents, gave them each one consumable reinforcer, turned away, and indicated by word or motion, "follow me." The staff members then returned to the colored line. Staff were instructed not to *pull* or *touch* the residents. If the resident followed to the line, the staff member would indicate where the resident was to stand on the line. Then the resident was reinforced: he was touched, the words "very good, stay here" were said, and he was given a consumable. If, after several requests, the resident did not follow, the staff member went to the next resident. The staff leader with the whistle blew it again when three minutes had elapsed, and each of the residents who remained on or near the line was given another consumable. The number of residents earning the second reinforcer was counted on each training session. This sequence was repeated ten times at irregular intervals each day until the number of residents coming to the line ceased to increase.

When this plateau was reached, the residents were ready for the next portion of the shaping procedure: to teach the residents to come to the line "on call" rather than being sought out. (The reason for "seeking out" on the earlier training sessions was to give the residents the opportunity to learn that reinforcers could be expected.) Again the staff took their positions at the head of each line, and the whistle was blown. The staff called each resident by name to come up to the line. If the resident came, he was reinforced immediately upon his arrival: he was touched and told to "remain here" while being positioned on the line and then given a consumable reinforcer. The whistle was blown at the end of three minutes or less, depending upon the time at which all the residents had been reinforced once. The residents remaining on or near the line were then reinforced a second time. Those receiving a second reinforcer as well as those receiving a first reinforcer were recorded for each of the training sessions.

When the number of residents coming and remaining in position reached a constant level, these residents were responding nearly 100 per cent of the time. Subsequently, the duration of time elapsing during each training session was progressively increased. In addition, residents were given a consumable only when the whistle was blown the second time, thus eliminating the consumable reinforcer for "coming to the line." The duration of time between the first and second whistle was increased gradually. Consequently, the resident also had to wait to be reinforced. The "waiting" interval was expanded approximately five to ten seconds per training session until the duration reached one minute. After reaching one minute, the interval was expanded fifteen to twenty seconds each training session. Only those residents who waited without pushing, shoving, or shouting were reinforced when the whistle was blown a second time. After the number of residents waiting quietly for four minutes during successive training sessions reached a plateau, Building Block II was started.

FOLLOWING

Building Block II ("follow me") was a natural extension of Block I, since many activities required movement of the residents from their living area to another area on the ward or on the grounds. The residents were to be taught to follow a leader with a minimum of noise, without wandering, and without aggressive interaction. The same staff-resident ratio as in Block I was maintained. The same equipment was used with the addition of another visual discriminative stimulus, a colored and shaped marker (wand) for each group. Again, teaching this behavior was *not* done at times when it was mandatory that the residents move to another area.

Each staff member took his position on the colored line and carried a wand, colored to match the line. When the whistle was blown, the residents approached the line, waited quietly, and were led from the day room area. After the staff said, "follow me," residents who did not follow were not forced or pulled along. Upon arrival at the predetermined destination, the residents were given a consumable. Any wanderers were returned to the ward with a minimum of pulling; they did not have any other social interaction with the staff until the other ward residents returned. Initially, the distances covered were not more than ten yards outside the ward area. These distances were gradually increased as the number of training sessions progressed. To further increase the amount of behavior under control, the reinforcement was given *only* upon return to the ward.

The Block I program was started on one ward of Maple Building in October of 1968. The resident response of "lining up" increased from 53 per cent on the first day to 80 per cent on the tenth day, reaching 100 per cent on day seventeen. The percentage "waiting" four minutes increased from 24 to 56 per cent. In Block II the residents' response, "coming to the line, staying four minutes, going to another area, and returning," increased from 41 to 88 per cent by day sixteen. The patients not responding were programmed individually. They too responded once a reinforcer was identified.

After the initial program was operating successfully on the first ward, other Maple wards instituted the same programs and achieved comparable results. Following the experience in Maple Building, programs were instituted in the same sequence in Cedar Building, again with comparable results.

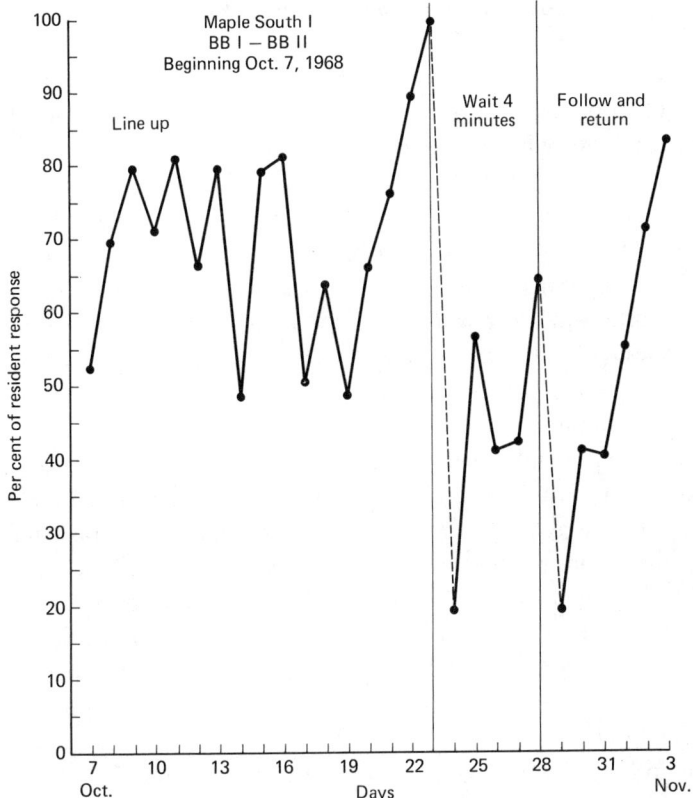

Figure 3-1. Per cent of residents responding during Building Block I procedure which required that the residents come on instruction and the development of behavior of Building Block II which required that the residents come on instruction and wait for four minutes before being reinforced.

The completion of Building Blocks I and II made possible the introduction of other more complex programs, including hand and face washing, toileting, staying dressed, and table manners.

WASHING

In the next step, Building Block III, the behavior desired of the residents was lining up, following the staff to the washing area, and using a "washing mitten" to wash their own faces, ears, neck, and hands. The equipment was the same as that used in Blocks I and II plus the mitten wash cloth and a few fragrant bars of soap. The opportunity to use the soap was reinforcing for many of the residents, who acquired the behavior rapidly.

After the staff members were positioned, each group of residents was led to the wash area. The staff leader assisted the "trainer." One staff member remained on the ward area. To maintain "coming and waiting" behavior, the residents were given a consumable reinforcer just before the command "follow me" on the average of once out of every twelve times the statement was made. On arrival at the wash area, one resident was admitted to the room containing sinks. The trainer in the wash area told the resident to approach the appropriate sink. In view of the resident, a consumable was dropped into the washing mitten. The mitten was held open at the top so that the resident had to put his hand in to obtain the reinforcer. In most cases, the resident withdrew his hand from the mitten after he had grasped the reinforcer. A second reinforcer was then held out so that the resident could see it; as he watched, the reinforcer was "palmed," but it appeared that the consumable had been placed in the mitten. The mitten was held open for the resident, and immediately after he placed his hand in the mitten he received a consumable from the trainer. As the reinforcer was delivered with one hand, the trainer's other hand grasped the wrist of the mittened hand and placed the hand in the warm water in the basin. The trainer then indicated to the resident by motions and words that he should put the wet mitten on his face (the resident *was not forced* to place the mitten on his face). If the resident touched the mitten to his face, another consumable was delivered immediately, thus ending the first training session for this resident. After taking the mitten off, the resident was directed back to the area where the others in his group were quietly waiting. The next resident followed the same procedure. The duration of time in the wash room did not exceed five minutes per resident on any session. Session time was recorded and

WARD-WIDE PROGRAMS FOR CHILDREN

SEQUENCE I
Shaping sequence for face-washing program

1. Approaches sink
2. Puts on mitt
3. Dips mitt in water
4. Touches mitt to face
5. Washes face partially
6. Washes entire face
7. Uses soap when handed him
8. Uses wash cloth
9. Uses was cloth and soap
10. Washes self thoroughly
11. Dries self after washing

used as a rough index of the efficiency with which Block III was being learned.

Later, those residents from each group who responded to the program most rapidly were admitted to the wash room and the earlier steps in the sequence were not reinforced. Finally, the resident was reinforced only for washing his face in a manner approximating the complete behavior.

Building Block III was initiated in November 1968. Fifty-eight per cent of the residents touched the mitten to their faces. Three months later, all of the residents approached the sink and put on

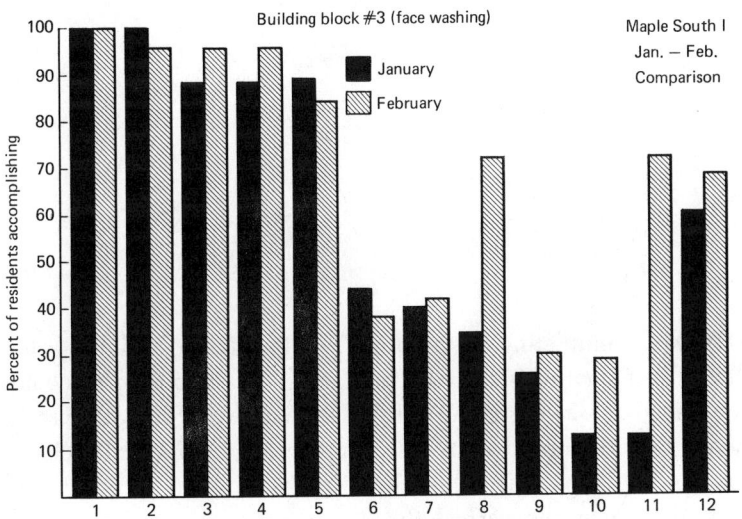

Figure 3-2. Comparison of per cent of residents accomplishing steps during training of face washing for two consecutive months. The eleven steps of this program are listed in Table 3-1.

the mitten. Ninety per cent dipped the mitten in water, touched the mitten to their faces, and washed their faces partially. Less than half the residents washed their entire faces. Thirty-eight per cent of the residents used soap when it was handed to them, 33 per cent progressed to a wash cloth rather than using the mitten, and 28 per cent used a wash cloth and soap. At this time, only 12 per cent of the residents in the program washed their faces entirely and dried themselves after washing. Within the next thirty days, the percentage of residents using wash cloths increased to 70 per cent. Those who washed their faces entirely had doubled, and those who dried after washing increased to 71 per cent.

One year later the program was altered to include twenty steps in the training sequence rather than eleven. Some residents accomplishing a later step in the sequence did so without completing all the preceding steps. For example, one resident, Phillip, accomplished the steps checked below:

SEQUENCE II
Twenty-step face-washing procedure

X	1.	Approaches sink		11.	Washes face thoroughly
	2.	Puts plug in drain	X	12.	Washes ears
X	3.	Runs water		13.	Washes neck
	4.	Picks up soap		14.	Rinses wash-cloth
X	5.	Washes hands		15.	Rinses soap off face, neck, ears
X	6.	Picks up mitten or wash-cloth			
	7.	Puts cloth in water	X	16.	Dries face
	8.	Wrings out wash-cloth		17.	Dries neck
	9.	Soaps wash-cloth		18.	Dries ears
X	10.	Washes face partially	X	19.	Empties sink
			X	20.	Dries hands

Without completing all the steps, Phillip exhibited much of the desired behavior of Block III. There were only two residents who responded at a level significantly lower than that of the other residents. Robert learned steps 1, 6, 7, and 10 which formed a chain for face washing *alone*, while Ricky learned only to approach the sink and pick up the wash cloth.

Two wards in Maple Building began the face-washing program the first week in November 1968. After two months all of the residents approached the sinks when called; 70 per cent washed their faces partially and 60 per cent washed and dried themselves completely. Five months after the program began, 92 per cent of the residents on one ward and 85 per cent of the residents on the other had learned the entire sequence.

ELIMINATING FOOD GRABBING

After Building Block I was functional in Maple Building, *the next staff-determined priority* was to eliminate the residents' "food grabbing" behavior. The goal for the group (eighteen residents) was to have them eat in the dining room without stealing food from each other's plates during the meals. The program design included entry to the dining room as they learned in Block II. Habitual "food grabbers" were seated as close to the entrance as possible. The main portions were served first, and dessert was served last. The floor and tables were cleaned before serving dessert. If a resident grabbed food from another resident's plate, his meal was interrupted and he was sent to the day room area. Residents were weighed weekly. If a resident lost two or more pounds, he was reported to the responsible physician who determined if he should continue on the program. Each meal interrupted was recorded.

This program started in November 1968. The number of resident meals *during* which grabbing occurred in the initial phase of the program averaged 4.4 per day (out of a possible 54). The number of interruptions decreased, until three months later grabbing occurred during only .64 resident-meals per day. The residents' weekly weight records revealed that four of the residents lost two pounds or more during the first four months. Only one of the four had a substantial loss (seven pounds).

Four months later, the staff began recording the number of times a resident grabbed food *after* completing all but dessert. This was in addition to the number of times he "grabbed" during the main portions. The resident was removed from the dining area

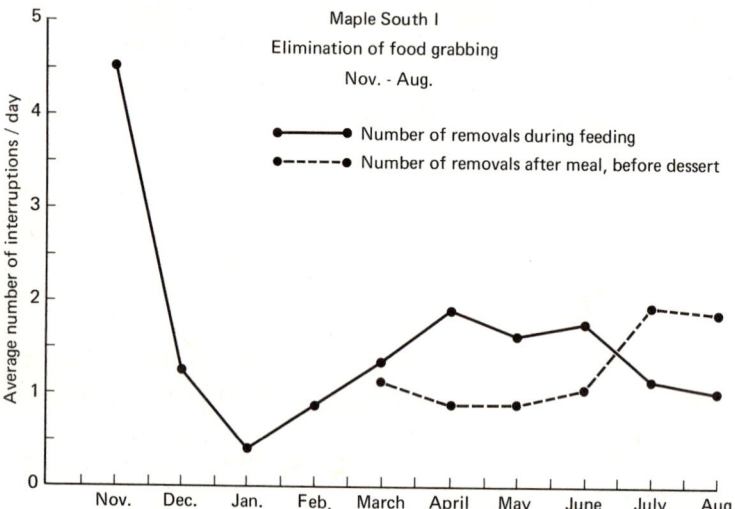

Figure 3-3. Solid line indicates average number of meal interruptions (removal of resident from dining room) and reflects decreased frequency of food grabbing since removal was contingent on emission of food grabbing behavior. Dashed line indicates average number of contingent removals occurring after completion of main course but before dessert.

at either time; if he had completed the main portions, he missed dessert. During this month, removal from the dining room averaged 1.39 resident-meals per day. The number of removals after the main portion accounted for 1.14. Surprisingly, most of the residents gained weight. One boy recorded a weight loss of nine pounds since the first week in March. During the next three months, the average number of meal interruptions remained about the same. Interruptions after the main portion ran slightly lower.

One resident, Charles, was not responding to the standard program. During the first two months, Charles grabbed food at more meals than any other resident: thirteen times in November and seventeen times in December. The standard meal interruption program was unsuccessful with this boy because he usually grabbed *after* he ate the food served him. Besides, he gulped his food in large, rapid mouthfuls. After his food grabbing reached a high of twenty-three meals, Charles' food was divided into six portions. The portions were served one at a time. If Charles did not grab from other residents' plates while eating one portion, he received the next portion, verbal praise, and physical contact. From January to February he lost five pounds, but his physician recommended that he be continued on the program. By the end of April all the weight loss was regained *plus* seven pounds. On the special program Charles grabbed only four times between February and March. He then returned to the standard program. Over the next five months he grabbed food ten times, a significant reduction from the first three months of the program when he had grabbed

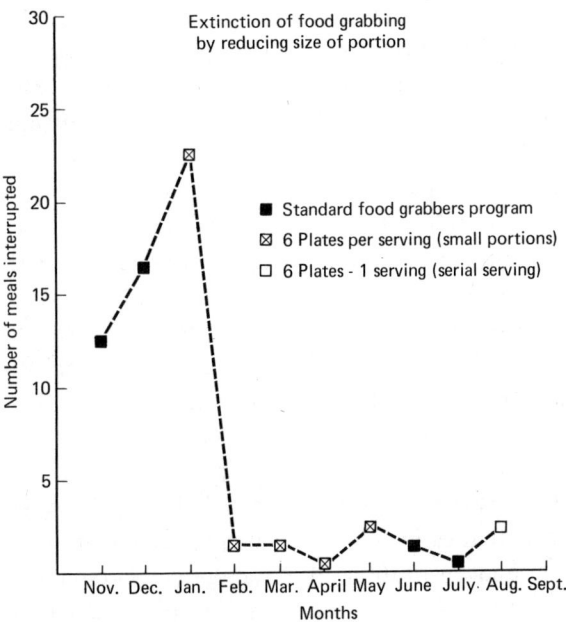

Figure 3-4. Graph indicating ineffectiveness of removal contingency for one resident and subsequent successful elimination of food grabbing behavior using a contingency based on portion size.

food fifty-three times. An interesting sidelight was that Charles, who often regurgitated after meals, ceased having this problem.

TIME STUDY

Before further behavior modification programs for the residents were initiated in Cedar Building, a time study was obtained on each ward (North and South). The purpose of the study was to compare staff-resident interactions before and after the institution of temporary saturation staffing and structured programming. Four twenty-minute periods were sampled each day on each ward. Each of these four samples was taken during different hours. Two samples were obtained in the morning and two in the afternoon. Hours for sampling were selected to include *only* those periods when both residents and staff were in the day rooms. The samples were obtained on three consecutive days by an observer who did not interact with residents or staff. The staff were told that the observer was rating resident behaviors. After the time study, ten psychiatric technician trainees were brought into the building for sixteen consecutive weeks. Standardized programming was initiated on each of the wards. The trainees' activities were directed by nursing education personnel in cooperation with the unit program director and ward charges. In addition to their work assignments, the psychiatric technician trainees received concurrent lectures in behavior modification theory and application. Two weeks following the trainees' departure, a second time study was obtained. In the second study, the samples were taken the same way as the first.

Comparison of the two time studies revealed changes between the original ward activities and those occurring after temporary saturation staffing and institution of structured programming. The number of technician-initiated verbal interactions increased; the number of technician-initiated physical contacts increased slightly on one ward and decreased slightly on the other. Both verbal interactions and physical interactions initiated by the residents decreased in both units. The number of industrial therapy resident-worker initiated verbal interactions increased on one ward and decreased on the other; the number of physical interactions initiated by the resident-workers decreased in both units. The most noticeable change occurred in the incidence of disruptive behaviors: verbal and physical disruptions decreased by a large percentage in both units.

ELIMINATING UNDRESSING BEHAVIOR

One program for residents of Cedar Building was designed to eliminate "undressing" behavior. Baseline data (the cumulative total of four spot checks per day) revealed that every day an average of fifteen residents were unclad or partially unclad, the result of removing or ripping their clothes. The procedure used to eliminate their problem was to *differentially reinforce being dressed*. In the morning, each resident was dressed and given a consumable. If, at the time of one of the spot checks, a resident *had* torn or removed her clothing, she was redressed. The staff would wait until the next time a spot check occurred and reinforce the resident if she was still dressed. Verbal praise, staff attention and contact, and consumables were used as reinforcers, depending upon each resident. During the first two weeks of the program, there was an average of eight girls undressed at the time the "check" was made each day. This average fell during the next four weeks, but climbed back up to eight unclad girls during the seventh week. The number decreased to four or five unclad girls each day from the eleventh through the fourteenth weeks. By the seventeenth week the average number of girls who were unclad or partially unclad at the check times dropped to less than three per pay. From the nineteenth through the twenty-first weeks of the program, undressing occurred on the average less than once a day. By the twenty-sixth week, no girls were unclad at the times of the checks. The program was continued another fifteen weeks. Undressing occurred at a much lower frequency than at the start

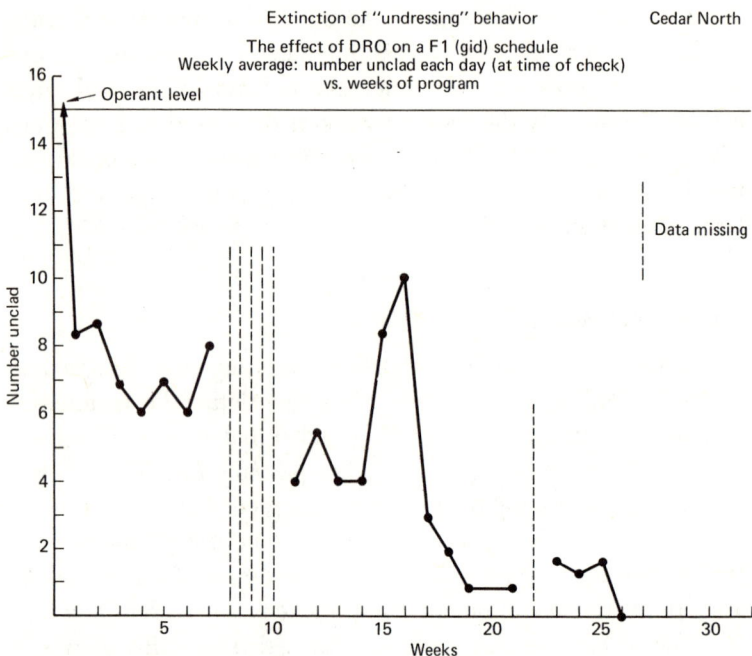

Figure 3-5. Decreased frequency of the appearance of unclad residents as the result of a procedure which differentially reinforced being dressed.

of the program. Less time was invested redressing unclad girls, fewer clothes required mending or discarding. The staff, no longer uneasy about permitting visitors on the ward, had more time to spend teaching increasingly complex behaviors.

TOILET SCHEDULING

Several months after the program to eliminate food grabbing was well under way in Maple Building, Cedar Building established a similar program with roughly similar results. Cedar Building instituted a number of other behavior modification procedures in addition to the elimination of food grabbing. Some of these were individual while others concerned the entire ward or building population. Mopping floors and wiping furniture consumed much of the staff's time since many of the residents were not toilet trained. Had better toilet training taken place, staff time could have been used for other training purposes. Each time a resident had an "accident," showering and redressing in clean clothes was necessary. The toilet scheduling program was intended to reduce the frequency of accidents and move residents in the direction of independent toileting. Specific times were designated in the morning, afternoon, and evening for toilet training. This procedure was followed consistently every day to maintain the schedule and strengthen the behavior. Building Blocks I and II were used to get the residents to the bathroom and then take their turn

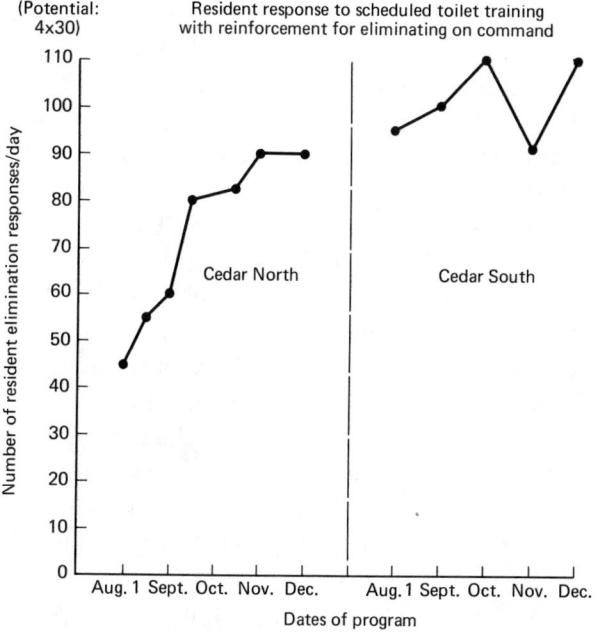

Figure 3-6. Increasing frequency of the number of appropriate elimination responses resulting from scheduled toilet training. Though not illustrated, a correlated decrease in the frequency of "accidents" occurred.

on the stool in an orderly manner. The program involved shaping techniques: these residents were reinforced for (1) entering the bathroom; (2) sitting on the toilet; and (3) voiding. When a resident did void on schedule, she was reinforced with praise and an edible. If she sat for any length of time and did not void, she was not reinforced and was asked to return to the day room. The data from one ward depict a major change in the frequency of scheduled elimination from August to December 1969. In August, when the program began, there were only 45 responses per day (out of 120 potential responses). In December, there were 90 responses or a twofold increase per day. A similar improvement, though not as large, was noted on the other ward. The residents there began the program at a higher level.

BATHING

In April of 1969, Maple Building instituted a bathing program for the residents. Each staff member was assigned two or three residents with whom to work. Each boy was worked with individually and taught to do as much for himself as possible. The behavior was shaped gradually in sequential steps. The procedure was similar to that of the face-washing program. Data were collected for the number of steps each boy would complete and whether he was cooperative, uncooperative, or showed no interest. When the program began, only twelve of the eighteen residents included in the program were cooperative; only four of these could perform half the steps in the sequence. Four boys were uncooperative but could complete some of the steps; two boys showed no interest in self-bathing. After six months some improvement was evident. Nine boys completed half the steps; six of the nine could perform more than six steps in the chain. There were only two boys having difficulty; one was uncooperative but still accomplished four steps. The other boy completed two steps though he still showed no interest in self-bathing per se. Of the group, 75 per cent of the Maple south ward residents showed

---

Bathing Evaluation   Name _____   Date _____

Directions: Check below the level at which the resident is now functioning. Mark only if he can accomplish the step. Do not add any additional comments.

( ) Undresses
( ) Gets in tub by self
( ) Uses wash-cloth
( ) Uses soap
( ) Starts to wash self
( ) Washes self completely
( ) Dries self
( ) Dresses

( ) Completes entire bathing procedure (steps 1-8)
( ) Puts soap and wash-cloth away, cleans tub and area after bathing
( ) Cooperative
( ) Shows no interest
( ) Uncooperative

Staff Initial _____

---

progress. Billy showed the most progress, going from step three to seven in the six-month period. As a result of the program, on both wards the boys are more self-sufficient at bathing. The staff can now attend to one resident's toileting while "supervising" another boy as he bathes.

Besides the bathing program, the Maple staff instituted other self-care programs, including shaving and toothbrushing. In the latter program, only half the boys did an adequate job with supervision in February 1969. By April, over three-fourths of the boys (79 per cent) were doing well with electric toothbrushes.

Token systems

A basic problem in shaping complex behavior in severely or profoundly retarded children is to develop effective, durable reinforcement. Consumable and recreation-type rewards show large individual differences. A possible solution to this problem is token reinforcement. There is much evidence to suggest that tokens have been very effective in training self-help and social responses in severely and profoundly retarded residents.

Watson, Lawson, and Saunders (1965a) illustrated the value of poker chips as tokens. At Columbus State School they trained fourteen severely and profoundly retarded males (mean C.A. = 11.0, mean I.Q. = 23.1) to operate a vending machine for candy or visual/auditory stimuli. The subjects were allowed to choose the primary reinforcements holding highest incentive value for them. The machine-operating response was strong and lasting. The staff found it easier to teach a profoundly retarded child to operate a machine than to trade tokens at a store. A machine also provides a reliable and objective method to assess reinforcement preferences and incentive value (Watson, Lawson, and Saunders, 1965b).

Auxter (1969) used secondary reinforcement to establish muscle coordination and play behaviors in retarded and emotionally disturbed children. Ten boys (aged nine to twelve years) progressed from marble tokens to token money to social reinforcement. For some of the boys, proficiency charts provided the incentive. With automated or human exchangers, tokens have proven useful secondary reinforcers for some populations.

In a special cottage program instituted at Parsons State Hospital and Training Center in Kansas, retarded girls with I.Q.'s ranging from 20 to 45 were taught self-care and social skills through token reinforcement (Girardeau and Spradlin, 1964). The girls earned tokens by exhibiting productive behaviors, e.g. dressing, face washing, hair combing. The tokens were exchanged at a small "store" for candy, hair clips, perfume, crayons, and paper.

An extensive ward-wide token economy program was established at Anna State Hospital, Illinois, which provided a pattern for other institutions (Ayllon and Azrin, 1968). The environment there was an open system. For many of the patients (who had been hospitalized for a long time) the strongest reinforcers were activities outside the ward, e.g. movies, dances, visits, employment. Thus, a closed system was not only impractical, it was impossible.

The Anna State Hospital experiment provided several guidelines for subsequent token economies in other institutions: (1)

The ward staff should teach only those behaviors that will continue to be reinforced after training. (2) The staff should observe each individual to discover what he does when the opportunity exists. These activities may be reinforcers (Premack, 1959). (3) Tokens can be used to bridge the time delay between the appropriate response and the primary reinforcer. (4) Residents should be given a clear understanding of the behavior expected of them. (5) Initially, the residents' behavior may need to be shaped.

Recent reports indicate diverse applications of token reinforcement programs. At Dixon State School in Illinois, token reinforcement programs administered by psychiatric aides have been successful with the mentally ill and the retarded and have relieved the administration problems of operant programs due to the shortage of professional personnel (Brierton, Garms, and Metzger, 1969). The Dixon staff maintained graphs for a twenty-eight-resident cottage, enabling the investigators to identify periods during which performance was relatively poor. Any declarations in performance could be compared with a day-by-day history of the changes introduced during the project as well as with other events impinging on the program. The data also provided information which was used to solve some of the problems inherent in a token economy. The Dixon project clearly demonstrated that aides could handle token exchange responsibilities. The investigators identified two factors which result in a drop in performance: (a) environmental changes deliberately introduced by the experimenters; and (b) token satiation. These factors have to be considered before a token economy can be extended. The Maple and Cedar staffs in Green Acres Unit at Faribault State Hospital have done this.

AT FARIBAULT

Using techniques similar to those established in institutions previously mentioned, a ward-wide token economy program called Building Block IV was established. In one ward nineteen severely and profoundly retarded male residents were chosen. They had a paucity of behaviors necessary to maintain personal hygiene and very few social interactions. One of the goals of the token program was to help them to become more independent and also more cooperative. Building Block IV was designed in accord with the principle of positive reinforcement for appropriate behaviors. It utilized some of the behaviors taught in Blocks I and II.

Initially, the behaviors to be reinforced on a priority basis were defined in considerable detail. It was expected that shaping methods would be involved. The level of "correct performance" or accomplishment required of each resident depended on his functional level at the time the program began. The requirements became more stringent as the program progressed. Chaining was also employed extensively.

The specific behaviors were grouped into classes, as follows:

Industrial therapy behaviors

Makes own bed
Mops floor
Sweeps floor
Moves furniture
Cleans furniture
Does errands

Resident care behaviors

Helps dress others
Helps with baths
Helps brush teeth
Ties shoes for others

Cooperative behaviors

Shares toys
Plays with others

Compliant behaviors

Comes to caller
Goes to hall on request
Goes to dorm or bed on request
Goes to dining room on request
Carries tray without spilling

Self-care behaviors

Goes to bathroom
Puts on clothes
Laces shoes
Washes face
Washes hands
Brushes teeth

After the behaviors were defined and grouped, the staff selected specific behaviors having high or low strengths and collected baseline data. The residents remained in their assigned groups. No particular behavioral characteristic was used for grouping. It was stipulated to the staff before the start of the program that no *current* resident privileges could be rescinded nor any medical services curtailed. Finally, a geographic area was specified for initial exposure to the token economy.

To establish the "value" of the token, one staff member was placed at Position A. He would call, "_____, come over here." If the resident who was called complied, he was given a token. Records were kept for compliance, token dispensation, and token exchange under trial-run conditions. After the resident received the token, a second staff member in Position B (initially next to Position A) took the token from the resident and exchanged it for a reinforcer, usually a consumable. The distance between Positions A and B was progressively increased with each training session. B moved toward the "company store" while A remained in the initial position. The rate of movement for B depended upon maintaining a constant level of resident response for exchanging tokens. When B finally arrived at the "company store" area, a display-exchange cabinet offering a variety of items was used.

Initially, tokens were not distributed unless they were going to be redeemed immediately. As the training sessions progressed, increasingly longer delays occurred between token dispensation and opening the "company store." After resident token retention reached one hour, token distribution began for some of the specific behaviors already listed. Token reinforcement was not undertaken for all behaviors at once, but only for those which were already occurring at relatively high strength. The list was expanded to include priority behaviors (staff opinion) after the token economy was running smoothly as demonstrated by the residents' token retention and token exchange rates.

When the program began in December 1969, all residents came when called. Thus, each received a token and exchanged it immediately. After the token retention distance exceeded 25 feet, one resident failed to exchange the token, but only during the morning training session. When the distance between A and B reached 39 feet, two other residents responded at a lower frequency. By the fifth week of the program, when the distance between A and B had reached 120 feet, only two residents were failing to respond 100 per cent of the time.

Five months later, the boys were receiving tokens for additional behaviors. Hair combing, washing, dressing, bed making, and eating behaviors were recorded daily for each boy. The records were then translated into token payments. Token reinforcement appeared to have a favorable effect on the residents' behavior. Between 60 and 90 per cent of those receiving tokens redeemed them following a thirty-minute delay interval.

In February 1970 the Cedar staff instituted a token economy program for some of their girls. Twenty-five older residents (also severely and profoundly retarded) who were chosen for the project learned the value of a token. Twenty-three of the twenty-five retained them consistently for ninety minutes after traveling 97 feet. When the program began, over 80 per cent of the girls already came when they were called, and 75 per cent retained and traded the token for consumable reinforcement. Five weeks later, 96 per cent of the girls were receiving tokens, and 88 per cent exchanged them for a consumable. At the end of five weeks *all* the girls came when called and received a token. The token exchange behavior increased to 90 per cent. At the time of this writing the staff still conducts token sessions and operates the "store." Some individual programs are being designed and others are in process.

Two girls were placed on individual token programs. Each girl earned a token for washing sinks, a token for helping put shoes on another resident, and a token for helping dress another resident. During the first week, Virginia, one of the residents, earned four tokens and Cheryl earned three. The girls were allowed to redeem them immediately if they wished. Cheryl washed sinks and dressed patients during the second week, earning nine tokens. Virginia earned six tokens performing the same tasks. During the second week they had to retain their tokens for one hour before exchanging them at the "store." During the third week the required token retention duration was increased to two hours. Cheryl earned ten tokens, but Virginia earned only five. In addition to washing sinks and dressing residents, other reinforceable behaviors have increased. Extra tokens can be earned for assisting with bathing or drying other residents and also for cleaning the rug with the carpet sweeper. It is possible for each of the girls to earn five tokens each day or a weekly total of thirty-five.

Aside from the progress made in Maple and Cedar, the hospital has also instituted an industrial therapy resident-worker token economy program. This has been done successfully at other institutions with several types of residents, including the retarded. Although some institutions have charged tokens for "food" or for a "place to sleep," the Faribault program allows the working residents to earn tokens at the work site which are exchanged for scrip (a provisional certificate of money) later in the day at their living quarters, and finally, the scrip is exchanged for actual money in the patients' bank accounts. Thus, the working residents receive reinforcement immediately at the work site and social reinforcement upon arrival "home," and they have the opportunity to learn money handling, counting, and banking procedures in preparation for coping with the real world when they are discharged.

As a result of the individual and group programs, the youngsters progressed from being helpless "custodial patients" to more self-sufficient, independent, and "socialized" human beings. Various people visiting Maple and Cedar Buildings during ensuing months noticed the marked change in resident behavior. The lack of "hanging and tugging" behavior is particularly impressive as are the improved living conditions. The change in attitude toward work and toward the residents is much improved. The atmosphere of these buildings has changed. Each of the improvements noted favorably by an "outsider" is a reinforcer for the Green Acres staff.

References

Atthowe, J. M. Ward 113 research and service program: staff orientation and procedure manual for administering the token-incentive program. An unpublished manuscript written at Veterans Administration Hospital, Palo Alto, California, October 1964.

Auxter, D. Operant conditioning of motor skills for the emotionally disturbed. *American Corrective Therapy Journal,* 1969, *23* (1), 28-31.

Ayllon, T., and N. H. Azrin. *The Token Economy.* N.Y.: Appleton-Century-Croft, 1968.

Brierton, G., R. Garms, and R. Metzger. Practical problems encountered in an aide-administered token reward cottage program. *Mental Retardation,* 1969, *7* (3), 40-43.

Girardeau, F. L., and J. E. Spradlin. Token rewards in a cottage program. *Mental Retardation,* 1964, *2* (6), 345-51.

Lloyd, K. E., and W. K. Garlington. Weekly variations in performance of a token economy psychiatric ward. *Behavior Research and Therapy,* 1968, *6* (4), 407-10.

Lucero, R. J., D. J. Vail, and J. Scherber. Regulating operant conditioning programs. *Hospital and Community Psychiatry,* 1968, *19* (2), 53-54.

Premack, D. Toward empirical behavioral laws: I. positive reinforcement. *Psychological Review,* 1959, *66,* 219-33.

Watson, L. S., R. Lawson, and C. Sanders. Generalized or token reinforcement with severely and profoundly retarded children. Paper read at AAMD, Miami, 1965(a).

———. Primary reinforcement preferences of mentally and profoundly mentally retarded children in a generalized reinforcement context. Paper read at APA, Chicago, 1965(b).

4
A behavior modification program for behaviorally retarded institutionalized males

JOHN GRABOWSKI AND TRAVIS THOMPSON

Introduction

Most large publicly supported institutions to which retarded individuals are committed have on their grounds a building which houses the "worst" residents. This building is viewed differently from different vantage points. It is frequently feared by staff and residents alike in other buildings, who in one case fear being sent to work there or in the other fear punishment by confinement there. It may be the source of intriguing tales for staff members who do work in the building. Eager newspapermen may exploit an institution's "worst" building for a story based on the conditions in the "snake pit." This may have beneficial effects or more commonly will lead to further suppression of the fact that the building exists, and it may even lead to barring visitors. To whatever extent possible, buildings of this sort are ignored by those who may be responsible for their existence. On occasion the problems of individual residents may be dealt with by a few staff members at various levels and/or of various disciplines.

Conditions in the "worst" building can be most effectively changed when it is acknowledged as a disaster area. In 1969 Dakota Building at Faribault State Hospital exhibited many of the symptoms of the "worst" building syndrome. It was the object of fear, intriguing stories, newspaper exposés, and occasionally the constructive activities of some staff members.

THE ESTABLISHMENT AND MAINTENANCE OF THE "WORST" BUILDING

The development and maintenance of the behavior of residents confined to a building such as Dakota are not the result of an undefinable process. Historically, the prevailing attitude has been that custodial care is the only reasonable treatment for the profoundly or severely mentally retarded (see Chapter 1). That is, these residents received food and clothing, and the staff maintained relatively sanitary conditions through frequent mopping of floors and equally frequent changing of residents' clothing. Residents were usually confined to Dakota Building as a result of assaultive, destructive, or self-injurious behavior and lack of self-care skills. The repeated transferring of problem residents to Dakota Building produced an impossible situation. Most of the residents in the building were outcasts from other buildings and only infrequently was admission to the hospital followed by immediate confinement in Dakota Building. The introduction of a resident, who had perhaps engaged in only one maladaptive episode, into a brutal environment had predictable effects. The resident either learned to counteract brutality in kind or became self-abusive, isolated, and passive. The repetition of this sequence produced a building inhabited almost exclusively by such residents.

The problem was compounded by the fact that the staff training program was oriented to custodial and medical care (i.e. dispensing a wide range of tranquilizing drugs and treating assault or self-induced trauma*), so that on-ward time was consumed primarily by medical and custodial care. Once classified as se-

* It is interesting to note that the phrase "symptomatic treatment" often leveled at behavior modification techniques is better exemplified by the care and treatment programs presently existing in many state institutions, that is, the philosophy which consists of caring for the hyperactivity with drugs, bandaging the cuts and bruises, but not dealing with the environmental and behavioral factors leading to the medical problems.

verely or profoundly mentally retarded, a resident was much less likely to be discharged or transferred to another building. Professional staff members providing special services were hardly eager to establish treatment programs for such residents because of the behavior problems they presented. Even those residents who were not assaultive urinated or defecated in their clothing, did not wear clothing, or masturbated incessantly. Their maladaptive behavior was obviously incompatible with engaging in activities outside the building or with effective training within the building. Even if this attitude did not prevail, professional staff members are reinforced by the progress of their patients, and the rate of progress of such residents was insufficient to reinforce the staff.

CHANGE

The medical director and the program coordinator, with the support of a new hospital administrator, initiated the recovery plan for Dakota Building. While administrative backing is essential in the initiation of programs, it is consistent support from the building staff that ensures establishment and continuation of the programs. Cooperation from this group was not instantaneous. Over the years, the staff in Dakota Building had been required to carry out numerous evaluations and had been asked to initiate a variety of limited therapeutic procedures with individual patients or groups. When the expected success was not forthcoming, the designer of the plan departed and the staff resumed the previous system. Repeated incidents of this sort served only to strengthen the view that "nothing could be done." Consequently, the staff members were initially resistant to changing the custodial care system which had been no less effective than the many "special" procedures which had been periodically introduced and terminated. Only through the cooperation of the building nurse and the social worker and the evidence of progress achieved did the staff find continued effort worthwhile. It became clear to the staff that the strategy of the promoters was to modify the program as a function of results. Failures in a given area resulted not in termination of the whole program (as some had hoped) but instead in alteration of procedures. Though resistance reappeared periodically, substantial gains were achieved.

A COMPARISON

Numerous investigations have demonstrated the applicability of behavior modification methods to training institutionalized behaviorally retarded patients (Bensberg, 1965; Lindsley, 1964; Roos, 1965; Gray and Kasteler, 1969). These programs have generally involved special wards or cottages with specifically selected and trained personnel. Additionally, the administrative staff responsible has had substantial control of consequences for appropriate and inappropriate staff behavior. Few large state institutions are able to institute such well-controlled programs. Problems are generated by redirection of financial resources, inadequate staffing, and administrative regulation. Our intention was to determine the feasibility of developing a program for chronically institutionalized, profoundly retarded residents which could be implemented with existing staff and facilities in a typical state institution. The basic approach was to systematically reinforce adaptive behaviors socially and with food or beverages, and to extinguish maladaptive behavior or to reinforce incompatible responses.

The problems faced in this situation were not basically different from those involved in establishing programs in other buildings with other groups of residents. They were, however, more severe due to the past history of the patients and staff in the "worst" building and the attitudes of other staff in the institution toward this building.

Program

PROGRAM GOALS

The goals of the program were to eliminate maladaptive behavior and establish or strengthen adaptive self-help behavior sufficiently to transfer some patients to higher-functioning wards or conceivably to sheltered environments outside the institution. For many residents the goal was to create a prosthetic environment which provided the opportunity to engage in a wide range of activities which would serve as reinforcers, that is, to increase the range and availability of reinforcers and the behaviors leading to them.

PROGRAM SETTING

The physical environment consisted of a building with an area of 13,300 square feet divided into two large wards (one having beds, labeled the dormitory, the other having chairs and referred to as the "day room"), a dining area, several offices, and eight side rooms used for isolating assaultive or destructive patients. All but one of these rooms were converted to patient training rooms. A large table, sufficient chairs, and a desk and supply cabinet were placed in each room. The room which had served as a dining area was subsequently converted to a recreation area with an obstacle course for gross motor coordination programs and related activities.

STAFF

The basic staff consisted of seven technicians who conducted the training, one registered nurse, one social worker, and two consultants. The registered nurse attended to the patients' medical needs and served as on-line program manager. The social worker aided in providing supplies and services, contacted residents' relatives regarding the program, and investigated placement opportunities for the residents. The consultants designed the program, specified behavioral goals, and described the steps necessary to reach those goals.

An average of fifteen technicians covered the three shifts each day in the building, manning training rooms and providing ward coverage (the number ranged from twelve to eighteen during the year). The services of the occupational therapy, special education, and recreation departments had previously seen small use in this building and an effort was made to enroll them. In the present program, these special services provided ten hours per week of staff time. The over-all staff-to-patient ratio in this building was 1 to 4 as compared with an institution staff-to-patient ratio of 1 to 3.23. Included in the staff figure are janitorial, kitchen, maintenance, and nursing service employees. The actual number of technicians working directly with patients was approximately 1 to 10 during the day, 2 to 67 in the evening, and 1 to 67 at night.

RESIDENTS

The age of the sixty-seven patients ranged from eighteen to sixty years and the mean duration of hospitalization was 19.1 years. The I.Q. of eighteen of the patients was not measurable, and of the remaining forty-nine the mean I.Q. was 23.4. All of the patients had previously been transferred to the building following extended periods in other institutions or buildings and all had been in Dakota Building for at least two years. Transfers were generally due to destructive and assaultive behavior, lack of basic self-care behavior, and/or self-destructive behavior. The most frequently occurring maladaptive behaviors are listed in Table 4-1. In addition to some congenital deformities, most of the residents had deformities or deficits which had been incurred during hospitalization. These included blindness and deafness (other or self-

Table 4-1. N- Maladaptive behavior most common in chronically institutionalized, profoundly retarded individuals. General categories include: self-abuse, assaultive and autistic self-stimulatory behaviors, and those behaviors generated by lack of self-maintenance behaviors.

1. Spitting
2. Biting (self and others)
3. Hitting (self and others)
4. Scratching (self and others)
5. Head-banging
6. Homosexual activity
7. Ingestion of inappropriate objects
8. Feces smearing
9. Rectal digging
10. Throwing objects
11. Uncontrolled urination and defecation
12. Pestering staff and patients inappropriately
13. Pacing
14. Posturing
15. Food grabbing (from other patients)

inflicted), traumatic lesions and scars, and postural abnormalities of the trunk and extremities. The etiology of retardation included congenital syphilis, head injury, and birth trauma, but for the majority of the patients the cause was unknown.

MATERIALS

A series of constructive activities modified from those developed by Larsen and Bricker (1968) were used. Additionally, activities suggested by technicians were rewritten in a standard format and were included with the available training materials. For each constructive activity a behavioral goal, a series of successive steps for reaching the goal, and a test for determining whether the criterion had been met were specified. The concept of "backward chaining" or strengthening behaviors through successive approximations to the terminal behavior was used in each activity. The activities programmed are presented in Table 4-2 and two sample programs are shown in Table 4-3. The materials required for each activity were constructed or developed by the technicians or were purchased when family donations permitted. Programs for individual behavior problems were designed by the consultants and communicated in writing to technicians. With the exception of the materials describing methods of shaping various behaviors, no materials other than those generally available were used. Each

Table 4-2. Patient training materials given to technicians included a description of the terminal behaviors, pre-test, suggested training program, post-test, and a recording sheet. These activities included:

1.	Sitting quietly in chair (facing table)	13.	Building puzzles
2.	Toileting	14.	Coloring
3.	Toothbrushing	15.	Playing with ball
4.	Hand washing	16.	Playing with wagon
5.	Bathing	17.	Imitation of movements
6.	Shaving	18.	Imitation of mouth movements
7.	Hair grooming	19.	Imitation of sounds
8.	Eating correctly	20.	Imitation of words
9.	Putting on shirt (buttoning buttons)	21.	Stringing beads
10.	Putting on pants	22.	Learning numbers and counting
11.	Putting on socks	23.	Learning and naming colors
12.	Putting on shoes (tying shoelaces)		

Table 4-3. The two simple program outlines presented indicated the general format of activity instructions. In each case the steps involve shaping the terminal behaviors through successive approximations.

A. Activity: Toileting

1. Lead the resident to the toilet, help him remove his pants and sit down. Require him to sit until he defecates and/or urinates. Reinforce him.
2. Lead the resident to the toilet. Instruct him to remove his pants and sit. Reinforce him. Require him to sit until he defecates and/or urinates. Reinforce him.
3. Lead the resident to the toileting area. Instruct him to walk to the toilet, remove his pants, and sit. Reinforce him. Require him to sit until he defecates and/or urinates. Reinforce him.
4. Stand some distance from the toileting area. Instruct the resident to go to the toilet. When he has done so and removed his pants and is sitting, reinforce him. Require him to sit until he defecates and/or urinates. Reinforce him.
5. Instruct the resident to go to the toilet and return. Reinforce him when he has completed the sequence.

Note: (1) carry this procedure out at regular intervals. As the behavior develops, begin to increase the interval between toileting periods.

B. Activity: Printing letters, numbers and drawing shapes

1. Use a heavy cardboard stencil and large pencil. Draw a line through this stencil and instruct the resident to trace the letter. Reinforce him.
2. Use a thin stencil. Repeat step one.
3. Print the letter. Instruct the resident to trace it. Reinforce him.
4. Print the letter as a dashed line. Instruct the resident to print the letter following the lines. Reinforce him.
5. Repeat step four but gradually reduce the size of the dashes until the resident can print the letter on instruction. Reinforce each correct response.

Note: Use these steps but different stencils to train drawings of circles, squares, and other shapes or outline drawings of objects.

room was provided with puzzles, coloring books, crayons, paper, flash-cards, and other activities designed to develop necessary skills (e.g. eye-hand coordination, color discrimination) which would facilitate training of self-care behaviors.

In addition, a supply of marshmallows, candy bars, and other edibles to be used as reinforcers were locked in cabinets. Locking the cabinets was found to be necessary since one of the most rapidly established behaviors of these allegedly untrainable residents consisted of cabinet-opening and "robbery."

STAFF TRAINING

The staff's prior training was of six months' duration, and included bed making, drug dispensing, and remotivation therapy. However, it did not include exposure to behavior modification (at the present time the official institution-wide training program includes training in behavior modification). Five weekly one-hour classes were devoted to the principles of behavior modification, the goals of the program, and discussions of individual patients' behavior. Quizzes were given at the end of each lecture. Some technicians obtained further information through the use of a beginning text on human operant conditioning (Reese, 1966). The satisfactory completion of the quizzes and programmed materials as well as the successful modification of one behavior of a patient were the specified requirements leading to a "merit increase" in pay.*

RESIDENT TRAINING

The residents were in heterogeneous groups of eight to ten with one technician for approximately seven hours each day. The use of heterogeneous groups, though not essential, appears to maximize the likelihood of success. Residents exhibiting fewer maladaptive behaviors may be taught to aid in the training of other residents. Additionally, if the residents are grouped by problem or severity of problem, one staff member is placed in the unfortunate position of having such a troublesome group as to deter the most ardent behavior modifier.

Self-care activities were trained early in the day (e.g. bathing, toileting, and dressing). Activties designed to establish other be-

* Merit increases have since been discontinued by the Minnesota State Civil Service.

haviors were implemented during the remainder of each daily group session.

Initially the patients ate meals in a large dining room. Some residents were seated separately because of persistent food grabbing and other maladaptive behaviors. Arrangements were later made to have the meals brought to the training rooms and this facilitated training of self-feeding behavior.

The technicians were instructed to train the residents to dress themselves (Table 4-2, activities 9-12). Residents were first trained individually in the training rooms. As training progressed, the technicians took the residents to the rooms each morning and required self-dressing.

Verbal behavior training was not stressed early in the program. However, as behavioral control developed, the training of mouth movements, sounds, and words was emphasized to a greater degree (Table 4-2, activities 18-20).

The development of self-care behaviors had the result that various special services (e.g. Special Education, Occupational Therapy, and Speech Therapy) provided more time to the Dakota Building staff on techniques of training and development of patients' skills.

Grossly disruptive and assaultive residents had in the past been placed in seclusion in the rooms which were converted to training rooms. This procedure was largely discontinued and the only consequence for disruptive behavior was brief exclusion from the training room. Furthermore, since the residents were devoting most of their time to constructive activities, there was limited opportunity for destructive behavior.

The maintaining consequences for staff were threefold: (1) improvement in patient behavior, often making the residents more pleasant and enjoyable to work with; (2) records of numbers of patient activities programmed by each technician were publicly plotted daily (this was later discontinued); and (3) administrative recognition, attention from consultants and visitors, and perhaps most importantly, positive feedback from the building nurse.

Results

THE "WORST" BUILDING ONE YEAR LATER

In April of 1970 the Dakota Building behavior modification program had been in existence for one year. It was not a year of constant improvement but rather one with periods of improvement and occasional plateaus in progress. However, the general trend was improvement at a rate higher than anyone had anticipated. The changes which will be discussed are not only those in patient behavior but in the attitude and behavior of staff at all levels. Additionally, program alterations as a function of residents and staff changes will be considered.

PATIENT BEHAVIOR CHANGES

The first major aspect of resident behavior dealt with was toileting. Among several reasons for this were (1) the amount of time spent cleaning feces and urine off the floors and the residents decreased the amount of time available to work with other aspects of patient training; (2) the staff was more likely to work with residents who were clean and toilet trained; and (3) it was a behavior which, if developed, the authors considered likely to sway those among the staff who were resistant to the behavior modification methods. When the program began, 65 per cent of the residents did not toilet themselves. A program involving frequent and regular trips to the toilet was instated. Within a few weeks most residents consistently waited until the group went to the toilet. Thus, under these contingencies the residents were reinforced for appropriate toileting behavior (with social and tangible reinforcement). As the residents adapted to the toileting procedure, the interval between toileting sessions was increased. At the end of one year 81 per cent of the residents toileted themselves, 18 per cent required reminding, and one resident thought to have medical problems was often incontinent (subsequently a staff member was able to eliminate incontinence in this patient as well and the medical "excuse" was found to be unnecessary).

This is one example of the procedures used and the results obtained. Most important is the fact that the toileting procedure itself did not emphasize elimination of the maladaptive behavior. Rather, the stress was placed on reinforcing the adaptive behavior. That is, regular toileting with consistent contingencies ultimately led to the once or twice daily toileting patterns found in most normal adults and was achieved simply by reinforcing a behavior incompatible with urinating and defecating inappropriately. Additionally, without specifically developing procedures to deal with rectal digging and feces smearing, these and related behaviors were eliminated (though the subject is indelicate it should be apparent to the reader that regular toileting precludes the presence of the necessary fecal material which leads to the "related behaviors"). Other behaviors were similarly eliminated by emphasizing the establishment of adaptive behavior (i.e. reinforcement of incompatible behavior). Several of these will be discussed briefly.

Before the behavior modification program began, 50 per cent of the residents either wore no clothing or were partially clothed (for example, wore pants only). The staff carried clothing procedures beyond simply dressing the resident and training him not to remove the clothing. The basic hospital outer clothing consists of zipperless, pocketless pants with elastic waistbands and pullover shirts and slippers with only a modicum of style. The staff involved in group training sessions arranged to obtain shirts, slacks, and shoes which fit well and were attractive. A number of residents who had been resistant to wearing "hospital clothing" rapidly learned to dress themselves and wear clothing, when other clothing or choice of clothing was provided. The clearest example of the extent to which the residents' behavior is correlated with the environment has to do with the type of clothing worn and the periods during which it was worn. Early in the first year of the program it was not uncommon for residents to be entirely dressed during the group training sessions and then revert to a condition of partial or total undress when on the ward. In the past residents wearing clothing were frequently accosted by others who would rip the garments. To avoid these unpleasant contacts some residents simply disrobed partially or entirely and were then not disturbed by "clothing rippers." This pattern continued during the program's early stages. However, when the residents returned to the training rooms where clothing ripping did not occur, these same residents dressed themselves and remained dressed until returned to the ward. In this regard a further example of the extent to which the residents learned about aspects of the environment was that later in the program some residents wore their "good" clothing in the training room and changed to "hospital clothing" when they returned to the ward. Thus, being dressed had become reinforcing, but the discrimination which developed was not unlike the one many of us share, that is, when at work we wear suits and ties, uniforms or dresses, but while at home we wear casual attire. Again the basic procedure consisted of providing substantial reinforcement for one behavior, in this case wearing clothing, and essentially no reinforcement for another behavior, not wearing clothing. The ripping of other residents' clothing also decreased, presumably because more reinforcement was available for engaging in other behaviors which were incompatible with clothing ripping. After one year, 91 per cent of the residents were usually totally clothed and 9 per cent were partially clothed ("partially" at that point had come to mean the wearing of a shirt and slacks but not shoes).

Similar results were obtained with self-feeding behavior. Before the program began, approximately 40 per cent of the residents did not feed themselves. Many of those who did feed themselves used the expedient technique of taking all the food on their tray in their hands and stuffing it in their mouth. Rapid eating may seem maladaptive to those who are not familiar with the situation. However, in many cases failure to eat rapidly resulted in loss of food to other residents who did eat rapidly and then proceeded to grab food from others. A variety of procedures, including double portions at meals, brief time out from the meal situation, or providing a meal in a series of small quantities (thereby lengthening the period required to consume the food), may serve to decrease the frequency of food grabbing. In specific situations any one of these may be the most reasonable solution. The present program was carried out without emphasis on the maladaptive behavior of food grabbing. Reinforcement of appropriate eating behavior essentially eliminated the problem. After one year 95 per cent of the residents were able to feed themselves using at least a spoon and in many cases using additional utensils. At the end of the year, one confirmed food grabber continued to engage in his favorite avocation. This behavior was subsequently eliminated using a systematic time out procedure.

Perhaps the most difficult behavior to establish was speech. In buildings such as Dakota, speech per se is typically not reinforced by patients or staff. When speech does occur it is frequently echolalic (that is, a resident is addressed "Hi Mark" and promptly responds with "Hi Mark"). Bizarre vocalizations and echolalia are occasionally reinforced by others. Presumably one source of reinforcement is the feedback or self-stimulation which results from such vocalizations. This aspect may not be unlike the humming or whistling behavior of normal adults. However, it was sometimes observed that these vocalizations caused other residents or staff members to retreat and that the vocalizations often increased in frequency in the presence of others. This, of course, is another instance of an apparently inappropriate and maladaptive behavior which, if considered in terms of the existing environment, is not only adaptive but may have survival value. Eliminating such vocalizations, which have served the patient effectively for years, is difficult.

It should be possible to decrease bizarre vocalizations and echolalia by developing effective verbal behavior. However, specifying the steps in training speech is more difficult than specifying those associated with other behaviors, and the procedure itself is difficult. In the present program emphasis was not placed on training speech during the first year. Yet some staff had success training speech: at the onset of the program 94 per cent of the residents were described as having no speech and at the end of one year 43 per cent used some words correctly. Subsequently a number of residents developed a substantial vocabulary. This was due in part to a greater emphasis on speech development after the first year of the program. Some residents had been able to speak with a degree of facility before their extended confinement in an environment which reinforced speech progressively less as regression to successive buildings occurred. Therefore, to an unknown extent the general change in the environment and re-establishment of the reinforcers for engaging in speech probably contributed to improvement in this area. Recruiting the aid of a speech therapist has increased the interest of the staff in developing this behavior and has led to further improvement.

Various other self-care behaviors have also been established to a greater or lesser degree, including shaving, bathing, and toothbrushing. Additional skills, such as color discrimination and eye-hand coordination, have been developed through the use of puzzles and similar activities. Acquisition of these behaviors facilitates acquisition of self-care behaviors and ultimately provides a basis for establishing behaviors involving more complex tasks and jobs similar to normal everyday activities.

In the preceding discussion there has been only minimal mention of the aggressive and assaultive behaviors which develop as an integral part of residents' repertoires in buildings such as Dakota. There is no doubt that a substantial portion of the medical care in such a building is required by wounds that patients suffer at the hands (or mouths) of other patients. These wounds are inflicted, for instance, when one resident sticks his finger in the eye of another resident or sinks his teeth into the fleshy bulb of another resident's nose. Prior to the behavior modification program, one patient in Dakota Building who used his teeth in this manner had been a candidate for teeth removal to lessen the damage produced by the bites. The final institutional solution was a frontal lobotomy. The case history informs us that shortly after the resident was returned to the building after "succesful" neurosurgery he severely injured another resident by biting him. Similar episodes have not occurred since the third month of the behavior modification program. As all institution staff know, and as others have heard, consequences of the assaultive behavior which is unpleasantly common in institutions are isolation, restraints, or seclusion. These restrictive measures are considered a necessary part of the operating procedure for many buildings in many institutions. If for no other reason, the Dakota Building project can be considered a success because of the elimination of such behavior and its usual consequence, seclusion. No specific procedures were used to eliminate aggressive behavior. Rather, a regimen of positive reinforcement was established which provided the residents with the opportunity to obtain reinforcers for adaptive, personally and socially useful behaviors. Before the program began approximately 45 per cent of the residents frequently engaged in assaultive behavior and there had been 2400 patient hours of seclusion each month for episodes of aggression (see Figure 4-1). That is equivalent to keeping four people in seclusion twenty-four hours a day each month. No residents were placed in isolation for assaultive behavior after the first six months of the program.

The program has been evaluated in terms of changes in residents' self-care behaviors, changes in total resident hours in seclusion for assaultive behavior, and individual cases. There are other indirect measures which indicate progress. These measures include drug use (for example, the prescribing of major tranquilizers), damage to the building and furniture, frequency of acute medical emergencies resulting from self- or other-inflicted trauma, and transfers of residents to other buildings or institutions.

When the program was initiated, 79 per cent of the residents received daily doses of tranquilizers. At the present time 54 per cent of the residents receive tranquilizing medications. The dosage has been substantially reduced for an additional 19 per cent

A BEHAVIOR PROGRAM FOR INSTITUTIONALIZED MALES

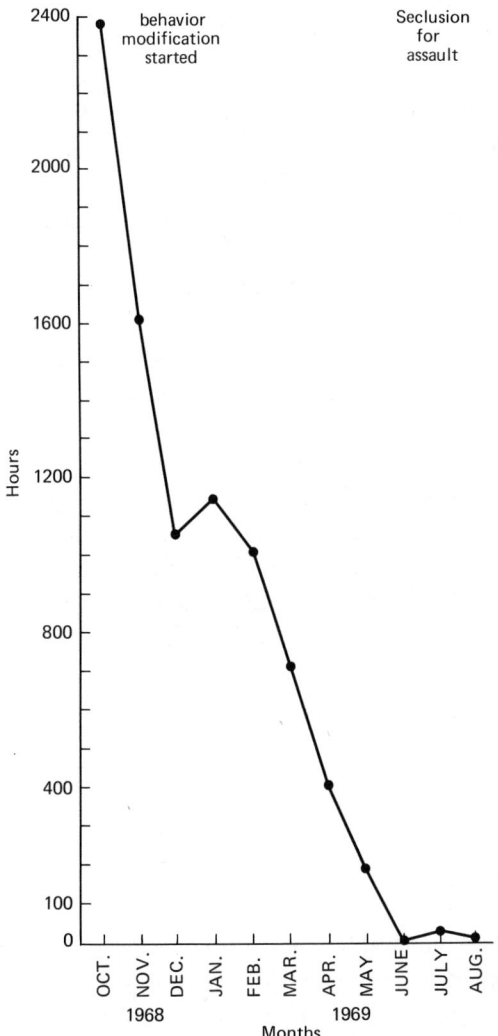

Figure 4-1. The number of hours patients were placed in seclusion for assaultive behavior per month. The behavior modification project was initiated in October 1969 (arrow). The baseline seclusion time (2400 hours per month) was equivalent to 3.3 patients placed in seclusion full time.

of the residents. Therefore, a decrease in dosage or elimination of tranquilizers entirely has been possible for 44 per cent of the residents. The implications of such reductions should be obvious. The heavy sedation which was once considered essential for control of behavior is no longer necessary in many cases. In fact, staff requests for reduced medication have become common since training is facilitated when residents are not subdued by medications.

The number and severity of medical problems have been reduced substantially. During a ten-month period preceding the program, an average of 6.5 serious injuries occurred each month in the building. The mean number of injuries per month was 1.0 after the program's second year.

When the program was initiated there were sixty-seven residents in the building. Subsequently, eight residents were transferred to other institutions, ten residents were transferred to other buildings within the institution housing higher-functioning individuals, six residents who were higher functioning and showed little progress were transferred to another building, and three blind residents were transferred to another program. As residents were moved to other buildings or institutions, new residents were introduced to the building and thirty-one of these individuals are now progressing satisfactorily in the program.

CHANGES IN STAFF BEHAVIOR

The most substantial behavioral change observed was in the on-ward staff responsible for carrying out the programs. It is clear that many of the building staff members were not previously engaged in developing the patients' skills, not because they were uninterested but because the existing staffing patterns, and absence of support for training patients, simply did not permit such activities. There was resistance initially, of course, and the prevailing attitude was that "these patients can't learn." Due to peer pressure, staff members who may have taken a different view were not vocal in their support of the program. Indeed, there were days when the consultants almost agreed with the prevailing staff view, but for different reasons. Given the opportunity and procedural suggestions, however, the staff successfully demonstrated that something could be done. At times the competition was substantial, with staff arguing about their respective successes. At other times, particularly when plateaus had been reached, there were lapses into the more traditional view that some new activity could not be learned by one or another patient. However, the tenor of these comments made it clear that changes had occurred. For example, when the program began a staff member would state that "Bill can't learn how to toilet himself," while at the end of the first year when Bill was able to toilet, dress, feed himself, say some words, and engage in a variety of activities the same staff member might say, "Bill can't be expected to sit and work six or seven hours a day." In other words, when complaints did occur at the end of the first year, it was evident that the level of activities discussed had changed substantially. Evidence of the interest exhibited by the staff and their desire to train the patients and improve conditions is exemplified by the fact that a number of staff members contributed additional time for which they could not be paid, or purchased from their own funds materials for use in working with the patients.

Several general comments regarding the effectiveness of staff can be made. Female staff members were generally more effective than male staff members in this building which housed male patients. Men who had worked in the building for long periods prior to program instatement tended to be less effective than those who began working in the building at or after program onset. Finally, with a few major and notable exceptions, younger staff members seemed to be more interested and effective than older staff members (though one of the most effective was a woman who had worked in the institution for twenty years and yet was more than willing to implement change and see it occur).

FINAL COMMENTS

The Dakota Building program was developed within the bounds of the generally available funding and staffing capabilities of a large state institution with a chronically institutionalized population. It became apparent early in the program that vast changes could be made in patient behavior if it was possible to alter staff behavior. In the usual institutional setting there are relatively few of the expected reinforcers available for staff. The technicians are poorly paid, pay increases are hard to get, and administrative and union regulations interfere with scheduling of time off or days off with pay.

In Dakota Building the primary function of technicians before the program began had been custodial care, and therefore the program constituted a major change in their work routine. This change met with considerable resistance, which diminished only when most of the self-care training had been completed.

The fact that training of patients was most effectively carried out by female technicians was in part related to the past history of the patients with male technicians. That technicians who began working in the building at or after program onset were more effective than technicians who had been working in the building previously is to be expected, since the behavior patterns maintained in the past by technicians were largely maladaptive. It is especially noteworthy that female technicians were not only able to function in this environment but actually excelled, since, before this program began, no females were allowed in the building without at least one male technician as an escort.

Establishing special rooms and patient groups for each technician seemed to improve technician performance. Visits by administrators, tours by groups of visitors, and the generally more favorable publicity also helped. Most importantly, the progress of the patients became reinforcing, as did the opportunity to suggest new programs and obtain supplies for use in the training rooms.

The fact that the behavior of profoundly retarded, chronically institutionalized patients was brought under effective stimulus control became evident in several ways. The increase in the number of patients engaging in adaptive behaviors and the substantial decrease in the rate and variety of maladaptive behaviors in the training rooms were striking. The contrast in the behavior of patients in the training rooms and on the ward was marked. At an early stage in the program, technicians began to open the training rooms at 7:00 a.m. and to close them briefly for coffee breaks and lunch. Subsequently many patients remained in the training rooms from 7:00 a.m. until 2:30 p.m. When not in the training rooms, each patient group was returned to the ward, where some removed their clothing and began engaging in many of the maladaptive behaviors previously seen in both situations. After several months many patients, when returned to the ward, would continue to wear clothing but changed into loose fitting pullover shirts and pants. At present the majority of patients remain clothed in the ward area, toilet themselves, and do not engage in grossly maladaptive behaviors; but many do pace the length of the ward, rock, or exhibit other autisms.

Finally, several other changes, which were not specific goals of the behavior modification program, have developed along with it. These include regular sleep patterns, fewer incidents of nocturnal enuresis, and fewer incidents of self-inflicted physical trauma. The number of patients' injuries requiring suturing and/or hospitalization have greatly decreased, and damage to furniture and equipment has been eliminated. Additionally, there has been a decrease in the use of major tranquilizers and barbiturates for behavior control.

The most important single finding of this project has been that it is possible to reduce or eliminate the vast majority of assaultive, disruptive, and objectionable behaviors without directly arranging consequences for those responses. In virtually every instance the frequency of such behaviors varied inversely with the frequency of constructive activities. As reinforcement was programmed contingent on constructive activity, the time devoted to constructive activity increased and time spent engaging in maladaptive behavior decreased. However, the effect seemed to be more than replacing one activity with another, since even when the patients were merely sitting at their tables in the training rooms, the frequency of maladaptive behaviors remained low. This suggests that the stimulus conditions associated with constructive activity and high frequency of positive reinforcement exercise control over behavior, much as the stimulus conditions of the large locked ward area seemed to set the occasion for grossly maladaptive behavior.

References

Bensberg, G. (Ed.). *Teaching the Mentally Retarded: A Handbook for Ward Personnel*. Atlanta: Southern Regional Education Board, 1965.

Gray, R., and J. Kasteler. Effects of social reinforcement and training on institutionalized mentally retarded children. *Amer. J. ment. Defic.* 1969, *74*, 50-56.

Larsen, L. A., and W. A. Bricker. A manual for parents and teachers of severely and moderately retarded children. *IMRID Papers and Reports*, 1968, 5 (22), J. F. Kennedy Center for Research on Education and Human Development, Nashville, Tennessee.

Lindsley, O. R. Direct Measurement and Prosthesis of Retarded Behavior. *Journal of Education*, 1964, *147*, 62-81.

Reese, E. *The Analysis of Human Operant Behavior*. Dubuque, Iowa: Wm. C. Brown Co., 1966.

Roos, P. Development of an Intensive Habit-Training Unit at Austin State School. *Mental Retardation*, 1965, *3*, 12-15.

Thompson, T., and S. Arhelger. "*Changes: Behavior Modification for the Profoundly Retarded*," a film produced by Sensory Systems, Inc., 4314 Abbott Ave. South, Minneapolis, Minnesota 55410.

5
An intensive teaching unit for severely and profoundly retarded women

GEORGE BIGELOW AND ROLAND GRIFFITHS

Introduction

In July 1969 Iris Building was opened as a residential intensive teaching unit to develop improved behavioral skills within the population of chronically institutionalized, severely and profoundly retarded women at Faribault State Hospital.

The patients were generally drawn from Holly Building—which housed the lowest functioning and most severely disturbed female residents in the institution. Holly was the women's equivalent to Dakota Building (described in Chapter 4).

The Iris program provided intensive teaching for these residents by incorporating them into small groups (about twelve at a time) and employing behavior modification procedures in an enriched environment with a high staff-patient ratio. It was designed to maintain an active teaching program throughout the day. The improved treatment available in Iris was made possible by the improved physical facilities, the increased number of active ward staff, increased attention by rehabilitation therapists, increased medical attention, increased supervisory attention, and especially by the effective application of behavior modification procedures.*

* The Iris treatment project was made possible through a Hospital Improve-

The aim of this intensive treatment unit has been to improve the behavior of the residents to a point where they could be moved into buildings with higher-level residents. Here the residents would require less custodial care and would continue to have opportunities for further improvement.

Intensive teaching units

In recent years, institutions for the retarded have found themselves with an increasing proportion of severely or profoundly retarded residents. In 1960, 26 per cent of the residents at Faribault State Hospital were in this category. By 1970, this proportion had risen to 84 per cent.

These are the residents who are most often neglected in therapeutic efforts with the retarded. In fact, it has often been assumed (e.g. Stevens, 1964) that such profoundly retarded individuals are incapable of improvement—regardless of the treatment approach. As a result, most state institutions have provided only custodial care for these residents (see Chapter 1).

But now the institutional atmosphere is changing. Effective teaching procedures exist, but require implementation. Administrators find themselves with the problem of how to get these teaching efforts to the residents effectively and efficiently. On those rare occasions when an institution has additional funds or staffing to invest in treatment programming, it is tempting to place these resources in the existing ward facilities and hope for improvement. An alternative to simply broadening existing programs is to establish an intensive teaching unit.

Intensive units are treatment areas in which a concentrated effort is applied to a specific teaching technique. Such units may

---

ment Project grant (MR 02170-01) from the U.S. Public Health Service to Faribault State Hospital. Application was made for the grant by Arnold Madow, Chief Psychologist, and Roger Johnson, Medical Director. Mr. Madow has supervised operation of the program through Mrs. Winifred Myers, Unit Director. The authors serve as behavior modification consultants, and each spends one day per week working in the project.

take the form of a classroom which residents visit several times weekly to be taught a small number of skills or activities, or they may take the form of a complete residential area where groups of residents receive constant instruction in numerous activities. Whatever their form, intensive units are oriented both in principle and in practice toward a teaching goal, which is pursued within a structured therapeutic framework.

Intensive units are in contrast to the conventional approach, which is characterized by erratic teaching efforts involving a variety of different teaching techniques applied within the normal institutional setting. Intensive units provide more organized, more directed, and more consistent teaching efforts, which occur in a distinctive therapeutic setting. The concept of stimulus control, discussed in Chapter 2, suggests that a radical change in stimulus conditions during the intensive teaching period should make it considerably easier to change the residents' behavior. The establishment of an intensive teaching facility within an institution can fulfill the need for the extraordinary teaching attention which is demanded by severely and profoundly retarded residents.

TEACHING VERSUS MAINTENANCE OF BEHAVIOR

Intensive teaching units generally involve only short-term participation. That is, they are usually not permanent residential placements. This is because the intensive nature of the units is necessary only for teaching, not for maintenance of the improved behavior which can be accomplished in a non-intensive setting.

Lindsley (1964) points out that acquisition of a behavior is often confused with its maintenance, although quite different sets of conditions are required in the two situations. The fact that the conditions necessary for learning (or teaching) a behavior are often quite different from those necessary for maintaining the same behavior is the key to the strength of intensive teaching programs.

In an intensive unit an environment is created in which a group of residents *acquire* several specific skills through concentrated teaching. After the residents have accomplished these goals, they are graduated to a non-intensive program which is adequate to *maintain* their improved behavior. The intensive facility is then able to accept a new group of residents into its teaching program. In this way, intensive units are well suited for developing improved behavioral skills in successive groups from a large resident population.

Retention. The acceptance and implementation of intensive teaching programs for the severely and profoundly retarded have undoubtedly been delayed by fears that the participants would not be able to retain what they learn—resulting in a waste of the treatment effort. Such fears may be voiced as suggestions that retardates are distractible or suffer from such severe memory deficits that they would soon lose whatever skills they had acquired.

Research by Belmont and Ellis (1968), Ellis and Anders (1968), and Haywood and Heal (1968) suggests that these fears are exaggerated. Most convincing of the ability of participants in intensive teaching programs to retain what they have learned is a report by Leath and Flournoy (1970) of a three-year follow-up to an intensive teaching program. They concluded that behavior-shaping techniques have positive long-range effects on a variety of self-help and social skills. The significant gains registered in the teaching period were generally maintained over the three-year period, though the intensive teaching was discontinued.

REVIEW OF INTENSIVE PROGRAMS

A review of recent literature suggests that intensive teaching units are receiving increased acceptance as an effective means of treatment—especially for the severely and profoundly retarded. Although many papers stray embarrassingly far from objective description or assessment, a summary of published reports provides some perspective on the functioning of these units.

Tobias and Cortazzo (1963) reported on the operation of an

Occupation Day Center for severely retarded children. The program stressed teaching skills which were thought to be necessary for independent living, such as grooming, occupational skills, and food preparation. Although the authors failed to state their teaching procedures explicitly, they mentioned the development of small-group programs. The program was successful as measured by a questionnaire distributed to the parents of the children.

Davis (1969) has described a Hospital Improvement Project (HIP) in which 160 severely and profoundly retarded adults were provided with a regular schedule of activities. The program consisted primarily of arts and crafts taught in small-group settings. The average class size was seven and the average participation per week for each resident was three hours. Scoring procedures for the activities indicated that 80 per cent of the residents manifested measurable progress relating to task difficulty.

A number of more ambitious programs have attempted to provide constant instruction in intensive live-in units with severely and profoundly retarded children. Colwell (1969) described the "amazing changes" that occur in self-help activities when operant procedures are systematically applied in a cottage setting. Also without quantification, Roos (1965) described a similar teaching unit employing operant conditioning methods. Secondarily to teaching self-help skills, the unit was effective for training staff and developing novel teaching procedures and equipment. Roos emphasized the importance of the team treatment approach and the involvement of the hospital administration in implementing such a program.

In the introduction to their *HIP Activity Manual*, Miller and Trainor (1968) described a Hospital Improvement Project-sponsored intensive habilitation program for severely and profoundly retarded children. The residents were divided into groups of ten to twelve each and ward staffing was increased to provide one group leader and one relief person for each group on both morning and afternoon shifts. The authors described improvements in a wide range of resident behaviors, and attributed some of the success of the program to the development of a team treatment approach to teaching.

Gorton and Hollis (1965) described a cottage unit for severely retarded girls, six through twelve years of age at Parsons State Hospital and Training Center. The staff involved in the project participated in lectures, films, and discussions on behavior modification principles. Teaching included a variety of self-care skills, feeding, training, and development of motor skills.

Of these studies, undoubtedly the most satisfactory methodologically was reported by Kimbrell, Luckey, Barbuto, and Love (1967). A seven-month intensive habit-training and social development program for severely and profoundly retarded girls was established. The residents lived in groups of ten in dormitories equipped with toys and developmental equipment. The environment was simplified to meet the needs of the girls (Kimbrell, Kidwell, and Hallum, 1967), who were encouraged in play, group participation, and self-help activities by the use of operant conditioning procedures. The residents made statistically significant progress over their comparison groups in skills measured by a modified version of the Vineland Social Maturity Scale. In addition, the trained residents required only half the amount of laundry used by peers who received conventional institutional care and treatment. A follow-up study indicated that the gains registered in the teaching period were maintained after three years without formal teaching (Leath and Flournoy, 1970).

Summary. Unfortunately, descriptions of intensive units have generally been less than explicit. As a consequence, detailed objective evaluation is impossible. Too much information has been omitted from these reports to allow them to serve as unequivocal models for future intensive programs, or even to allow the sorting out of desirable from undesirable program characteristics. Among the questions requiring further elaboration and evaluation are: (1) Which specific behaviors can most readily be taught? (2) How much actual teaching time should be involved each day? (3) What size should the teaching groups be? (4) Should more than one staff member be involved in teaching a particular activity? (5) How can staff best learn effective teaching techniques? (6) How can resident progress best be evaluated?

Despite these drawbacks, it is clear that an effective technology for teaching even the most severely retarded is being developed. All of the projects so far reported have used small-group teaching situations, and of those authors who have described their teaching techniques, all have used the principles of behavior modification (Gorton and Hollis, 1965; Ross, 1965; Kimbrell *et al.*, 1967; Colwell, 1969; Miller and Trainor, 1968). The mental retardation literature leaves little room for doubt that behavior modification represents the most successful approach yet known to teaching the severely and profoundly retarded. Effective procedures have been reported to teach toileting, feeding, dressing, grooming, motor skills, speech, and complex work skills. Hollis and Gorton (1967), Watson (1967), and Nawas and Braun (1970a, b, c) provide excellent reviews.

STAFF-RESIDENT INTERACTIONS

Intensive teaching units seem to be characterized by an increased number of staff-resident interactions. They have relied heavily on small-group situations. Teaching has been done either individually (Roos, 1965) or in small groups (Tobias and Cortazzo, 1963; Gorton and Hollis, 1965; Davis, 1969). Some of the more ambitious projects have employed small-group living arrangements (Colwell, 1969; Kimbrell *et al.*, 1967; Miller and Trainor, 1968). The increased number of staff-resident interactions takes on further importance when it is realized that one of the most important principles of behavior modification is that attention can be an extremely effective and durable reinforcer. Increasing the number of staff-resident interactions is often equivalent to increasing the total amount of reinforcement that each resident receives.

The principles of behavior modification also suggest that changes in *which behaviors* are reinforced should also characterize effective teaching situations.

Gorton and Hollis (1965) indicate that in traditional (e.g. custodial-care) situations staff members usually give attention to those residents in imminent danger of self-destructive acts, those who are overtly aggressive, those who are the object of aggressive acts, those who have soiled themselves, or those who destroy their clothing. A behavioral analysis of this situation suggests that the staff in custodial-care settings is inadvertently reinforcing undesirable resident behavior.

Descriptions of intensive units suggest that the nature of these staff-resident interactions is altered in a critical way. Instead of paying attention to inappropriate behavior, the staff on intensive units begins to give attention to those residents engaged in constructive activities. Inappropriate behavior is increasingly ignored. In behavioral terms, desirable behavior is reinforced while undesirable behavior is extinguished.

We feel that this change in the nature of the staff-resident interactions is critical to the success of intensive units. Consideration of the reports from intensive units to date suggests that there are at least three major reasons for this systematic change in the nature of staff-resident interactions.

First, and most important, is the fact that most of the staff members in intensive units have been instructed in the application of behavior modification procedures. They must learn to reinforce desirable behavior and to ignore undesirable behavior.

Secondly, a number of intensive units have physically restructured the ward and teaching areas to facilitate improved staff-resident interactions. Basically, these efforts have been oriented toward making it easier for the residents to engage in desirable behavior—thereby making it easier for the staff to reinforce this desirable behavior. Efforts in this area involve what is often called an "enriched environment" and what Lindsley (1964) calls "prosthesis"—environmental changes which provide greater support for and direction toward proper behavior (e.g. providing recreational opportunities versus custodial care in a barren environment).

A third and more subtle factor which appears to influence the nature of staff-resident interactions is the change in staff attitude that occurs as teaching progresses. When staff members learn to use effective behavioral procedures, they become more optimistic about the residents (Davis, 1969; Miller and Trainor, 1968; Roos, 1965). They themselves begin to develop techniques to improve behavior; they rely less upon behaviorally active drugs. They come to view themselves as teachers rather than caretakers. They begin to reinforce residents with whom they previously had only unpleasant interactions.

Overview of the Iris Program

FACILITIES

Iris is an old three-story building constructed in 1902. Both the main and top floors have one dormitory room holding about eight beds each. All three floors have a variety of rooms used as teaching areas. Two of these rooms, known as Day Activity Centers (DACs), contain educational toys and materials. Several other rooms are equipped with materials for teaching specific skills, e.g. use of eating utensils, grooming skills, gross motor skills. Meals are served in a cafeteria in a neighboring building.

These facilities are quite spacious by institutional standards. Under normal conditions, this building would house two to three times as many residents as it currently does as an intensive treatment unit.

STAFFING

During each of the two regular work shifts (6:30 a.m.-3:00 p.m. and 2:30 p.m.-11:00 p.m.) two ward staff members are on duty. Overnight one staff member is on duty. Monday through Friday, on a schedule which overlaps both shifts of the regular ward staff, a registered nurse (the building supervisor), an occupational therapy assistant, and a ward charge (who handles most administrative and paper work) are on duty. All three of these staff members participate in direct patient treatment, although much of their time is occupied by other responsibilities—medical, administrative, supervisory, etc. All staff members volunteered to work in this specialized intensive teaching program, and most had been working in the institution previously.

Generally, there is one ward staff member per six residents. This level of staffing (ratio of staff to patients) is about two to three times as great as is usual within the institution.

RESIDENTS

At any one time, the resident population in Iris Building numbers between twelve and fifteen. Between July 1969 and December 1970, thirty-three residents have participated in the Iris program. Twenty-five of the participants have been profoundly retarded (I.Q. below 25), and seven have been severely retarded (I.Q. between 25 and 40). One moderately retarded resident (I.Q. of 49), who presented a special behavioral problem, has also been treated. Chronological ages have ranged from twenty to forty-four, with most residents being in their twenties (though five have been over forty). Typically, these residents were institutionalized in Faribault State Hospital for twenty years prior to their entry into the treatment program.

The only strict requirement for entry into the Iris treatment unit is that the resident be sufficiently ambulatory to go up and down stairs and to walk to the cafeteria for meals. Those residents selected from Holly Building are a fairly representative cross-section of that building's population, with the exception that the most aggressive residents have so far been omitted. The three residents selected from other buildings have been chosen because they displayed severely disruptive behavior which could not be controlled elsewhere.

PROGRAM GOALS

Specific program goals are essential. The Iris treatment program focuses on a wide range of specific behavioral goals. The aim is not to improve the quality of the residents' behavior within just one particular area (e.g. toileting) as many previous programs have done, but rather to improve a wide range of the residents' behavior. The final goal is to develop in the residents appropriate behavior to serve them *throughout the day*. If residents are not provided the opportunity to fill their day with desirable behaviors, then disruptive behavior problems may develop and the gains made in specific teaching activities may be lost.

Thus, Iris residents are generally being taught a variety of different skills simultaneously. The three major areas upon which the programs focus are: (1) self-care skills; (2) activity ability; and (3) non-disruptiveness. Each of these areas includes a variety of specific programs, as will be described. Not all residents are taught all activities. Teaching activities are selected which are relevant and useful for individual residents.

Self-care skills. Teaching residents to be self-sufficient in routine daily activities is essential if institutions are to move beyond a custodial role. The Iris program concentrates on teaching a variety of self-care skills. These include dressing (putting on a shirt, putting on pants, putting on socks, putting on shoes, lacing shoes, tying shoes, buttoning, zippering), toileting, hand washing, bathing, toothbrushing, eating (using knife, fork, and spoon, eating at proper speed, and chewing food).

Activity-ability. The aim here is to provide the residents with the ability to occupy their time in some positive way. Educational, recreational, and vocational skills are all included within this category. Thus, a very wide range of activities is involved, and the specific ones chosen for teaching must depend upon the needs of the individual resident.

Some residents are taught simple sensory and motor skills (putting pegs in holes, shape discrimination, color discrimination, matching-to-sample, stacking rings or blocks). At a more advanced level, residents are taught to play with various toys (assembling puzzles, coloring, looking at a book, Tinker Toy-like assembly toys). They are taught to select recreational activities for themselves. Promising residents may receive teaching in talking or in naming objects. Household and vocational skills are also taught, including making beds, sweeping, mopping, folding laundry, washing sinks, wiping off tables. Learning these skills increases the chance that the resident will be able to live more independently within the institution, perhaps take on a payroll job, and perhaps ultimately leave the institution.

No limit has been placed on any individual. However, a progression has generally been followed where residents learn basic educational and recreational skills first, and are later given the opportunity to learn various helping skills. The aim is first to teach the resident things which make it easier for her to learn (cooperating, paying attention, sensory-motor skills), then to teach her to occupy her time recreationally, and finally to provide vocational skills.

Non-disruptiveness. Since many of the residents who participate in the program present behavior problems, the control and elimination of disruptive and destructive behavior is an important aspect of the program. In practice, however, this goal is generally achieved by developing positive behaviors from the above two categories to replace the misbehavior. Occasionally, programs have focused specifically upon some aspect of misbehavior—headbanging, grabbing food, or throwing furniture.

THE FUNCTIONING PROGRAM

Treatment Sequence. The investment of time, effort, and money in intensive treatment units is only justified if adequate attempts are made to ensure that the behavioral gains achieved will be maintained after the resident leaves the teaching unit. *Thus, it is essential that adequate behavior-maintaining programs be established in the buildings to which residents graduate.* The entire treatment program then becomes a sequence of buildings—with the intensive teaching unit being one step of the sequence.

The complete Iris treatment sequence is depicted in Figure 5-1.

INTENSIVE TEACHING UNIT FOR RETARDED WOMEN

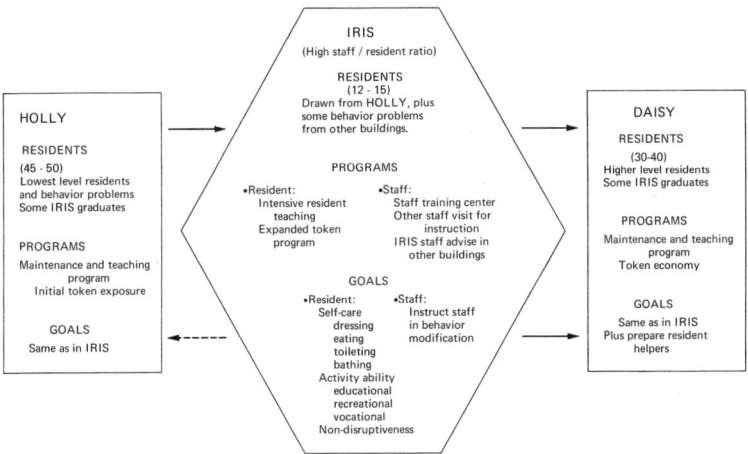

Figure 5-1. Graphic summary of the characteristics of the three buildings involved in the treatment sequence.

The treatment population originates in Holly Building, moves to Iris Building for intensive teaching, and subsequently is graduated into Daisy Building or into a special section of Holly. Specially designed behavioral programs are in progress in all of these locations. Behavior modification procedures, as described in Chapter 2, are used throughout.

This treatment sequence allows the intensive teaching unit to operate both effectively and efficiently. The sequential arrangement accomplishes two aims: first, it gives residents some familiarization with the teaching procedures *before they enter* the intensive teaching unit; and second, it guarantees that after graduation from the intensive teaching unit an adequate environment will be provided to maintain the improved behavior of the residents.

The typical situation in the pre-treatment section of Holly is twenty to thirty profoundly retarded and disruptive residents living together in a single large ward room. Another single room serves as the dormitory. It was possible to establish some preparatory teaching programs in this situation. The goals of this programming are the same as those described for Iris, but, because of the understaffing in this situation, teaching proceeds slowly. Basically, the residents become accustomed to the teaching procedures, they have the opportunity to fill part of their day with constructive activities, they improve somewhat in basic self-care skills such as toileting and bathing, and they receive their first exposure to token reinforcers which are exchangeable for treats. However, because of the continuing need for custodial care by staff in this area, only a relatively small portion of their day is devoted to learning.

If graduates from the Iris treatment program were returned to this situation, their deterioration would be very rapid, and the time and effort invested in Iris would be wasted. This is intended as no indictment of the staff in Holly; they do what they can in the situation which the state has provided. However, it must be realized when planning an intensive program that, due to the principle of stimulus control described in Chapter 2, deterioration will be rapid if individuals are simply returned to their pre-treatment environments.

The Iris graduates have been placed in situations which maintain their improved behavior, areas where staff spend little of their time in custodial chores and consequently are able to spend more time in active teaching. The physical arrangement in both Daisy and the special section of Holly is similar to that in Iris; there is a variety of different rooms rather than a single large room as in the pre-treatment section of Holly. Maintenance and teaching programs are in progress throughout the day in both of these graduation areas. These programs guarantee that staff members continue to work with the residents and reinforce them periodically for their improved behavior. Because of the lower staff-resident ratio, teaching necessarily proceeds more slowly in these areas than in Iris. The programs established are adequate to maintain the gains achieved in Iris, and in many cases additional progress is made.

The goals in these graduation buildings include those of Iris itself. In Daisy, these have been expanded to include preparing some residents to become paid helpers within the institution, which represents a further extension of teaching vocational skills. Daisy also operates a token economy for the residents similar to that described in Chapter 6. Throughout the day residents may earn tokens for a variety of desirable behaviors and subsequently exchange the tokens for other reinforcers.

Thus, the progression from Holly, to Iris, to Daisy represents an integrated treatment sequence, whereby residents receive basic preparation in Holly, intensive teaching in Iris, and subsequently graduate into Daisy where behavioral programs maintain the improved behavior and where continued teaching provides the opportunity for further learning and advancement toward independence.

Scheduled teaching. The therapeutic benefits of intensive units do not result simply from the increased staffing and improved facilities which are available, but from the educational and therapeutic interactions which occur between residents and staff members. A crucial aspect of intensive teaching programs is the arranging of these therapeutic interactions. They generally do not occur spontaneously at a rate sufficient to effect major behavioral improvements. Rather, they must be scheduled.

There are two aspects of resident-staff interactions which must be considered in scheduling: the quantity and the quality. The first of these refers simply to bringing the residents and the staff together in some structured situation, i.e. guaranteeing that interactions will occur. The second refers to teaching the staff the principles of behavior modification, i.e. guaranteeing that the interactions which occur will be educational and therapeutic.

The main technique for ensuring that structured interactions occur is the use of staff schedules. These are essentially daily work plans for individual staff members. A portion of a typical schedule for the Iris staff is shown in Figure 5-2.

The residents are divided into two groups and stay together in

114   ILLUSTRATIVE PROGRAMS

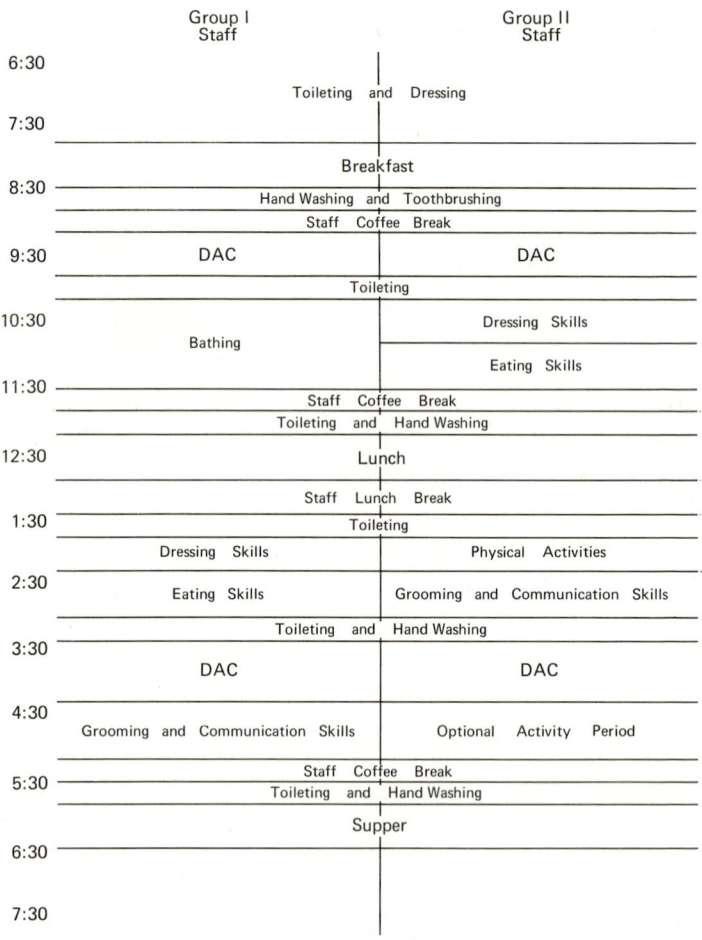

Figure 5-2. A sample daily work schedule for two Iris staff.

these groups throughout the day. During each work shift, one staff member is responsible for each of these groups. The staff schedule indicates what each staff member should be doing with each group of residents. This same over-all schedule is in effect seven days per week.

As the sample schedule shows, the residents' day is comprised of both regularly scheduled teaching periods (e.g. eating skills, dressing skills, Day Activity Center) and a variety of routine daily activities (e.g. meals, toileting, bathing). The routine activities are those which traditionally occupy staff in custodial-care institutions. In Iris these activities are handled as teaching periods.

For example, when the residents are awakened in the morning the idea is not simply to get them dressed and to breakfast. Staff members use this as a *very practical* time to teach the residents to dress themselves properly. *Staff members are careful never to do things for a resident that the resident can do for herself.* Rather, the staff spends its time teaching those residents who still need improvement. The same is true for other "routine" activities. When toileting, bathing, hand washing and toothbrushing are scheduled, these periods are used for the dual purpose of getting the task accomplished and teaching the residents to perform it themselves.

The staff schedules are intended to guarantee that each resident receives teaching in an appropriate range of activities. Individual teaching periods are kept short (one hour or less) to prevent boredom on the part of the residents and the staff. Since different activities are taught in different teaching rooms, activities are separated by the opportunity to move from one area to another. Within an activity period, such as eating skills or dressing skills or DAC, staff members are often free to select those particular activities which they feel are most appropriate for an individual resident. A variety of written programs is available for use in each of the teaching periods, and these generally correspond to the specific activities listed previously under "Program Goals." Written programs are also available to guide the teaching of the routine activities.

Throughout the treatment sequence written programs are used to provide staff with a procedural outline of how to teach an activity. These written programs ensure that all staff will approach a teaching problem in the same way, thus avoiding the possibility of different staff working at cross-purposes. Many of the activities are taught as backward chains—the last step of the task is taught first. This type of program, in particular, requires that a written outline be provided to the staff because it is the opposite of a common-sense approach. To further ensure that staff members approach the teaching task effectively, score records are kept on a number of activities. This allows staff to begin a teaching task at the level which is appropriate for each resident.

EVALUATION

The final test of any treatment procedure is the simple question of how well it works. Are the goals of the program accomplished? Do the residents learn the behaviors they are supposed to learn? Any treatment efforts which are tried require adequate evaluation for improvement and correction. If procedures are instituted without evaluation, the risk is simply too great that the effort will be wasted on ineffective techniques without the waste even being realized. Certainly, any procedure which has not been subjected to the test of objective evaluation should not be blindly copied by others.

Of the thirty-three participants in the Iris program, thirteen have not yet completed their intensive teaching period. Evaluation of the program is, therefore, based upon the twenty residents who have graduated. Several alternative procedures for evaluation will be considered.

Fates of treated residents. Examination of the fate or disposition of the participants is one rather general way to gauge the success of a treatment program. The specific goal of the Iris program is to prepare residents to function satisfactorily in buildings with higher-functioning residents.

Fourteen of the twenty residents who have completed have graduated to higher-level buildings. Five have returned to Holly Building where they reside in a special section which maintains a considerably improved level of behavioral functioning as compared to the pre-treatment section of Holly. One resident became ill shortly before she was to transfer to a higher-level building and died after several months of hospitalization.

Thus, judged on this very general criterion, the Iris program is successful in achieving its goal. The continued adequate functioning of these residents indicates that their behavior has been improved considerably. The following evaluation procedures provide a more quantifiable measure of this behavioral improvement.

Comprehensive ratings. To provide information on a broad range of the residents' behavior, the institution's "Social Skills Checklist" has been filled out both before and after the intensive teaching experience. This is a long series of questions about specific aspects of the residents' behavior. To evaluate the treatment program, forty-one items have been selected from the larger checklist which are relevant to the goals of the Iris program. These items include questions on toileting, bathing, dressing, eating, grooming, recreational and vocational skills, etc. The rating is done by a staff member who is familiar with the resident.

Pre- and post-test scores on this rating scale are available for sixteen residents and are shown in Table 5-1, along with the

Table 5-1. Scores and changes by each resident on comprehensive rating scale.

	Scores			Percentage change		
Resident	Pre-test	Post-test	Change	Per cent of pre-test	Per cent of total scale	Per cent of possible change
G.G	24	21	- 3	- 12.5	- 7.3	- 12.5
G.L.	32	30	- 2	- 6.2	- 4.9	- 6.2
R.F.	37	36	- 1	- .27	- 2.4	- 2.7
L.A.	33	33	0	0.0	0.0	0.0
B.R.	12	13	+ 1	+ 8.3	+ 2.4	+ 3.4
M.W.	21	23	+ 2	+ 9.5	+ 4.9	+10.0
J. G.	26	28	+ 2	+ 7.6	+ 4.9	+13.3
S.K.	16	21	+ 5	+31.2	+12.2	+20.0
D.L.	27	30	+ 3	+11.1	+ 7.3	+21.4
M.K.	15	22	+ 7	+46.6	+17.1	+26.9
J.R.	31	34	+ 3	+ 9.7	+ 7.3	+30.0
C.V.	9	24	+15	166.7	+36.6	+46.9
M.T.	21	32	+11	+52.4	+26.8	+55.0
J.K.	23	34	+11	+47.8	+26.8	+61.1
P.M.	21	34	+13	+61.9	+31.7	+65.0
S.G.	21	35	+14	+66.7	+34.1	+70.0
Average	23.1	28.1	+ 5.0	+21.6	+12.1	+27.9

amount of change occurring during the treatment period. The per cent of possible improvement for each resident is graphed in Figure 5-3. The "possible change" upon which this calculation is based is the difference between the pre-test score and a perfect score for those residents who improved, or between the pre-test score and a zero score for those residents who showed declines.

Twelve of the sixteen residents show improvement on the behaviors measured by this rating scale. Most of the residents not showing improvement had very high pre-test scores, indicating that this scale is not appropriate for evaluating their level of ability since there was little room for improvement. Clearly, the program is quite successful in improving the behavior of the participants.

Progress records. Continuous progress records of the residents' behavior changes over time provide the most valuable and detailed information concerning resident improvement. Such continuous records have been kept by staff for a limited number of behaviors. Though this is the most valuable type of record, it is

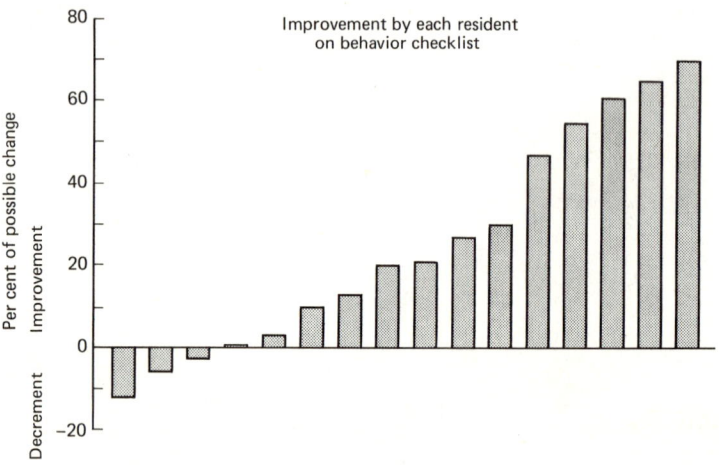

Figure 5-3. Per cent of possible improvement for each of the sixteen residents for whom pre- and post-ratings are available.

also the most time-consuming for staff during the teaching period, and also for supervisors in preparing the summary records. When continuous records are kept, it becomes possible to evaluate the success of a particular teaching effort after only a trial period. Teaching approaches which are not successful can then be improved before too much wasted effort is invested in them.

When a new group of residents enters the Iris program, one of the primary efforts is to teach proper toileting behavior. Figure 5-4 shows the decline in incontinence during residents' stay in Iris.

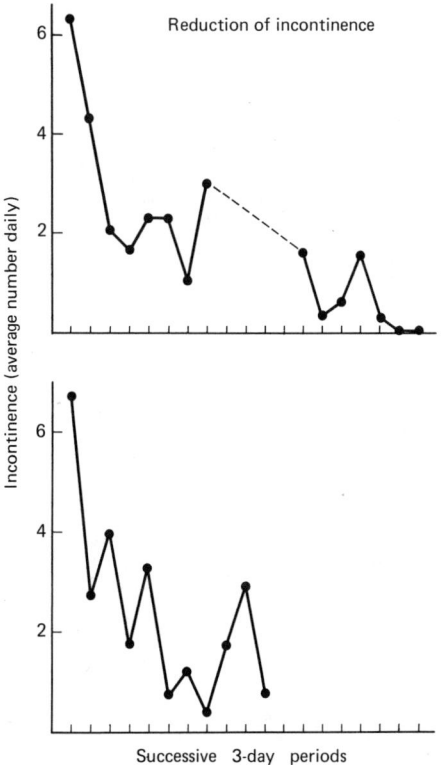

Figure 5-4. Each graph starts when a new group of residents entered Iris. Total incontinence (both urination and defecation including bed wetting) declines during treatment in Iris.

Continuous records have been kept of other routine self-care activities, including bathing, hand washing, and toothbrushing. Examination of the bathing records has not revealed any consistent evidence of progress, so the teaching program and the scoring arrangement are being revised. The hand washing and toothbrushing programs have been quite successful. Seventeen out of twenty residents attained perfect scores in hand washing, and eighteen out of twenty reached perfect scores in toothbrushing. Representative progress records for two individuals are shown in Figure 5-5 for hand washing, and in Figure 5-6 for toothbrushing.

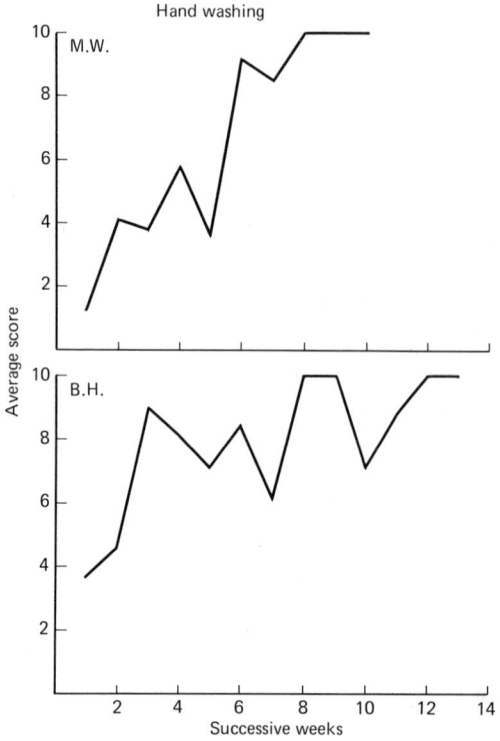

Figure 5-5. Representative score records showing improvement by two residents on hand washing.

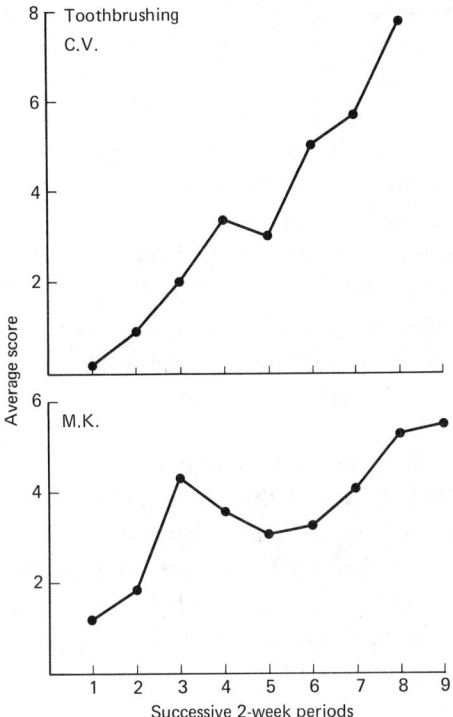

Figure 5-6. Representative score records showing improvement by two individuals on toothbrushing.

The rates and patterns of improvement may be very different for different individuals.

Detailed aspects of organization and implementation

BEGINNING THE TREATMENT PROGRAM

The problems involved in introducing behavior modification methods in Iris Building were quite different from those ordinarily faced when initiating such a program. Usually, the first task is to convert the staff orientation from custodial care to active teaching. However, in Iris Building staff members already had a predominant treatment orientation. They had worked hard with residents and felt that they could go no further without assistance.

During the initial three months that Iris became an intensive teaching unit, staff members became progressively frustrated. They indicated that they simply did not know what else to do with the residents. During this initial period the residents had experienced an enriched environment with increased staffing. The stimulation resulting from this treatment method, however, was not enough to produce the changes that were desired. To be sure, the residents were clean and neatly clothed, and their environment was clean and pleasant, but this was primarily the result of having enough staff to tend to these matters and was not due to any overwhelming change in the residents' behavior.

Staff members felt that with their current resources the treatment program had stagnated. It was at this point that behavior modification consultants began to serve the Iris program.

The diagnosis was clear. Iris had staff, facilities, and general goals but lacked effective teaching procedures. This was particularly interesting in view of the fact that the staff had participated in a traditional training program for institutional staff.

THE FIRST STAFF MEETING

It was decided that one general staff meeting could provide sufficient familiarization with the methods of behavior modification to allow the initiation of the first formal programs. Although the Iris staff was enthusiastic, a certain amount of skepticism accompanies the introduction of any new treatment method in institutions. The most telling reassurance to the staff comes from a demonstrable success (Nawas and Braun, 1970a). Therefore, we decided that initially staff members would use the new procedures only briefly during the day. Later, as they became more comfortable with the procedures and as they gained confidence in their efficacy, the staff could be asked to use behavior modification methods throughout the day.

There were four main objectives to the first general staff meeting: (1) introduction of the *methods* of behavior modification; (2) a behavioral *problem* for each staff member; (3) initiation of a special *demonstration program;* (4) initiation of a *scheduled teaching program.*

Methods. At the meeting each staff member received an outline description of behavior modification (Table 5-2). The discussion presented the general idea that behavior is caused by the environment and emphasized reinforcement as the major cause, how to analyze a particular situation for causes, and how to use reinforcement in teaching.

Problem. The staff also received an outline for analyzing resident behavior (Table 5-3). For the following week, each staff member was asked to analyze some behavioral situation and to design a program to improve the situation by using the principles of behavior modification. This sample program not only gave the staff some experience with objective analysis but provided feedback to the consultants on the staff's understanding of the principles of behavior modification.

Demonstration program. A demonstration program was designed to illustrate the effectiveness and simplicity of behavior modification. To make the demonstration meaningful an offensive behavior that annoyed the staff was chosen: the incredibly fast and sloppy eating behavior of one of the residents. This resident literally tried to cram all of her food into her mouth at the same time, which often resulted in choking and spitting food back up onto her plate. The program specified that the resident must swallow each mouthful of food before being allowed to lift her fork to her mouth again. While the program initially required constant staff supervision at meals, it was simple and successful—ultimately the resident was eating neatly with very little staff supervision.

Scheduled program. The staff was asked to spend two one-hour periods each shift working with the residents in the DAC teaching rooms. We started with just one highly structured, scored, and

Table 5-2. Reproduction of outline given to each staff member when first teaching the principles of behavior modification.

Procedure for altering behavior

The technique is called "behavior modification"

The basic concern is to improve the patient's *behavior*.

Behavior is caused and can be altered by changing some of these causes. A primary cause of behavior it its *consequence* — what happens following the behavior.

A basic principle is to *do whatever is effective* in improving the patient's behavior.
This requires:

1. You know which behaviors you want: i.e. that there are specific *behaviors to be strengthened*.

2. You know which behaviors you do not want: i.e. that there are specific *behaviors to be weakened*.

3. You are *counting* these behaviors so you can tell whether or not the patient is improving.

The basic technique has three steps:

1. *Pinpoint* : Describe the behavior in enough detail so that anyone who reads your description can count how frequently the behavior occurs. This is the *target behavior*.

2. *Count and/or chart* : Records must be kept to tell us whether the patient's behavior is improving or not.

3. *Change* some aspect of the behavioral situation which you think might affect the frequency of the pinpointed behavior.

How to approach a behavior problem:

Remember that *behavior is caused*.

Examine the behavioral situation:

    A.   Description of current behavior

        1. *Pinpoint* : specific enough to allow counting

        2. *Before* : situations or circumstances under which the behavior is most likely to occur.

        3. *After* : what happens following the behavior?

Could any of these events be serving as reinforcers?

    B.   Description of desired behavior

        1. *Pinpoint*

        2. *Before*

        3. *After*

Decide behavioral *goal* :

        1.   *Strengthen* a behavior by *reinforcing* it.

                Reinforcers should be delivered *immediately* following the desired behavior.

When a new behavior is first being learned, reinforcement should be delivered *consistently*, *every time* the desired behavior occurs.

Later, to make the behavior more durable, reinforcement should be delivered *Intermittently*.

2. *Weaken* a behavior by *extinguishing* it.

Extinguish a behavior by ignoring it, or preventing it from having a reinforcing consequence, e.g. time out.

The best way to weaken an undesirable behavior is to extinguish it while at the same time reinforcing some desirable alternative behavior to replace it.

Punishment may also weaken behavior, but use of this technique is discouraged.

Principles of *designing a program* :

Keep reinforcement frequent enough to maintain the performance of the patient.

Do not require too much. Initially, start with a task the patient can already do.

Gradually require more. Always increase the requirement slowly and gradually.

scheduled program to familiarize the staff with behavioral procedures. It was essential that the staff learn to dispense reinforcers properly, readily, and comfortably if further teaching was to be successful. The task chosen was teaching the residents to fasten and zip up zippers on coats. The program and scoring procedure was described explicitly and the staff was expected to score several residents on the activity each day.

TEACHING THE STAFF

Much of the consultants' initial effort in the Iris program was directed toward teaching the staff proper use of the principles of behavior modification. Part of the consultants' working day was spent working with staff in the ward situation. During periods of teaching activity the consultants demonstrated techniques and also made suggestions for improving staff techniques. Discussions with staff concerning resident behavior allowed the consultants to

Table 5-3. Reproduction of problem sheet which each staff member was asked to complete as part of initial training in behavioral procedures

Outline for approach to behavior modification

I   Resident

II General class of behavior

III Description of current behavior

   A. *Pinpoint:* specific enough to allow counting; indicate frequency of occurrence.
   B. *Before:* situations or circumstances under which it is most likely to occur
   C. *After:* what happens following the behavior?

   Could any of these events be serving as reinforcers?

IV Description of desired behavior

   A. *Pinpoint:* specific enough to allow counting
   B. *Before:* situations or circumstances under which it should occur
   C. *After:* what reinforcing consequence will follow the behavior and serve to maintain it?

V   Detailed procedure and program for developing the desired behavior.

make suggestions about handling particular behavioral situations which permitted further emphasis of particular techniques of behavior management. The rationale for all treatment programs was always explained to the staff.

Initially, the consultants wrote virtually all behavioral programs in Iris, including both ward-wide teaching programs and those designed to handle the disruptive behavior problems of individual residents. Since one of the goals was to develop a unit that would be totally self-sufficient, staff members were encouraged to suggest programs. When they were proficient at suggesting programs, they were encouraged to submit written programs for the consultants to review. Finally, staff members were encouraged to work individually with any resident on any teaching task of their choosing. Each staff member submitted a written description of his program along with a scoring procedure. Thereafter the staff members taught the resident daily and publicly graphed the results.

Suggesting, writing, and implementing such programs familiarized the staff members with the principles of behavior modification. As they became convinced that the procedures could radically alter the lives of the residents, the staff members grew increasingly concerned that effective treatment procedures be used. They also began to realize that improper use of behavioral principles affects the residents' behavior adversely and consequently causes problems for all the staff in the future. Therefore, staff members began to initiate discussions among themselves about the most effective procedures to use with certain residents. They became skilled in weighing the pros and cons of various approaches. In addition, whenever staff members saw a behavioral situation being handled improperly, they were quite inclined to speak up and make suggestions about how the situation could be improved. Although this may seem natural to the reader, it is, in fact, quite unusual within a state institution.

At the end of six months, there was little question that the Iris staff members had become very effective behavior modifiers. They could not only teach residents effectively, but they could scrutinize behavioral problems, write and carry out effective programs. Whereas initially the consultants had spent much of their time devising therapeutic programs, their role increasingly became that of scheduling staff and facilitating staff development of programs.

STAFF SCHEDULING

An often overlooked but extremely important factor in the successful functioning of an institutional building is the proper scheduling of staff time. A schedule indicates what the staff should be doing with the residents and when. Its importance lies in the fact that it helps the staff maintain a high level of therapeutic activity throughout the day.

The first changes in Iris Building were made with little appreciation for staff scheduling. The staff members were asked to increase the time they spent in the teaching rooms from about one to four hours each shift. This was simply too much. While teaching the profoundly retarded can be exciting and rewarding, it also is fatiguing. The staff was expected to spend too long a period in the same place with the same group of residents. Both the staff and the residents became bored. It became apparent that if teaching was to be effective in Iris, a better means of scheduling staff would have to be designed.

The problem of staff scheduling is that of deciding on an order of activities that will make teaching most enjoyable for the staff, while still maintaining a high level of effective teaching. It was decided that *variability* was an important aspect of staff scheduling. Instead of a few long teaching periods in the same room, many shorter teaching periods were scheduled in different rooms with different residents. A sample staff schedule is illustrated in Figure 5-2. During each shift, a given staff member is responsible for taking a group of girls to a variety of different program areas. There is a variety of written programs in each area (e.g. bathroom: washing, toothbrushing, toileting; eating room: use of fork, knife, spoon, tray, etc.) In each of these program areas the staff member has some degree of flexibility as to exactly which activities are taught.

Beyond scheduling variability throughout the day, a number of different procedures were attempted to ensure that the staff would spend the allotted time teaching in each of the program areas. For a while staff members were asked to record the times that they entered and left program areas on sheets posted near the doors. At another time, they filled out time records of how they spent their entire work day. At still another stage the number of scored activities by each staff member was recorded each day.

Although none of these procedures was optimal, the authors feel that some sort of measure of staff performance is desirable. It gives the consultants and administrators a realistic appraisal of what the residents are being taught as well as the opportunity to evaluate the effects of program scheduling. Such measures keep staff performance high and serve to remind staff members that their job is active teaching. If used constructively, the staff appreciates the feedback from such performance indicators.

EXPANSION OF PROGRAMS

As the staff became familiarized and skilled in the use of behavior modification procedures, the amount of programming throughout the day was extended. Various self-care programs were developed and scheduled.

Toileting periods were scheduled throughout the day. This was essential in teaching previously incontinent residents proper use of the toilet facilities. Incontinence usually occurs among residents because they are seldom, if ever, reinforced for using the toilet. Scheduling frequent toileting periods increases the chances that such residents will use the toilet and hence be reinforced.

A program was written for daily bathing in a bathtub. Previously the residents had been bathed by showering. Since the shower had hindered the ability of staff members to be effective teachers, they had viewed bathing as primarily a custodial task rather than a teaching activity. Along with the bathing program, instruction was given in undressing and dressing.

Other self-care activities taught were washing hands with soap and water (which was scheduled four times daily) and brushing teeth (twice daily).

One teaching room was used to teach eating skills. These programs included teaching residents to carry a cafeteria tray and to handle eating utensils properly. The staff developed several ingenious programs involving the use of eating utensils. Residents learned to use a spoon in a task which required them to spoon kernels of corn from one bowl to another. They learned to use a fork by moving balls of clay from one bowl to another, and a knife by cutting flat pieces of clay.

Special housekeeping activities were designed to prepare some of the more advanced residents to work as resident-helpers within the institution. These activities included sweeping, mopping, washing sinks, and wiping tables. Educational and recreational programming was also expanded during the DAC periods.

The expansion of therapeutic programming in Iris occurred gradually. New programs were added as they were developed. The aim, which was ultimately attained, was to establish effective therapeutic activities throughout the day.

THE DEVELOPMENT OF TOKEN SYSTEMS

Token use in Iris developed out of a program designed to control minor misbehaviors. Many of the residents first admitted to the unit engaged in a variety of aberrant self-stimulation activities such as rectal digging, nose picking, chewing on pieces of string, or continual picking at lint on their clothing. One of the staff members suggested a program to systematically reinforce residents for doing anything other than their particular type of misbehavior. This program was called DRO (Differential Reinforcement of Other Behavior) and involved reinforcing residents at the end of a fixed time interval if they did not engage in the specified undesirable behavior. Those residents who did misbehave missed out on reinforcement.

It was decided that the program would be facilitated if the residents were given immediate feedback when they misbehaved. Each resident was given a token necklace to wear at the beginning of each session. If a resident misbehaved during the session, her necklace would be taken from her. At the end of the session each resident who still had her token necklace could exchange it for a treat. The staff praised those residents who had tokens and ignored those residents who had misbehaved. After several hours of teaching, the residents learned how to use the token necklace appropriately. This greatly enhanced the effectiveness of the DRO program and enabled the staff to extend the reinforcement intervals from several minutes to fifteen to thirty minutes.

Once the residents learned the value of the token necklace, it was possible to expand the use of the token program to other periods during the day. For instance, tokens were used to improve resident behavior during meal times. Any resident who misbehaved during the meal would lose her necklace. At the end of each meal, residents with tokens traded them for a candy treat and were praised for being good.

A further extension of the token program involved using the token necklaces as positive reinforcers. When residents accomplished some desirable behavior, they received a token necklace. For instance, before meals residents were able to earn their necklaces for that meal by washing their hands.

Although token programs are becoming increasingly popular in institutional settings (Ayllon and Azrin, 1968), they have been used so infrequently with the severely and profoundly retarded that unfortunately they are often completely overlooked as a viable means of behavior control for such residents.

EXTENSIONS TO OTHER BUILDINGS

Before any residents graduated from Iris, it was necessary to establish adequate behavior-maintaining programs in the graduation areas, the next step in the *treatment sequence*. Since there are considerably fewer staff per resident in Daisy and Holly, the intensity of programming in these areas necessarily had to be lower than in Iris. The main emphasis in programs in these areas has been to keep the staff actively engaged with the residents. Staff schedules were prepared just as they were for the Iris staff. Because resident progress could not be expected to be very rapid, record keeping concentrated upon whether or not staff members were busy, and whether or not they were keeping the residents engaged in some activity. Less emphasis was placed upon the recording of resident progress. The procedures involved in initiating programming in Daisy may be instructive.

Before programming began in Daisy, the residents spent most of their time sitting idly in a pleasantly decorated day room. Few constructive activities were available. The initial programming efforts in Daisy were to encourage the staff to work at getting the residents actively engaged in some activity. Records were kept of

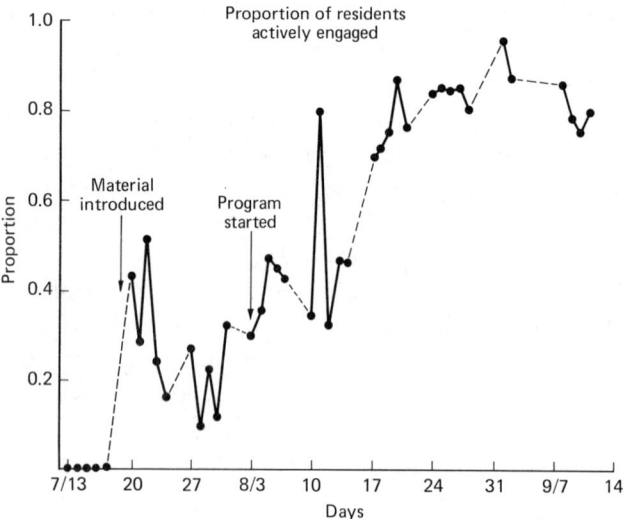

Figure 5-7. Proportion of residents actively engaged in the Daisy day room before programming started, after activities were made available, and after a reinforcement program was started.

the proportion of residents actively engaged. These were obtained by several daily spot checks and are grouped in Figure 5-7.

Initially, no residents were busy. The first change was to introduce some recreational materials (puzzles, toys, etc.) into the day room (i.e. providing a more enriched environment). Immediately, the proportion of busy residents jumped to 40 to 50 per cent. Over the next ten days, however, this dropped back to about 15 to 20 per cent. Apparently the initial increase was due simply to the novelty of having activities available. The enriched environment alone was insufficient to maintain a high level of participation.

At this point, a staff schedule was introduced which assigned one staff member to the day room with instructions to encourage and reinforce those residents who were actively engaged in activities. As shown in Figure 5-7, the proportion of busy residents quickly rose to about 85 per cent. Records of resident participation such as these can serve as an effective indicator of whether the staff is working with and reinforcing the residents.

Other programs in Daisy were oriented toward maintaining the specific behavioral improvements which had been produced in Iris. These included daily programming of various self-help skills, such as bathing, washing, and toothbrushing, as well as regularly scheduled recreational and educational periods. A token economy was started like the one in Poppy Building (Chapter 6), where residents earned tokens throughout the day which could later be exchanged in a "token store" for treats or special clothing. One of the higher level programs which was initiated in Daisy involved teaching residents to do a variety of housekeeping activities within the building. Residents who did well were given jobs as resident-helpers in other buildings. The main goal of this program was to move these residents to still higher-level buildings where they could live more independently and have greater freedom.

INTENSIVE UNITS AND BEHAVIOR PROBLEMS

If staff members have been well trained in the practice of behavior modification, intensive teaching units are particularly well adapted for the rehabilitation of behavior problems. One of the major strengths of the Iris treatment program was its ability to accept residents with particularly severe and disruptive behavior problems from other areas in the institution and restore them to a more effective level of functioning.

Resident J. O. One of the residents had a long history of extreme self-abuse. She was a head-banger, and had previously spent large portions of her days strapped by both arms and legs into a bed to prevent her from severely damaging herself. She was not verbal, and she appeared to have both speech and hearing defects.

When J. O. could no longer be managed in the regular ward, she was transferred to the acute medical hospital. In spite of changes in her medication, she continued her self-abuse and required restraints and periodic I.M.'s. After spending over a year in the acute medical hospital, she was transferred to Iris and behavior modification was attempted.

Not surprisingly, the history of her problem suggested that this severe and dangerously self-destructive behavior was being maintained by the staff attention that it inevitably produced. Typical chart notes indicated that the resident was being reinforced for becoming disturbed: "The technician stated that getting (the resident's) mind off her disturbed state by rubbing her back and neck or by taking her out in the cool air helps quite often."

The treatment program in Iris consisted essentially in ignoring the resident's self-destructive behavior while providing attention for more adaptive types of behavior. It was stipulated that whenever the resident began to get agitated or bang her head, all staff would totally ignore her. If she continued to bang her head for a few minutes, the staff was to put a football helmet on her head with as little interaction as possible. The specially prepared football helmet had a locking chin strap so that the resident was unable to remove it.

The rationale for this treatment was that the beginning of the self-abuse episode should not be successful in producing attention from the staff. Therefore it was required that she be immediately ignored whenever this behavior started. Although we decided that J. O. could safely experience the painful first burst of head-banging, she had to be protected from prolonged head-banging and possibly serious damage.

The severe head-banging in this resident, which had been a problem for years previously, disappeared within a few weeks. J. O. continued to have some loud temper tantrums; however, these also became much less frequent over her seven months' stay at Iris. Although previously she had been in Holly with the most disruptive female residents of the institution, she had improved to the point that she could now be transferred to a higher-level building.

Resident J. A. was a relatively bright (I.Q. 49), verbal resident who was seriously disrupting staff activity in Daisy Building. She had recurrent auditory hallucinations that bothered her to the point that staff members felt she "needed" someone to talk to many times each day. Typically, if no one would talk to her, she would become increasingly disturbed and disruptive on the ward and ultimately get attention.

When she was transferred to Iris, the staff was instructed to ignore her undesirable behavior and talk with her only about positive, acceptable types of activities. They were to terminate their interaction with her when she talked about becoming disturbed or mentioned her hallucinations. The improvement was immediate and dramatic. The hallucinations either stopped or no longer bothered her and she began to engage in more acceptable social behavior with both staff and other residents. After several months she took a part-time job as a resident-helper in the cafeteria, and in several more months she was transferred to one of Faribault's highest-level buildings, which houses resident-helpers and residents eligible for community placement. One day she approached one of the consultants and said, "Thank you for making me better. I always wanted to be better but I didn't know how to before."

Behavior problems in institutions usually develop because the resident receives attention for disruptive behaviors such as stripping, incontinence, pestering, head-banging, etc. Since such behaviors are annoying, the problem resident is generally disliked by the staff. Accordingly, the staff interaction with this type of resident is usually disapproving or punitive. With the behavior modification approach, the resident no longer receives attention for inappropriate behavior. As the resident becomes less of a problem, the staff begins to like him more, and accordingly, gives more attention to appropriate behavior. The effects are rapid and dramatic.

The successful treatment of behavior problems was an unexpected benefit of intensive units. Initially, we anticipated that Iris would be concerned almost exclusively with the slow acquisition of self-help and activity behaviors. Now it appears that the residents who have benefited most rapidly from the Iris project are those individuals who had once been functioning at a higher level but had deteriorated during their institutionalization. In terms of efficient use of treatment facilities (i.e. achieving rapid, major improvement after only short periods of treatment), this type of resident appears ideally suited for intensive treatment programs.

COORDINATION

The success of intensive teaching units depends upon cooperation at three separate levels: the hospital administrators, the behavioral consultants, and the building staff. A program's success is in jeopardy if any of these three groups fails to do their part.

Hospital administrators. Roos (1965) indicated that an intensive unit's success was greatly enhanced when the hospital superintendent emphasized direct participation and active facilitation in a program rather than the traditional "laissez-faire" attitude. There is no doubt that at Faribault the administration provided the initial impetus for program development throughout the institution. In the Iris program, the enthusiastic support from the institutional administration when coupled with the effective leadership of the unit director proved invaluable to the implementation of the program.

Behavioral consultants. Nawas and Braun (1970a) stressed the importance of the behavioral consultant in the development of behavior modification programs. The behavioral consultant works with both the building staff and the administration. In the building, the behavioral consultant writes programs, trains staff, and makes suggestions for scheduling staff. The behavioral consultant should serve as a liaison between the building and administration. It is the behavioral consultant's job to work with administration in developing future plans.

Building staff. Lastly, and no doubt most importantly, the building staff must do its part if a program is to succeed. As Nawas and

Braun (1970a) point out, a staff member may resist changes and sometimes actively but surreptitiously try to undermine the program. The staff understandably resents innovations that will necessarily disrupt familiar routines. On the other hand, a flexible, open-minded staff that is willing to try the techniques of behavior modification will greatly speed program development.

References

Ayllon, T., and N. Azrin. *The Token Economy*. New York: Appleton-Century-Crofts, 1968.

Belmont, J. M., and N. R. Ellis. Effects of extraneous stimulation upon discrimination learning in normals and retardates. *Amer. J. ment. Defic.*, 1968, 72, 525-32.

Colwell, C. N. "Amazing changes" in profoundly retarded. *Rehabilitation Record*, 1969, 10 (1), 10-12.

Davis, W. E. An approach to programming for severely and profoundly retarded adults. *Training School Bulletin*, 1969, 66 (3), 100-104.

Ellis, N. R., and T. R. Anders. Short-term memory in the mental retardate. *Amer. J. ment. Defic.*, 1968, 72, 931-36.

Gorton, C. E., and J. H. Hollis. Redesigning a cottage unit for better porgramming and research for the severely retarded. *Mental Retardation*, 1965, 3 (3), 16-21.

Haywood, H. C., and L. W. Heal. Retention of learned visual associations as a function of I.Q. and learning levels. *Amer. J. ment. Defic.*, 1968, 72, 828-38.

Hollis, J. H., and C. E. Gorton. Training severely and profoundly developmentally retarded children. *Mental Retardation*, 1967, 5 (4), 20-24.

Kimbrell, D. L., F. Kidwell, and G. Hallum. Institutional environment developed for training severely and profoundly retarded. *Mental Retardation*, 1967, 5 (1), 34-37.

Kimbrell, D. L., R. E. Luckey, P. F. Barbuto, and J. G. Love. Operation dry pants: an intensive habit-training program for severely and profoundly retarded. *Mental Retardation*, 1967, 5 (2), 32-36.

Leath, J. R., and R. L. Flournoy. Three-year follow-up of intensive habit-training program. *Mental Retardation*, 1970, 8 (3), 32-34.

Lindsley, O. R. Direct measurement and prosthesis of retarded behavior. *Journal of Education*, 1964, *147*, 62-81.

Miller, L., and M. Trainor. *HIP Activity Manual*, Pacific State Hospital, Pomona, California, 1968.

Nawas, M. M., and S. H. Braun. The use of operant techniques for modifying the behavior of the severely and profoundly retarded: part I. introduction and initial phase. *Mental Retardation*, 1970a, *8* (2), 2-6.

———. The use of operant techniques for modifying the behavior of the severely and profoundly retarded: part II. the techniques. *Mental Retardation*, 1970b, *8* (3), 18-24.

———. An overview of behavior modification with the severely and profoundly retarded: part III. maintenance of change and epilogue. *Mental Retardation*, 1970c, *8* (4), 4-11.

Roos, P. Development of an intensive habit-training unit at Austin State School. *Mental Retardation*, 1965, *3* (3), 12-15.

Stevens, H. A. Overview. In H. Stevens and R. Heber (Eds.), *Mental Retardation*. Chicago: University of Chicago Press, 1964, pp. 1-15.

Tobias, J., and A. D. Cortazzo. Training severely retarded adults for greater independence in community living. *Training School Bulletin*, 1963, *60*, 23-27.

Watson, L. S. Application of operant conditioning techniques to institutionalized severely and profoundly retarded children. *Mental Retardation Abstracts*, 1967, *4* (1), 1-18.

6
A token system for retarded women: behavior modification, drug therapy, and their combination*

O. LINDA McCONAHEY

Previous research with token systems
for the mentally retarded

Token reinforcement studies began experimentally in 1937 (Kelleher, 1966) when animals were first trained by food reinforcement to insert tokens into a slot. After the delivery of token was made contingent on a response such as bar pressing, the exchange interval (the time required to keep the tokens before exchange) and the exchange ratio (the number of tokens needed to exchange) were varied. Kelleher (1966) considered schedules of token reinforcement to be special cases of long behavioral chains,** in which the delivery of the token acts as a reinforcer at the end of each component.

Since their introduction, there have been many reviews of the therapeutic use of tokens in applied institutionalized settings (Atthowe and Krasner, 1968; Ayllon and Azrin, 1965; Ball, 1969; Birnbrauer and Lawler, 1964; Birnbrauer et al., 1965; Burchand, 1967; Hunt et al., 1968; Fischer, 1966; Lent, 1968; Lent and Spradlin, 1966; Liberman, 1968; Lloyd and Abel, 1970; Lloyd and Garling-

---

* This research was supported in part by U.S.P.H.S. Grant Number MH-05106 and U.S.P.H.S. Grant Number MH-08565 to the University of Minnesota.
** Technically called chained schedules (Ferster and Skinner, 1957).

ton, 1968; Perline and Levinsky, 1968; Phillips, 1968; Roberts and Perry, 1970; Winkler, 1970; Zimmerman *et al.*, 1969). Perhaps the most complete is *The Token Economy*, a book by Ayllon and Azrin (1968). These reviews describe the application of the principles of behavior modification to therapeutic and educational problems. In contrast to much of the literature on behavior modification dealing with a single reinforcer (e.g. food) employed to change the frequency of occurrence of a single response in one patient, the token programs involve many different terminal reinforcers for a variety of responses from many patients. Often the reinforcement contingencies are in effect twenty-four hours a day, seven days a week.

On a token ward the occurrence of low-frequency behaviors (such as personal grooming, social interaction, and constructive tasks) provides access to high-frequency behaviors (such as eating, recreation, and sitting) by means of the tokens. The assumption is made that a high-frequency behavior can act as a reinforcer for a behavior less likely to occur (Premack, 1959).

Tokens are introduced gradually by pairing their presentation with other reinforcers (usually edibles) and slowly extending the time and distance between the receiving of the token and its exchange for edible reinforcement. At first tokens are presented without requiring any specific behavior of the resident, but gradually the requirements to earn tokens increase until the behavior reaches the criterion chosen. In this way individual differences in learning and performance can be dealt with in the over-all token system.

Although the use of incentives for adaptive behavior is not new, the system generally present in mental hospitals was not workable even under ideal conditions since the giving of rewards was not systematized and was almost impossible to record or supervise. Most recording (when done at all) was retrospective; and when verbal reinforcement was used, the way in which reinforcement was given varied greatly, even if the words were the same. There was need for a specification of the appropriate behavior and the reinforcer in advance in order that there might be some consistency.

ADVANTAGES OF TOKENS

Tokens are valuable for several reasons:

1. The number of tokens earned can be quantitatively related to the amount of reinforcement.

2. Tokens are portable and can be carried by the resident away from the place of reinforcement. They also allow the response to be reinforced any time or place.

3. There is no maximum number of tokens a subject may possess. Therefore, satiation does not occur (i.e. the resident does not become "tired" of tokens).

4. Tokens can be made continuously available between the response and the terminal reinforcement, and thus bridge the delay between the response and the delivery of the reinforcer.

5. Tokens can be made durable and unique.

6. Tokens allow sequences of responses to be reinforced without interruption due to the delivery of a primary reinforcer such as food (Ayllon and Azrin, 1968).

Token systems, when instituted on a ward-wide basis, can provide a compromise between shaping programs for individual residents and a single program for the whole population. Zimmerman et al. (1969) studied a group of seven retarded boys using verbal instructions in which tokens were exchangeable for primary reinforcers after the sessions. They found this approach successful for all but the most severely retarded children in teaching instruction-following behavior. In contrast, Lent and Spradlin (1966) developed a token system for mentally retarded girls involving individual programs. It was highly effective where the ratio of staff to patients was large, a situation which, unfortunately, rarely exists in state mental hospitals. Because of staff shortage and lack of funds, a typical token program consists of broad guidelines for token earning for the whole population with special programs for individuals, as needed.

When dividing a ward into workable groups, one of two approaches is usually taken. The residents are either divided by degree of adaptive behavior and each group contains like members, or else each group is completely heterogeneous. There are advantages and disadvantages to each method. A homogenous group is easier to teach since all are at the same level, and as members progress they can be moved to higher-functioning groups. However, the members of each group have already been "branded" and the group leaders tend to expect much less from the low-functioning groups. The heterogeneous group is much more difficult to teach since there must be many levels of activities available simultaneously, but it carries the advantage of exposing low-functioning residents to high-functioning residents, and often the learning of adaptive behaviors is thereby accelerated. Lloyd and Abel (1970) described homogenous grouping on the basis of behavior in a psychiatric ward. They concluded that grouping might be unnecessary if rules could be established less arbitrarily. They also found that there was no relation between drug prescription, psychiatric diagnosis, age or length of stay in hospital and favorable progress under a token economy.

It might be questioned whether the contingent presentation of tokens is effective in changing behavior, or whether it is simply the increased number of staff and staff attention which alters resident behavior. Ayllon and Azrin (1965), Winkler (1970) and Lloyd and Garlington (1968) have shown that when no tokens were given contingent on performance, adaptive behavior decreased, and when tokens were given, but not contingent on performance, adaptive behavior decreased as well.

Ayllon and Azrin studied patients who had been on a token ward for eighteen months. The reversal of prior conditions caused large and abrupt changes in the numbers of hours of work on jobs by patients. Winkler (1970) showed that changes in patient behavior could not be explained solely by such factors as increased staff attention, extra luxuries, or increased expectations. He investigated the effects of (1) a brief period of token removal; (2)

presentation of non-contingent tokens; and (3) removal of fines in one area on positively reinforced behaviors, unreinforced behaviors, and fined behavior. All behaviors positively reinforced had improved over time, and both violence and noise (two unreinforced behaviors) had decreased significantly. When tokens were removed, all patients showed a decrease in performance (in this case shoe cleaning), and when tokens were reinstated, performance returned to baseline.

When tokens were presented non-contingently (for simple assembly-type jobs in the industrial therapy unit), work output dropped immediately.

During occupational therapy, fines were discontinued for noise, while being maintained on the ward. Noise and violence increased

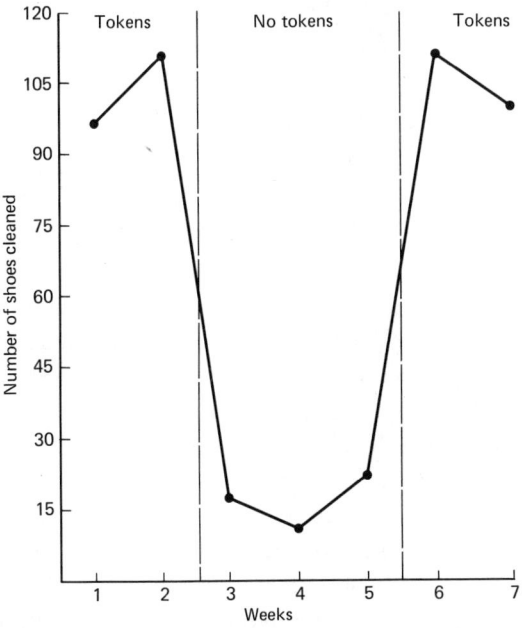

Figure 6-1. Number of shoes cleaned as a function of the presence and absence of positive token reinforcement.

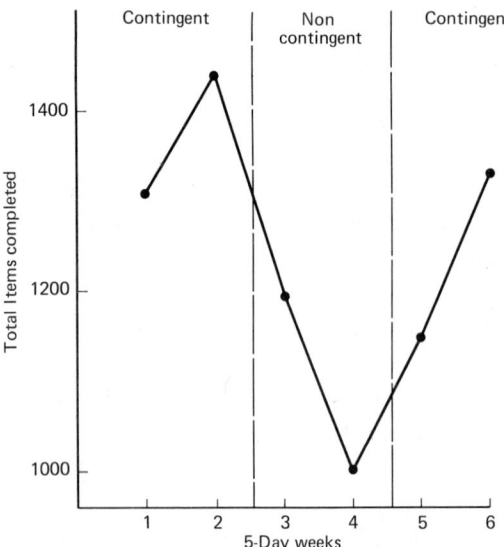

Figure 6-2. Work output as a function of the contingency and non-contingency of tokens.

in the unfined area (occupational therapy), but not in the fined area (the ward).

Lloyd and Garlington (1968) studied behavior associated with personal care and also found that behavioral ratings were consistently higher during contingent token application. Other manipulations at Faribault State Hospital, described in the second section of this chapter have also shown that the changes in behavior seen cannot be due solely to increased staff attention or expectation.

Token economies have been developed and have changed the behavior of both profoundly and mildly mentally retarded persons. Hunt et al. (1968) used tokens to reinforce appropriate personal appearance in exit-ward patients, those who were expected to be discharged within approximately one year. Using a system in which patients earned points for adaptive behavior, they reinforced appropriate dress both continuously and intermittently. Their results show that these procedures changed the appearance

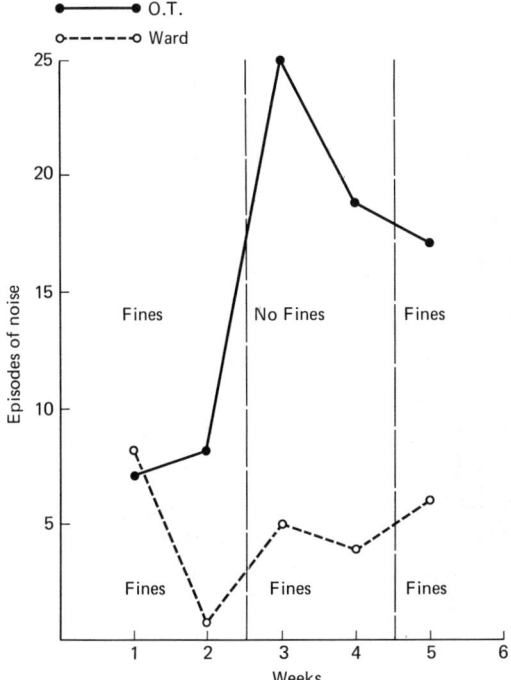

Figure 6-3. Unnecessary loud noise as a function of the presence and absence of fines.

of three-fourths of the patients, with the intermittent reinforcement procedure resulting in the best maintenance of the improved behavior after reinforcement was discontinued.

After reviewing many behavior modification projects in California, Liberman (1968) emphasized the need for adequate training of the staff in the rationale and use of reinforcement programs, as well as discussing individual versus group-wide programs. He concluded that the group-wide method is much more economical in requirements of staff number and time, while the individual method, as would be expected, seems to be most efficient in producing individual changes in behavior. Liberman also discussed the problems inherent in a ward-wide token program when escape from the contingencies is possible. Some solutions that have worked include placing token meters on doors to the outside in "open" buildings, repeated returning to the token ward after "elopement," periodic changing of the color of tokens and devaluation of previous colors in order to prevent hoarding, search and seizure and banking of excess tokens to prevent stealing, and punishment with mild electric shock to decrease the incidence of tantrums to avoid the contingencies (see Chapter 2 regarding the use of punishment).

Ball (1969) described the problems involved in establishing a token economy, including the demands on the staff, initial selection of the patients, and a description of the program by the ward nurse. Particularly, he stressed the necessity for adequate staff training and involvement in the program. Whether the token economy program ultimately succeeds is up to the psychiatric technicians and hospital aides—those who interact most closely with the patients and have the primary responsibility for their care.

Roberts and Perry (1970) placed *all* residents in The Mental Retardation Center, Pueblo, Colorado, on token economy programs. Using tokens and a point system, all behavior of every resident within the program was included. They solved the problem of an individual's personal funds by stating that "No U.S. money from any source may be spent on the institutional grounds." Dollars earned at jobs or sent from home must be banked to be spent off the grounds, and the privilege of getting off the grounds to spend them requires a certain amount of tokens to be earned.

Working with mildly retarded antisocial patients Burchand (1967) developed a Behavior Credit System (BCS) to deal with the effect of response cost (losing tokens for maladaptive behaviors). A BC sheet was posted each week. In order to earn a BC or maintain the maximum number of BC's (seven), a resident had to pay during the same day any response cost with which he had been charged. Prices and privileges were partially determined by the number of BC's a resident had. Residents with less than seven

BC's were required to pay additional tokens for each item purchased and were not eligible for "outside" privileges. In this way the problem of getting into "negative" token values is eliminated.

Token reinforcement has been used successfully in institutional classroom settings by Birnbrauer and Lawler (1964), Birnbrauer *et al.* (1965), and Perline and Levinsky (1968). Birnbrauer and Lawler taught severely retarded children who had never before functioned productively in a group setting to hang up their coats upon entering the classroom, take their seats quietly, and wait for their assignments. Eleven out of thirty-seven progressed to the point of working alone and persistently on programmed multiple-choice assignments. Birnbrauer *et al.*, working with mildly and moderately retarded children, discontinued token (point) reinforcement in order to determine if the tokens were essential to the relatively high levels of accuracy and rates of studying maintained. During the twenty-one-day non-token period they found:

1. five of the fifteen pupils showed no change in performance.

2. ten of the fifteen pupils either increased markedly in over-all percentage of errors or showed a decline in the amount of studying or an increase in disruptive behavior.

A token program for moderately and severely retarded women

Poppy Building is the residence of fifty-one women at Faribault State Hospital. The official description of the residents living there is "Females aged nineteen and over who are (a) ambulant, (b) totally toilet trained, (c) hyperactive, (d) or low functioning."

This is not accurate since some non-toilet trained residents and some who could not be considered "low functioning" but who presented sufficient behavior problems that they could not live in the "high functioning" buildings which had a more "open-door" policy did reside there.

The age range was 20-65 ($X = 33.2$) and the I.Q. range was 10-18 ($X = 34.8$). All of the residents have been diagnosed mentally retarded (profound to moderate) and 35 per cent received anticonvulsant medication. Fifteen per cent were diagnosed psychotic with mental retardation. All of the residents lived in the building. The building consisted of two large day rooms (ward areas), two large dormitories, one dining room, four bathrooms (one each in the wards and dormitories), eight small seclusion rooms (five of which were later converted to patient training rooms), an office, and a staff lounge area. Half the residents were assigned to the locked North ward and did not have free access to areas other than the ward during the day.

The token economy in Poppy Building was instituted in two phases. In the first phase twenty-five residents having no physical disabilities nor receiving anticonvulsant medication were chosen. These residents participated in a program from December 1969 to May 1970 in which the effects of behavior modification, drug therapy, and their interaction were investigated.

The following notes were made after my first several visits to Poppy Building in the fall of 1969:

> September, 1969, I paid my first visit to Poppy, primarily to observe the residents and the staff. For the first two months I did little in the way of actual preparation for the first study. I concentrated on getting to know the staff and the residents and letting them get to know me. If it is valid to look back now and generalize, I believe that the single most important thing I did was to go by myself into the wards. The staff seemed to accept my observations as accurate, I think because they were made on the ward in the normal setting in which the staff worked. I was not a consultant who asked for the resident to be brought to him in a calm and quiet office and suggested programs not feasible in the ward situation. I will never forget my initial impressions. As a stranger walking into the ward area, I was immediately surrounded by twelve to fifteen women, some half dressed, some smelling of urine and feces, some drooling, others talking, but all of them attempting to get my attention. I was poked, asked questions, touched, hugged, sworn at, pulled, kissed, punched, and gently patted on the behind. The staff member on duty stood by, somewhat amused, to see a consultant "getting her hands dirty." I, at the same time, while primarily terrified, was greatly impressed by the power of attention to these women and the possibilities of using it as a reinforcer. As I con-

tinued to visit the wards, I ignored all approaches to me and gradually came to be "a part of the furniture" and was able to observe the daily routine. The majority of the women spent the day sitting, some rocking, some walking aimlessly around, others sleeping on the floor. The television was on continually and several of the women sat in front of it, but none seemed interested in the programs. Occasionally a staff member would make available some games or toys or the recreation worker would gather a small group to work with. Staff members performed mostly custodial functions for the residents although they expressed interest in taking a more active role in teaching. Most of the staff members were less than enthusiastic about the use of tokens but agreed to "give them a try."

During September and October a series of five classes on behavior modification was conducted for the staff. These classes consisted of lectures covering the basic concepts of behavior modification (reinforcement, contingency, behavior elimination, etc.) with some discussion of schedules of reinforcement and the use of tokens as secondary reinforcers. Objectives were specified at each discussion and a quiz on the preceding material began each lecture. An attempt was made to include all of the personnel in the building who would be in contact with the residents, including the unit supervisor, the dining room staff, and the custodial staff. One requirement that was not in effect then, but which was used later and saves much explanation and frustration later on, was to have each participant modify one behavior of a resident. The staff member could select the resident and the behavior to be changed. He was asked to pinpoint the behavior (define it so that it can be counted), specify the terminal behavior, count the behavior to be changed over time (usually one hour per day), decide on a reinforcer, apply the reinforcer contingent on the desired behavior and continue to count over time (Lindsley, 1970). It seemed to work best if each step followed the lecture on that material. In this way questions could be answered about the mechanics of reinforcement and each staff member has had a preview of what he would be doing in the program as well as an opportunity to try it himself before the program began.

Table 6-1. Examples of data sheets used.

A. Preliminary behavior checklist

NAME
No. of tokens earned Sitting at table Table activity Assisting Ward work Off-ward work Special progress No. of tokens exchanged TV Walk Fine Coffee treat Special activity

B. On-ward activities — South

NAME
Brush teeth Wash face Dress on Shoes on Rocking Lying on floor Pestering staff Soiled Feeds self Uses utensils Aggression Self-abuse

C. Daily frequency checklist

												Names
Pesters												Bites staff
Talks residents												Throws object
Talks staff												Raises voice
Talks self												Verbal abuse, resident
Bites self												Verbal abuse, staff
Assists												Wet
Shares												Soiled
Takes												Smearing
Bangs head, object												Enters bathroom
Locked out												Hoards
Hits self												Lying down
Kicks self												Breaks furniture
Rocks												Bangs doors
Picks self												Enters clothes room
Hits body object												Not sitting
Hits self												Dress on
Hits residents												Shoes on
Hits staff												Dress clean
Kicks residents												Hair combed
Kicks staff												Abuse, object
Bites residents												
Throws object												
Bites staff												
Throws object												

D. Detailed behavior evaluation*

Outlines of behaviors covered
I. Self-care
A. Dressing
B. Eating
C. Grooming
1. Bathing
2. Toileting
II. Social skills
A. Comprehension
B. Speech
C. Numbers
D. Reading
E. Time
F. Money
G. Writing
H. Fine motor skills
III. Ward work
IV. Gross motor activities

* Copies of the DBE can be obtained by writing to the author.

During November one extra staff member was hired as a program supervisor and data collector. Although this position could be filled by an on-line staff member, having someone with no other duties than supervision of the programs facilitated the establishment of the programs and allowed more rapid and smooth progress. For the last two weeks in November, the residents were observed by this person, who will be referred to as the observer, and their behavior for one hour each day was charted through the use of a checklist (Table 6-1). On the basis of this rating, the residents were assigned to one of three groups, so that each group was heterogenous, containing equal numbers of most adaptive and least adaptive behaviors. The rest of the study was divided into five twenty-eight-day phases. Twenty-eight-day phases were selected to provide sufficient time for changes in drug states to approach a steady state and because twenty-eight days corresponds to the mean menstrual cycle length. It has been shown that psychiatric drug evaluation data on women should be plotted individually by day of menstrual cycle, rather than by calendar day, due to cyclic mood changes (Dimascio, 1968).

Days 1-28. All residents were gradually withdrawn from medication on days 1-14, leaving two weeks for residual effects to dissipate. Typically, in clinical drug evaluation studies ten days to two weeks is allowed as a drug washout period, although there is some evidence that a longer period is desirable with certain drugs (Olson and Peterson, 1960). But two weeks was the maximum the staff (used to reliance on drugs to control all maladaptive behavior) said they could tolerate. However, the length of the drug-free period was not emphasized and many of the staff did not recognize that individual residents were off medication. During the two drug-free weeks a detailed behavioral analysis was done on each resident by the observer (Table 6-1). This checklist consisted of 140 discrete behaviors that each resident *would* or *would not* do when asked and prompted by the observer. It did not necessarily have any relationship to what they actually did daily. The Nurses Observation Scale for Inpatient Evaluation (NOSIE) and the Clinical Global Impressions (CGI), two common measures in drug evaluation studies, were also employed at this time. These tests were repeated during the two weeks following termination of the study.

Days 29-57. The residents were randomly assigned to two groups, half receiving chlorpromazine (Thorazine) for twenty-eight days and half receiving a placebo of identical appearance.

Days 58-86. Both groups were switched from ongoing treatment to the opposite treatment (i.e. from chlorpromazine to placebo and from placebo to chlorpromazine).

Days 87-115. Repeat of days 29-57.

Days 116-144. Repeat of days 58-86.

The study used a double-blind design with neither the resident nor the observer knowing whether the resident was receiving active compound or placebo. The use of a cross-over design has several advantages:

1. Since each subject is his own control, the between-subject variation, which is usually the largest source of variation, is not a factor and hence the design is a more sensitive measure of drug effects.
2. Since no sampling differences occur between groups, relatively few subjects can be used and several dosage levels employed.

Its disadvantages are:

1. It assumes no carry-over effects.
2. It requires multiple testing.
3. One often cannot give all possible treatments to the same set of subjects. In this study the dosage varied between individuals but the active compound and placebo were matched and the number of capsules taken was constant for both drug and placebo.

A token system was employed to reinforce general constructive behaviors as indicated by concrete products (puzzles, stringing beads, color identification, etc.) and other behaviors readily verifiable by observation. The behavioral measures were recorded daily for one hour each morning and afternoon and during breakfast and lunch (see Table 6-1). Each behavior was explicitly defined so that it could be observed as a discrete response. Tokens were given immediately after completion of specified activities and were exchangable for articles and privileges at "the store" between 11:00 and 12:00 p.m. The number of tokens awarded was dependent on the length and difficulty of the task. Tokens were

initially introduced to the residents in one week. The procedure generally followed two aims:
1. Pair the token with a known reinforcer so that it acquires value to the resident.
2. Gradually increase the time and distance between presentation of the token and its exchange for a known reinforcer.

This is necessary to bridge the delay between receiving the token and exchanging it at the store. The procedure was as follows:
1. Give each resident a token and *immediately* take it back and exchange it for a known reinforcer. Edibles work well here (marshmallows, cookies, crackers, etc.) and a convenient time to do this is at the residents' coffee break. The procedure must be repeated at least four times.
2. Gradually extend the time between the token presentation and its exchange. For example, one staff member distributed the tokens and another followed one minute later making the exchange. The time delay was slowly increased. The increments depended somewhat on the residents' ability, but an increase of one minute each time, at least for the first two days, is not excessive.
3. Gradually increase the physical distance between the giving of the token and its exchange. This was also a good time to introduce a contingency. To do this, two staff members stood about five feet apart, one with tokens and one with treats. The first one said, "Come to me and get a token," and gave the token. The second one said, "Come to me and get a treat for your token," and made the exchange. This was understandable to some residents, but others had to be led through the steps at first. This was repeated several times, and the distance and the time were slowly increased until the tokens were given for approaching the first staff member on command and were exchanged about ten minutes later in another room or on another floor. As the time delay was increased, it became necessary to have a place for each resi-

dent to store the tokens. This has been accomplished in several ways. We used specially constructed token bags which were tied around the waist. These provided a place on the person to keep tokens which was relatively inaccessible to other residents. Other programs have used apron pockets, necklaces of tokens, trouser pockets, and tokens on key chains attached to belt. Several of these carry the disadvantage of being visible to the other residents and therefore more vulnerable to attempts at stealing. The token bags were distributed during dressing and collected at the store before lunch.

Each day was divided into:

1. Morning (6:30 a.m.-11:00 a.m.), during which there were specific reinforcement contingencies for each patient.
2. Afternoon (12:00 p.m.-3:00 p.m.), during which the patients remained on the ward without specific programmed reinforcement contingencies.

The morning began with the residents getting up, washing, and dressing. At first tokens were given for specific washing and dressing behaviors, but this proved difficult since during washing and dressing there were no places to put the tokens and little way for the staff to record the behaviors. For this reason and because it was observed that the resident who got up promptly, washed, and dressed efficiently was "punished" by having to wait thirty to forty-five minutes before breakfast, a cafeteria system was instituted at breakfast whereby the dining room was open from 7:00 to 7:30 a.m. for residents to enter, providing they had bathed and dressed. This system proved workable, allowing those residents who got up promptly, washed, and dressed to go to breakfast first. It also eliminated one more of the "herd" movements so common to institutions where the residents descend into the dining room en masse when the bell rings. In addition, it made possible more realistic reinforcement of good eating behavior as there were fewer people in the dining room at one time.

After breakfast the residents were reinforced for toothbrushing and bed making. In both cases the behaviors were broken down into discrete steps, each reinforceable by a token.

The rest of the morning was spent in patient training areas. The residents were divided into three heterogeneous groups as described previously. Each group met in a partitioned area in the day room. Specific learning tasks were assigned in each physical area. In one, grooming was taught; in the second, intellectual development (reading, number and color identification); and in the third, fine motor movements. One psychiatric technician was assigned to each activity area. During the morning the residents moved through each area, thus exposing each resident to three activities and three staff members. To facilitate grouping, each group was assigned a color: red, blue, or yellow. The distinctive token bags were the same for all members of each group and one staff member assigned to each group. For the first week, the red staff member repeatedly called together the "red group," reinforced them for coming to the table area, had them sit for a couple of minutes doing a simple task, reinforced them for sitting quietly, and let everyone get up and move about. Gradually the time required to sit was increased to fifteen to twenty minutes and the time to be up and walking around decreased to three to five minutes. This was accomplished by the end of the week for all three groups.

At the beginning of the third week after tokens were introduced, the separation into morning and afternoon sessions and the drug therapy began. At first the moving from area to area was confusing, but as the residents moved consistently clockwise in one group at a time, the moving came to be quietly and efficiently done. We discovered during this third week that certain residents had been traditionally assigned to a specific area in the day room. These residents became agitated when asked to move and tended to return to the original area. When this happened they were firmly returned to the correct area and reinforced for sitting there. This drifting behavior gradually disappeared.

A typical day for one resident was as follows:

A TOKEN SYSTEM FOR RETARDED WOMEN

6:30 - a.m.	out of bed
6:30 - 7:00 a.m.	bathe and dress
7:00 - 7:20 a.m.	eat breakfast
7:30 - 8:00 a.m.	brush teeth and make bed
8:10 - 8:50 a.m.	grooming area
8:50 - 9:10 a.m.	coffee break
9:10 - 9:50 a.m.	intellectual development area
10:10 - 10:40 a.m.	fine motor movements area
10:50 - 11:30 a.m.	store
11:45 - 12:30 p.m.	lunch
1:00 - 5:00 p.m.	on ward
5:00 - 5:30 p.m.	dinner
6:00 - 8:00 p.m.	on ward
9:00 - p.m.	to bed

The store consisted of a cupboard filled with priced items (see Table 6-2). Items costing the same amount were put on the same

Table 6-2. Examples of things tokens can be exchanged for.

A. Products
1. Magazine, books, crayons, scissors, pencils, writing paper
2. Food
    (a) Donut for coffee break
    (b) Candy, crackers, fruits
    (c) Extra coffee
3. Cigarettes
4. Jewelry
5. Clothes
6. Stuffed animals
7. Crafts: yarn, objects to be embroidered
8. Expensive items which can be rented on a daily basis — radios, watches, etc.

B. Privileges
1. Ball, jump rope to be used during exercise time
2. Special movies on ward
3. Extra coffee break
4. Walk outside of ward with attendant
5. Ten minutes with a social worker or occupational therapist or other staff member
6. Opportunity to listen to records alone for fifteen minutes.

Table 6-3. Examples of behaviors reinforced and their token exchange value.*

		Tokens to be given upon completion
A.	Grooming	
	1. Wash own face	1
	2. Brush teeth	1
	3. Put on shoes, dress, underwear	1
	4. Bathing within a reasonable time	1
	5. Not soiling clothes	1
	6. Keeping clothes on during the day	1
	7. Assisting others in grooming	2
B.	Ward work	
	1. Making beds	1 (1 for each 3 beds made)
	2. Dusting ward and halls	2
	3. Help in kitchen	3
C.	Constructive activities	
	1. Doing puzzle	3
	2. Reading aloud words from a book	3
	3. Making potholder	5
	4. Stringing beads	3
	5. Coloring in book	2
	6. Going to scheduled activities	1
D.	Other	
	1. Neat eating habits	1
	2. Following instructions by the staff members	1
	3. Taking medication	1

*The exact value to be used for each activity were determined both by the difficulty of the work, its duration, and by the ability of the individual patients. Ideally the values were assigned so that the slowest, least capable patient could receive at least one reinforcement per day.

shelves. The residents came to the store in groups, having already counted their tokens. They were taken one at a time to the cupboard, directed to the shelf which had things they could afford, and asked if they wanted to buy anything that day. A timer was set for one minute, and when the bell rang, the next resident was taken to the cupboard. Tokens were allowed to be saved from one day to the next, but a limit of two weeks of saving was set to prevent token hoarding.

The afternoons were staffed with the same personnel as the mornings. This was done so that one of the differences between morning and afternoon might not be the staff members available to pay attention to the residents. No specific instructions were given concerning the afternoon activities except that staff members should do those things that the staff had traditionally done during previous afternoons.

By using contingency management during part of the day and no specific reinforcement during the remainder, a daily control measure was obtained of the behavioral effect of discontinuing systematic reinforcement. An effort was made to observe comparable constructive and maladaptive responses in the morning and afternoon, but this was not always possible.

The foregoing describes typical multiple schedule design used in operant conditioning experiments to evaluate behavioral effects of drugs (see e.g. Boren, 1966; Thompson and Schuster, 1968).

DRUG THERAPY

Chlorpromazine was chosen as the experimental drug largely because of its current widespread use in treatment with mentally retarded persons, its purported history of success, and its relative safety (Mautner, 1959). It is a phenothiazine derivative and was one of the first major tranquilizers used in the management of anxiety and aggressive behavior. Chlorpromazine can be used over a wide range of doses with minimal toxic side effects. Recently there have been some studies on the effects of discontinuation of chlorpromazine therapy after both chronic and acute administration. While some have shown that intermittent drug therapy might be a feasible and desirable course for institutionalized residents as it saves money and forces a continued re-evaluation of each resident (Rothstein, 1960; Diamond and Marks, 1960; Gross et al., 1960; Good et al., 1958; Olson and Peterson, 1960, 1962; Zocchie et al., 1969), others have questioned this procedure because of the disruptive effects of a change-of-drug state (Overton,

1966; Stewart, 1962; Otis, 1964). These studies suggest caution in the use of high doses of tranquilizers in chronic patients when a lesser dose would be adequate, since maximal stimulus change with associated behavioral change might be expected to occur between the high-dose drug state and the non-drug state. Heistad and Torres (1959) suggested that the changes in drug state may interfere with previously learned behavior by changing significant aspects of the internal stimuli for specific emotional responses.

Results

DRUG EFFECTS

An analysis of variance showed no significant differences between the results obtained during chlorpromazine therapy and during placebo therapy for all subjects taken over each of the behaviors observed. However there was significantly greater variablility in the afternoon (non-operant sessions), suggesting the possibility of specific drug responders. Several individual residents showed

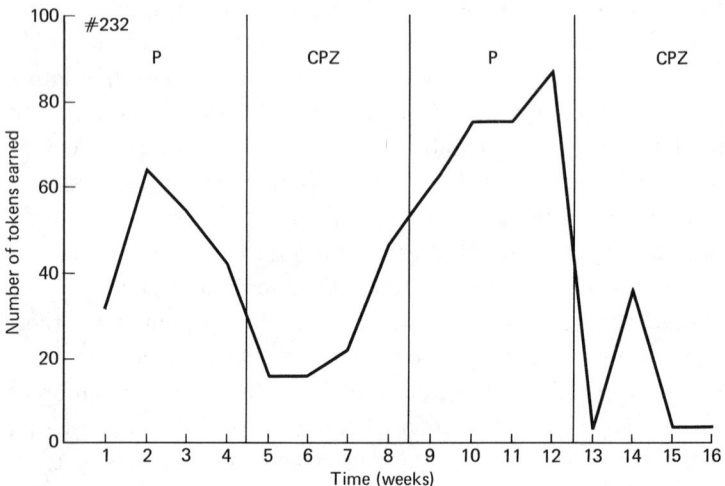

Figure 6-4. Number of tokens earned as a function of drug therapy.

A TOKEN SYSTEM FOR RETARDED WOMEN

replicable improvements on one or two of the fifty behaviors recorded while receiving chlorpromazine, however no family of related responses appeared to be specifically sensitive to chlorpromazine, nor were any sub-group of residents specifically responsive to the drug. The token earning behavior of one such responder (see Figure 6-4) shows the depression of tokens during both the chlorpromazine therapy periods with a sustained rise in earning tokens during each placebo period.

OPERANT EFFECTS

The pre-test and post-test score differences on the NOSIE, CGI, and Detailed Behavior Evaluation (DBE) were compared. Figure 6-5 summarizes the results of t-tests performed on the different scores and Figure 6 shows the improvement between pre- and post-test. The NOSIE post-test scores were significantly higher

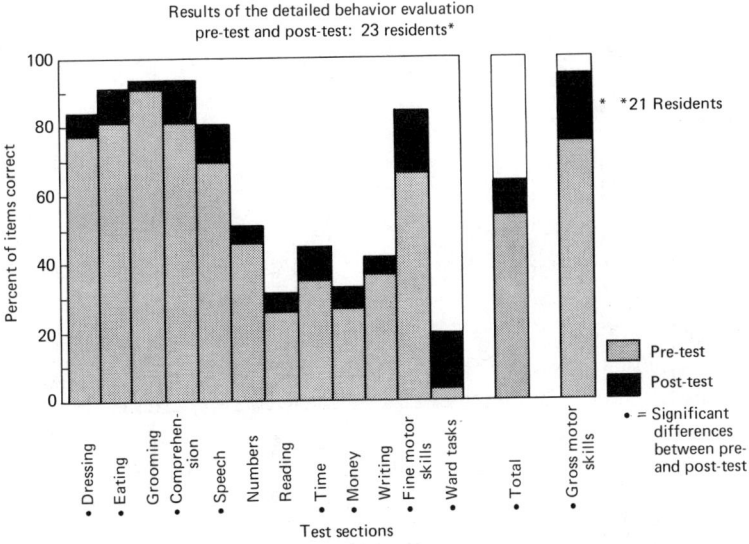

Figure 6-5. P values of t-tests of significance performed on the difference score between pre- and post-tests.

for all twenty-four residents (an increase from a mean score of 166.9 pre-test to 171.8 post-test, p = 0.002). The DBE showed an increase from a mean score (N = 24) of 73.1 to a mean score of 85.3 on the post-test, p = 0.002. The greatest improvement within the DBE was in gross motor skills, fine motor skills, ward work, verbal comprehension, eating, grooming, speech, and time sense (p = 0.002). Significant improvement was also seen in dressing (p = 0.01) and money comprehension (p = 0.05). The CGI post-tests were significantly different from the pre-tests in the direction of improvement (p = 0.002).

The morning and afternoon behavioral trends were strikingly different. In general, adaptive behaviors were more frequent in the morning (when they were specifically reinforced) and mala-

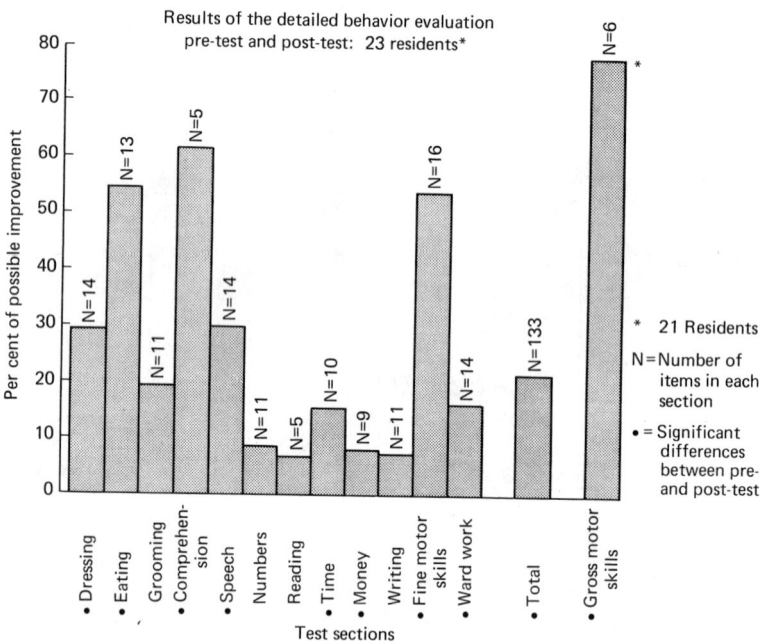

Figure 6-6. Improvement expressed as the per cent of items correct on pre- and post- tests.

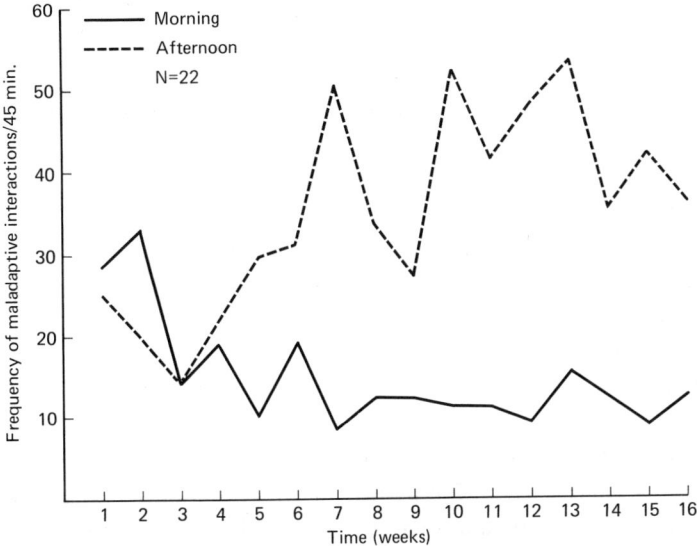

Figure 6-7. Number of maladaptive interactions (raising voice, verbal abuse toward other residents, talking to oneself, pestering) as a function of morning (operant) and afternoon (non-operant) sessions.

daptive behaviors more frequent in the afternoon. An analysis of variance was done on those twenty-five behaviors which occurred often enough to be analyzed. Of these, twenty-four showed significant differences. There were more adaptive behaviors occurring in the morning (operant) and more frequent maladaptive behaviors in the afternoon. Carrying a food tray without spilling, going directly to one's seat, using a spoon correctly, sitting properly in a chair while eating, talking to staff members, assisting others, having shoes on, hair combed, and a clean dress when checked, and sitting at a table working constructively occurred significantly more often in the operant sessions. Talking to one's self, rocking, hitting other subjects, raising one's voice, verbal abuse of other subjects, and lying on the floor occurred significantly more often in the afternoon. The relative frequencies of maladaptive interaction behaviors (raising voice, verbal abuse toward other residents, talking to one's self, pestering) are shown in Figure 6-7. These behaviors decreased in the morning from a total of 28.5 occurrences in the first week of the study to 12.8 occurrences in the sixteenth week, while the same behaviors observed in the afternoon increased from 25.5 to 36.6 during the same period. Stereotyped behaviors were more frequent in the afternoon. Rocking occurred almost twice as often in the nonoperant period (morning, 128.6 occurrences; afternoon, 207.6 occurrences). Both lying on the floor and hoarding showed the same frequency distribution with hoarding three times as often in the afternoon and the frequency of lying on the floor in the afternoon eight times the morning rate.

Figure 6-8 shows the frequency of talking to staff members in the morning and in the afternoon. Over-all, 870.1 patient-staff interactions occurred in the morning while 682.6 occurred in the afternoon. The only adaptive behavior which appeared more often in the afternoon was talking to other residents: morning, 290.6 occurrences; afternoon, 613.1 occurrences.

The number of tokens earned by the subjects showed a significant increase over time from a total of 3714 earned the first week to a total of 6723 in the final week (see Figure 6-9). This repre-

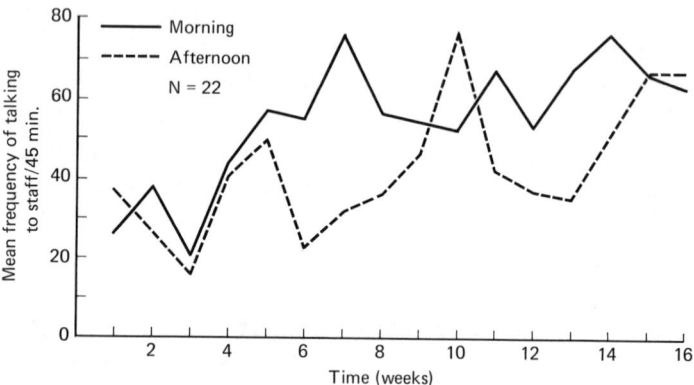

Figure 6-8. Number of resident initiated resident-staff interactions as a function of morning (operant) and afternoon (non-operant) sessions.

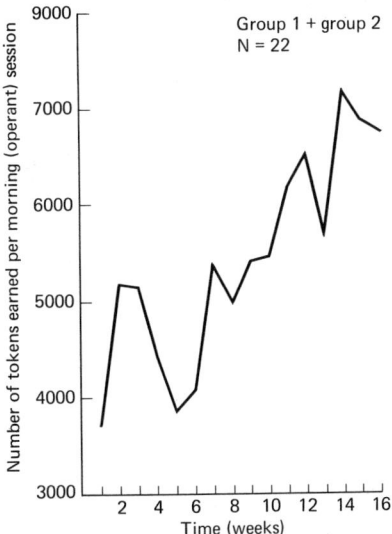

Figure 6-9. The number of tokens earned per morning session (N = 22).

sents a rise in the mean number of tokens earned by a subject each day from 33.8 to 61.1.

One means of comparing the effects of chlorpromazine and behavior modification is to look at their relative contribution to the frequency of an observed behavior. The total number of times all subjects were observed to be sitting at a table working constructively was calculated for the four conditions of:

1. placebo + no contingencies
2. placebo + contingencies
3. chlorpromazine + no contingencies
4. chlorpromazine + contingencies

The totals obtained were respectively 150, 985, 151, 975, (see Figure 6-10). The same values were calculated for the frequency of raising one's voice and were placebo + no contingencies, 179; placebo + contingencies, 54; chlorpromazine + no contingencies, 161; and chlorpromazine + contingencies, 48 (Figure 6-11).

Several other measures have indicated the success of the program in encouraging the use of behavior modification on methods

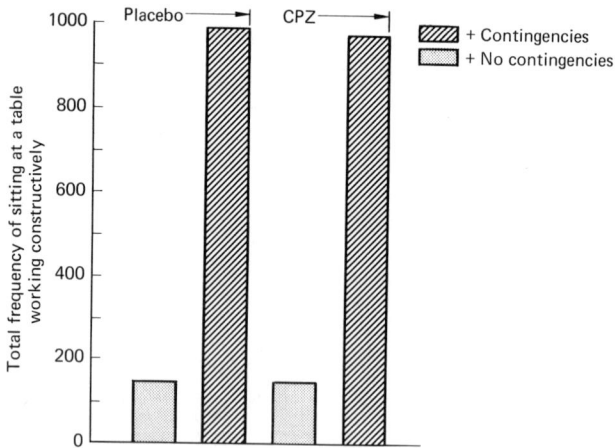

Figure 6-10. The total frequency of observations on which residents were sitting working constructively during 45-minute teaching periods (N = 22) under four conditions: (1) under no drug (placebo) and no behavior modification (no contingencies); (2) placebo plus contingencies; (3) chlorpromazine without contingencies; and (4) chlorpromazine plus contingencies.

rather than reliance on drugs for behavioral control. The seclusion time (Figure 6-12) decreased from 285¾ hours per month in January 1970 to 74¼ hours in May 1970. Seclusion time further decreased to 23½ hours in November 1970, while the number of residents on drugs stayed low (nine in November 1970 as against sixteen before the study). During the six months after the study the residents were maintained on lower doses of drugs (6441 mgm total/day before the study, 3754 mgms/day for twenty-four residents after the study, or a decrease from 268.4 mgm/resident/day to 156.4 mgms/resident/day six months after the termination of the study.

Discussion

The results obtained well illustrate the necessity of controlling behavioral therapy during a study of the behavioral effects of psychoactive compounds. As indicated both by the pre-test and post-test, the efficacy of the compound used as judged by behavioral measures would have been very different for the operant (morning) and non-operant (afternoon) periods. The results also give a

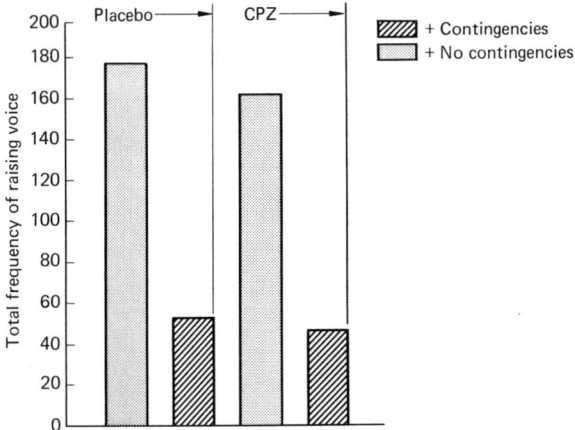

Figure 6-11. The total frequency of observations on which residents raised voice (N = 22). (See legend of Figure 6-10 for key.)

clear indication of the relative importance of using a systematic program of reinforcement of adaptive behaviors as opposed to chlorpromazine as a primary means of behavioral control. The failure of chlorpromazine, one of the most widely used drugs for controlling hyperactive, assaultive behavior in institutionalized retardates, to exercise any consistent behavioral effect, raises several questions. It appears that the chronic use of such compounds with many retardates for behavior control may be unwarranted. Further, these findings indicate that an effective behavior modification program can have more favorable effects, both in increasing adaptive behavior and decreasing maladaptive behavior, than chlorpromazine therapy. Removal of the drug seemed to have little or no adverse effect when contingency management was in effect. Hence, the efficacy of chlorpromazine in either increasing adaptive or decreasing maladaptive behavior in retardates seems questionable.

The pre- and post-test scores and graphs of daily frequency behaviors indicate that the behavior modification program was effective in increasing over-all both the frequency of daily adaptive behavior and the number of adaptive behaviors the residents could complete upon request. The greatest improvement was in

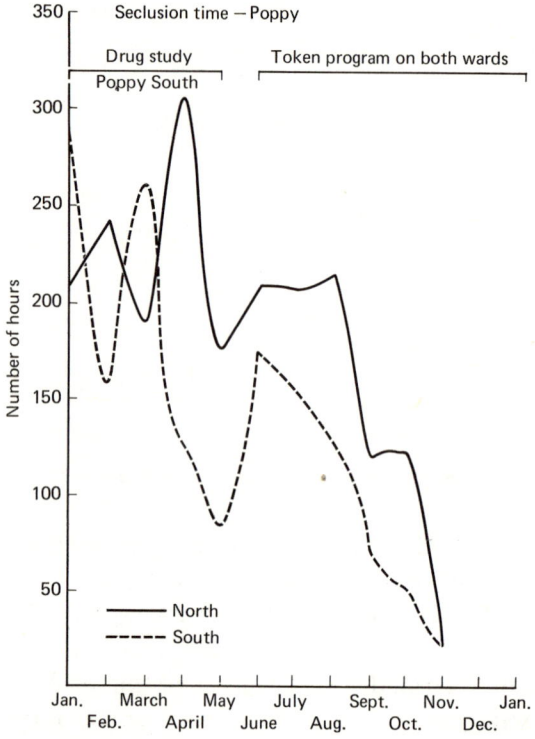

Figure 6-12. The number of resident hours of seclusion. (One resident hour refers to one hour during which a resident was locked in a seclusion room, usually due to assault.)

fine and gross motor movements. The former result was not unexpected as it included activities which the staff enjoyed teaching, such as coloring within lines, stringing graduated sizes of beads, and completing puzzles. The reason for the large improvement in gross motor activities (skipping, jumping, catching a ball) is more obscure since these activities were not specifically reinforced. This observed outcome may be due to a number of factors: (1) generalization from the skills learned in the fine motor movement teaching sessions; (2) increased attention span and hence increased capacity to listen to and follow directions; (3) an over-all lower drug level and thereby a decrease in possible ataxic effects.

The frequency of adaptive behaviors increased faster and remained higher in the morning (operant) sessions. Such activities as sitting at a table, engaging in a constructive activity, talking to staff, having appropriate clothes on when checked, eating correctly, bathing correctly, and keeping neat were observed consistently more frequency in the morning for all residents when these behaviors were specifically reinforced. The afternoon provided the same opportunity for these behaviors to occur (the tables were there with activities and staff members available) but participation was not specifically reinforced. The lack of generalization of adaptive behaviors from the morning to the afternoon is not surprising if one considers the change of stimulus conditions between the morning and the afternoon. Although all of the behavioral recording was done while the residents were in the same day room location, the stimulus conditions of the large divider sections and the presence of the token bags were specific to the morning. Since these were the only two major changes in the stimulus conditions, and the same number of staff members was available to the residents in the afternoon, the possibility that increased staff availability was the major reason for improvement in behavior can be discounted.

The results also show that the program was effective in decreasing the number of maladaptive behaviors in the morning operant sessions. Aggressive acts, both verbal and physical, stereotyped behaviors such as rocking, and other behaviors which would normally interfere with learning (lying on the floor, talking to self, and hoarding) decreased rapidly during the morning. These behaviors remained at a very low or near zero rate, while the same behaviors in the afternoon occurred at a higher frequency, and in some cases (talking to self, raising voice) showed an overall frequency increase.

The concurrent decrease in both the average number of milligrams of drug used to maintain each resident and the number of hours of seclusion per month for the building indicated that the program has been effective in teaching alternate methods of dealing with aggressive behaviors (see "Results," Figure 6-9). At the termination of the drug study the staff voted to continue the behavior modification program and extend it to twenty-four hours a day. Six months after the termination of the study only nine of the twenty-four residents were receiving medication, and the use of seclusion remained low.

THE DEVELOPMENT OF A TOTAL TOKEN ECONOMY

The second phase of the program extended the token economy to twenty-four hours, seven days a week, and added twenty-five more residents. The twenty-five new residents lived on the North ward of Poppy Building and 70 per cent of them were epileptics. The mean I.Q. was 33.0 with a range of 13-60, and the age range was 20 to 58 (mean 34.8).

Tokens were introduced in the same way as previously discussed, the procedure taking about one week. After their introduction the whole building was on a token economy twenty-four hours a day. Because of the lack of staff and in order to incorporate recreation and occupational therapy staff into the program, patient training areas were operated only two hours a day for each resident. The North ward residents were tested and divided into three heterogeneous groups for patient training. The schedule was as shown in the table.

The schedule was followed Monday through Saturday. On Sunday there were church activities available during the morning and movies or other programs during the afternoon.

The program required a minimum staff of five to run smoothly, although it has functioned with three staff members and two resident-helpers (higher-functioning residents who have been trained as assistants). Of the five required, each supervised one patient training area and was responsible for the ward activities. Since this program grew out of the smaller program, it incorporated much of it, but there were several additions and corrections which will now be discussed. First, the token system was ex-

A TOKEN SYSTEM FOR RETARDED WOMEN

NORTH SIDE				SOUTH SIDE			
6:30 -		a.m.	Get out of bed	same as North side			
6:30 -	7:00	a.m.	Bathe and dress	"	"		
7:00 -	7:30	a.m.	Breakfast	"	"		
7:30 -	8:00	a.m.	Brush teeth and make beds	"	"		
8:00 -	10:00	a.m.	On-ward activities	8:00 -	10:00	a.m.	Resident training
10:00 -	11:30	a.m.	Recreation or O. T.	10:30		a.m.	Store
12:00			Lunch				
1:00 -	3:00	p.m.	Resident training	1:00 -	2:30	p.m.	Recreation or O.T.
3:00 -	3:30	p.m.	Store				
3:30 -	5:00	p.m.	On-ward activities	2:30 -	5:00 p.m.		On-ward activities
5:00 -	5:30	p.m.	Supper	same as North side			
6:00 -	9:00	p.m.	On-ward actvities and actvities outside the building	"	"		
10:00		p.m.	To bed	"	"		

tended throughout the night. This was done by having the night psychiatric technician note hourly those residents who were not in bed. This was easily done since the technician made rounds hourly through both dormitories. At the end of the night, the number of times that each resident was in bed when checked (a possible eight) was totaled and the resident was given that number of tokens. Because each resident did not have a locked place to put her tokens and because stealing tokens had been a problem, the tokens were removed each night at bedtime and returned before breakfast.

The patient training areas were moved to three old seclusion rooms on the ground floor of the building. They were brightly painted and furnished with a round table, chairs, and a cupboard or chest of drawers. These rooms had been used previously for work with the North ward residents. Each room was assigned an activity and only the materials relevant to that activity were kept there. The three areas of training were grooming, intellectual development, and social-cooperative behaviors. Arts and crafts was eliminated as an activity for patient training and was delegated to the ward activities. Social cooperative behaviors was added in an attempt to teach such behaviors as sharing and assisting and helping, since we failed to teach these behaviors in the other areas. These behaviors seem to be the most difficult to teach, requiring imagination in creating activities which are not competitive but require cooperation. A simple beginning was made in adding objects to an open box. Starting with two residents, each was required to place his object in the box before either was reinforced. The number of tokens earned was the same as the number of participants. The number of participants was slowly increased to include all members of the group. The same kind of behavior was taught with puzzles, bead stringing, picture drawing, ball passing, etc. In this kind of activity, peer pressure becomes an important factor, as everyone's reinforcement depends on each participant's cooperating.

Reading, using primarily the Peabody Rebus Reading Program (Woodcock, 1966), and color and number identification were taught in the intellectual development area. At the request of the staff, underarm and leg shaving and nail clipping took up one-half the time spent in the grooming area. This grooming used to be done at bedtime, when there were fewer staff, and resulted in going-to-bed activities beginning shortly after supper. The remainder of the grooming time was used to teach manners, hair care, and bathing behaviors. The program was arranged so that the residents rotated through the various areas, entering each two times a week. For example, the red group had grooming on Monday and Thursday, intellectual development on Tuesday and Friday, and social cooperative behaviors on Wednesday and Saturday.

The store was located in a fourth former seclusion room and

was available to each group of residents daily following their training time.

The on-ward activities took place, of course, on the ward itself. Because of the lack of staff and physical space, they took the place of three resident training groups. A table was set up on the ward with chairs around it and residents were reinforced for sitting there and participating in arts and crafts activities. Tokens were given for sitting quietly at the table and for completing simple activities. Tokens were also earned for doing work on and off the ward at this time (for example, making beds, running errands, dusting, sorting clothes). Tokens were charged for watching TV, going outside for a walk, going to out-of-building activities, and for maladaptive behavior such as hitting or kicking others or turning over furniture. Fines were permitted two times in a row, after which a time out procedure was employed. This was to avoid negative token values. Time out is literally time out from reinforcement (see Chapter 2). One room, designated as the time out room was used. The resident was told what she had done wrong and that she must go to time out, led from the reinforcement area to the time out room with as little physical contact and verbal scolding as possible, put into the room, and the door (which contains a one-way mirror) shut. The time in, resident's name, and time out were recorded on the door. The duration of time out was five minutes or as soon after a five-minute interval as the resident became quiet. A staff member remained near the door for the duration of time out. This prevented "forgetting" someone in time out and employing time out as seclusion, as commonly practiced in state institutions.

Recreation and occupational therapy have been incorporated into the token program. Residents pay two tokens for the opportunity to go to recreation or occupational therapy and receive tokens for participation there. Although they are encouraged to attend, no one forces them to do so, thus permitting each resident a choice. If a certain resident has never attended recreation, it is up to the recreation worker to determine why, to change the activities available, or to work more closely with the resident and encourage his participation. Because the occupational therapist and recreation worker could not work with twenty-five residents simultaneously, these activities were made available to one group at a time. Generally, all of those who were not eligible for occupational therapy on one day were eligible for recreation. This permitted each resident to go to occupational therapy once on Monday, Tuesday, or Wednesday and to recreation two of those three days. On Thursday the occupational therapy and recreation workers together planned large group activities and on Fridays they worked separately with individuals who do not function well in a group or who have special difficulties. The incorporation of occupational therapy and recreation into the token program has been a tremendous improvement over the previous system. The building staff knows exactly when the residents will have recreation and occupational therapy and can plan to complete their other activities before that time. Each resident, if she has two tokens, can elect to go to recreation or occupational therapy and for some this has been the first time for either activity in the history of their stay at the institution. Knowing which residents are eligible each time has made the planning of specific activities easier for the recreation and occupational therapy workers.

During the night, at meals, during the patient training and onward activities, and at recreation and occupational therapy, records are kept of the numbers of tokens earned and spent and the behaviors engaged in (see Table 6-3). Although these sometimes seem a burden for the staff, they permit the only accurate record of the number of tokens actually earned, allow for continuity of progress from one day to the next, indicate to the staff what is happening during the night (rather than, "she was restless all of last night"), and give information as to what the store should stock. Every three months all of the residents are tested on a series of grooming, reading, and social cooperative measures. On the basis of these tests new activities are initiated and old ones dropped or intensified.

The emphasis throughout the token program has been on positive reinforcement and teaching competing behaviors for maladaptive behaviors. Fines are used only for those behaviors which are physically harmful to the resident or to others or which cannot be ignored. Included are such behaviors as hitting or kicking others, throwing furniture, or persistent loud screaming.

The staff members seem to be pleased with the program. They have the option every three months of discontinuing or changing it in any way. Each week there is a one-hour meeting with the building staff, the unit director, the recreation worker, the occupational therapy and the psychology consultant. At this time problems about the general program and about specific residents are brought up. Minutes of the meetings are typed and distributed to all of the staff, informing them of any problems and the decisions reached.

References

Ayllon, T., and N. Azrin. The measurement and reinforcement of behavior of psychotics. *Journal of the Experimental Analysis of Behavior*, 1965, 8 (6), 357-83.

―――. *The Token Economy*. New York: Appleton-Century-Crofts, 1968.

Atthowe, J., and L. Krasner. Preliminary report on the application of contingent reinforcement procedures (token economy) on a "chronic" psychiatric ward. *Journal of Abnormal Psychology*, 1968, 72 (1), 37-43.

Ball, Thomas S. (Ed.). *The Establishment and Administration of Operant Conditioning Programs in a State Hospital for the Retarded*. California Mental Health Research Symposium, No. 4, 1969.

Birnbrauer, J. S., and J. Lawler. Token reinforcement for learning. *Mental Retardation*, 1964, 2 (5), 275-79.

Birnbrauer, J. A., M. M. Wolf, J. D. Kidder, and C. E. Tague. Classroom behavior of retarded pupils with token reinforcement. *Journal of Experimental Child Psychology*, 1965, 2, 219-35.

Boren, J. J. The study of drugs with operant techniques. In W. K. Honig, (Ed.), *Operant Behavior: Areas of Research and Application*. New York: Appleton-Century-Crofts, 1966.

Burchard, J. D. Systematic socialization: a programmed environment for the habilitation of antisocial retardates. *Psychological Record*, 1967, 17, 461-76.

Diamond, L. S., and J. B. Marks. Discontinuance of tranquilizers among chronic schizophrenic patients receiving maintenance dosage. *Journal of Nervous and Mental Disease*, 1960, *131*, 247-51.

Dimascio, A., and R. Shader. Behavioral toxicity of psychotropic drugs. *Connecticut Medicine*, 1968, *33*, 617-20.

Ferster, C. B., and B. F. Skinner. *Schedules of Reinforcement*. New York: Appleton-Century-Crofts, 1957.

Fisher, J. Reinforcement theory in psychological treatment: a symposium. California Mental Health Research Monograph, Number 8, 1966.

Good, W. W., M. Sterling, and W. H. Holtzman. Termination of chlorpromazine with schizophrenic patients. *American Journal of Psychiatry*, 1958, *115* (1), 443-48.

Gross, M., I. Hitchman, W. Reeves, J. Lawrence, and P. Newell. Discontinuation of treatment with ataractic drugs. *American Journal of Psychiatry*, 1960, *116*, 931-32.

Heistad, G. T., and A. A. Torres. A mechanism for the effect of a tranquilizing drug on learned emotional responses. *Medical Bulletin*, University of Minnesota, 1959, 518-27.

Hunt, J. G., L. C. Fitzhugh, and K. B. Fitzhugh. Teaching "exit-ward" patients appropriate personal appearance behaviors by using reinforcement techniques. *Amer. J. ment. Defic.*, 1968, *73* (1), 41-45.

Kelleher, R. T. Chaining and conditioned reinforcement. In W. K. Honig (Ed.), *Operant Behavior*. New York: Appleton-Century-Crofts, 1966.

Lent, J. R. Mimosa cottage: experiment in hope. *Psychology Today*, 1968, *2* (1), 51-58.

Lent, J. R., and J. Spradlin. Cottage demonstration project. *Project News*, Parsons State Hospital and Training Center, 1966, *2* (7).

Liberman, R. A view of behavior modification projects in California. *Behavior Research and Therapy*, 1968, *6*, 331-41.

Lindsley, O. Personal Communication, 1970.

Lloyd, K. E., and W. K. Garlington. Weekly variations in performance on a token economy psychiatric ward. *Behavior Research and Therapy*, 1968, *6*, 407-10.

Lloyd, K. E., and L. Abel. Performance on a token economy psychiatric ward: a two-year summary. *Behavior Research and Therapy*, 1970, *8* (1), 1-13.

Mautner, H. *Mental Retardation*. New York: Pergamon Press, 1959, Ch. 3.

Olson, G. W., and D. B. Peterson. Sudden removal of tranquilizing drugs from chronic psychiatric patients. *Journal of Nervous and Mental Disease*, September 1960, 252. Vol. 131.

———. Intermittent chemotherapy for chronic psychiatric inpatients. *Journal of Nervous and Mental Disease*, 1962, *134*, 145-49.

Otis, L. S. Dissociation and recovery of a response learned under the influence of chlorpromazine or saline. *Science*, 1964, *143*, 1347-48.

Overton, D. A. State-dependent learning produced by depressants and atropine-like drugs. *Psychopharmacologia*, 1966, *10*, 6-31.

Perline, I. H., and D. Levinsky. Controlling maladaptive classroom behavior in the severely retarded. *Amer. J. ment. Defic.*, 1968, *73*, 74-78.

Phillips, E. L. Achievement place: token reinforcement procedures in a home-style rehabilitation setting for "pre-delinquent" boys. *Journal of Applied Behavior Analysis*, 1968, *1*, 213-23.

Premack, D. Toward empirical behavior laws: I. positive reinforcement. *Psychological Review*, 1959, *66*, 219-33.

Roberts, C. L., and R. M. Perry. A total token economy. *Mental Retardation*, February 1970, 15-18.

Rothstein, C. An evaluation of the effects of discontinuation of chlorpromazine. *New England Journal of Medicine*, 1960, *262*, 67-69.

Stewart, J. Differential responses based on the physiological consequences of pharmacological agents. *Psychopharmacologia*, 1962, *3*, 132-38.

Thompson, T., and C. Schuster. *Behavioral Pharmacology*. New Jersey: Prentice-Hall, 1968.

Winkler, R. C. Management of chronic psychiatric patients by a token reinforcement system. *Journal of Applied Behavior Analysis*, 1970, *3*, 47-55.

Woodcock, R. *Peabody Rebus Reading Program*. Circle Pine: American Guidance Service, 1966.

Zimmerman, E. H., J. Zimmerman, and C. D. Russell. Differential effects of token reinforcement on instruction-following behavior in retarded students instructed as a group. *Journal of Applied Behavior Analysis*, 1969, *2*, 101-12.

Zocchie, A., T. T. Tourlentes, S. L. Pollack, and D. Haim. Intermittent phenothiazine therapy with chronic patients. *Archives of General Psychiatry*, 1969, *20*, 726-28.

III
Special applications

7
Changing the behavior of the retarded in the special education classroom

WILLIAM H. FULLMER

Special education, like most education programs, is being challenged. It is being asked to explain its role in educational development. It is being asked to explain what can and cannot be done for children with special learning problems, how special educators can accomplish these learning changes or why they cannot, and what alternatives might be available. These questions are difficult to answer when one's goals are vague and when the procedures used are more vague, but this need not be the case. New methods are being developed which emphasize a systematic approach to structuring children's educational development. These methods, based on behavior modification principles, are now being taught in a few teacher education programs, but in general teachers become aware of them only through the grapevine or through in-service training programs. The present chapter exposes the reader to behavior modification methods applied to the special education classroom. Much of what is discussed resulted from the author's involvement in a special education program operated within a large state institution.*

* The establishment of Behavior Modification in the Special Education Program at Faribault State Hospital was made possible with the cooperation of Orv Berg, Director of Rehabilitation; Mrs. Mabel Gates, Unit Director; Delbert Knack, Principal; and the Special Education teachers.

Some applications of behavior modification

Behavior modification methods have been employed to reduce disruptive kinds of behavior. Bostow and Bailey (1969) used a combination of reinforcement and time out from reinforcement to decrease the aggressive behaviors of a seven-year-old child. The child would hit, bite, kick, or butt other people from twenty to seventy times per half hour. He had received two tranquilizing drugs which proved ineffective. However, when he was placed in a time out area for two minutes immediately following each aggressive encounter and was reinforced with milk and cookies for behaving in a non-aggressive manner, the child's aggressive behavior was nearly eliminated within two days. In another study Homme *et al.* (1963) noted that a group of pre-school children frequently ran around in general *rough-house* activity, even when they were instructed to sit and pay attention. Homme arranged for those *more likely* behaviors to be made available contingent on *less likely* behaviors such as sitting, studying, and paying attention. If the children sat and paid attention for a short time, they were given a signal to get up and run around. By gradually increasing the length of the work time and decreasing the length of the rough-house time, a very orderly classroom developed (an orderly classroom need not be free of all rough-house activities). What is equally important is that threats and punishment were not needed. The children would attend to the teacher for longer and longer intervals when this resulted in their having the opportunity to run and play.

At times it is difficult to induce students to follow instructions, sometimes because instructions are unclear, but most often because there is no immediate advantage to following them. Schutte and Hopkins (1970) observed that a group of kindergarten students followed instructions approximately 60 per cent of the time. When the teacher "paid attention" to those students who followed her instructions (that is, praised the children either while they were carrying out the instructions or immediately afterward), instruction-following increased to over 80 per cent. Similar effects were found in a classroom of retarded boys all showing "attentional deficits" (Zimmerman *et al.*, 1969). The frequency of following instructions increased when this kind of behavior was reinforced with praise from the teacher. The frequency increased even further when following instructions earned tokens that could be exchanged for goodies (i.e. candy, balloons, toys).

In each of these studies a form of disruptive behavior was reduced or attentional behavior increased. Clearly such disruptive or non-attentional behaviors interfere with the learning of new activities in the classroom, and thus the teacher must change these behaviors before advancing into her planned curriculum. The techniques described are directly applicable to the classroom. The teacher may not have "milk and cookies" available as reinforcers, but there are many other things in and around a classroom that would work as well. Token or point systems, *praise,* and a host of "preferred activities" are typically effective reinforcers when used correctly. Correct use means, among other things, presentation of the reinforcer *immediately* following the desired behavior. Giving Johnny a treat at the end of class and telling him he was a good boy today is just not enough.

Behavior modification has also proven effective in developing and maintaining a variety of academic behaviors. Wheeler and Sulzer (1970) trained an eight-year-old speech-deficient retarded child to respond to picture forms with complete sentences. The picture forms were cards from levels #P and #3 of the Peabody Language Development kit. Initially the child responded to these cards with incomplete sentences, but could identify objects in the pictures. The child was then reinforced with tokens for giving a complete sentence description of the picture. If he made an error, he was given a prompt by the teacher which he would then imitate, finish the rest of the sentence and be reinforced. After five thirty-minute sessions the child responded to the five training cards at 83 per cent correct, and to two cards not used in training at 100 per cent correct. After approximately thirty training sessions the child was tested on six new cards that he had not seen since the initial test. He now responded to these cards with a complete sentence 70 per cent of the time. The authors concluded, "since the response was rapidly developed to stimuli (cards) with which training had been given and to stimuli with which no training had been given, it can be said that a functional response class or generative language had developed."

Guess (1969) used reinforcement techniques to train retardates in the correct use of plurals. Two thirteen-year-old boys with I.Q.'s of 40 and 42 used only singular word forms although they could produce the /s/ and /z/ sounds. The author first trained receptive plurals (i.e. pointing to one or a pair of objects) by reinforcing correct responses with tokens. Incorrect responses resulted in the teacher saying "no," and then starting another trial. The receptive plurals were acquired very rapidly, but probes to see if this would help expressive plurals (i.e. saying the plural form) proved negative. *There was no generalization.* A procedure was then used which was identical to the first one except that the boys had to respond verbally instead of pointing. Reinforcement of correct expressive plurals (e.g. coin/coins; truck/trucks) again resulted in rapid acquisition. Along with showing that reinforcement is effective in the training of language skills, this study suggests that there may be little or no carry-over (generalization) between receptive and expressive language.*

Imitation is another type of behavior that has been shown to be affected by reinforcement. It can be used very effectively in the classroom to initiate a new response and is probably often used accidentally in this way. Studies by Baer, Peterson, and Sherman (1967) and Baer and Sherman (1964) demonstrated that children would learn to imitate both general motor and vocal responses of a model when correct imitations were reinforced. Once the imitative behavior was established, a new response model was typically

* For a more detailed description of language training see Bricker and Bricker, 1970.

imitated correctly too, even when this new response was not reinforced. When imitation was no longer reinforced, it decreased to almost zero. Clearly, reinforcement was necessary to maintain the class of imitative behaviors.

These studies demonstrate the effectiveness of reinforcement techniques in strengthening various academic responses in retardates. In each case the behavior improved when it was reinforced and deteriorated when it was no longer reinforced. Similar techniques were applied in the special education classrooms at Faribault State Hospital.

Implementing behavior modification in the classroom

Behavior modification programs were introduced into one section of the school program operating within the institution. All of the students were institutionalized residents living in an administration unit composed of four buildings. Almost all of these residents were in their teens, and the I.Q. range was roughly 25 to 65 with the mode near 40. With approximately forty residents per building, there were about 160 students in this section of the school program. At one point in the recent history of the institution, there was a great deal of emphasis on including a large number of residents in school, an approach having substantial fiscal benefits. The disadvantages were sufficient, however, to bring about a change in favor of higher-quality education. The number of residents receiving classroom instruction was decreased and the number of teachers for this section was increased. The result was eight teachers to work with a little less than 40 per cent of the unit population (about sixty residents). Class size was between six and ten residents, who were in school from ten to twenty-five hours a week.

A series of meetings was held with the teachers to present some of the principles underlying behavior modification, to correct some misconceptions, and to identify some of the problems the teachers were having in their classrooms. Behavior modification principles were discussed in general terms (i.e. technical terminology was not stressed) and in the context of human behavior. Each teacher was to decide whether she wanted to increase or decrease the likelihood of a certain behavior. If she wanted to decrease the occurrence of some disruptive behavior she could use extinction, time out from reinforcement, or reinforcement of behaviors incompatible with the disruptive behavior. Extinction typically meant withholding teacher attention or ignoring the behavior, since teacher attention was the most likely source of reinforcement. If the teacher wanted to increase the occurrence of some behavior, she could use some form of reinforcement. Again, teacher attention was stressed, and the use of consumables (candy or cereal), play activities, and various token systems were also discussed. In addition, several studies were reviewed which showed how teacher attention could affect specific behaviors of the students. The discussion of these consequences of behavior led to an interesting question. *If the way in which a teacher responds to specific student behaviors can have such a great effect on the subsequent performance of those students, should the teacher respond to them in a somewhat haphazard manner, or should she plan how she will react (plan contingencies) so as to determine the likelihood of subsequent behaviors?* The growing body of knowledge in the behavioral sciences strongly suggests that the latter is essential, even though it magnifies the responsibility of the teacher, and of education as a whole.

While introducing the reinforcement principles, it was not uncommon to hear, "Oh, I use that all the time." Further questioning indicated that indeed some teachers did use rewards and other consequences, but seldom in a systematic and contingent manner. That is, everyone got a treat at the end of class regardless of how they performed during the class. And in relation to ignoring inappropriate behavior, many suggested that they did not attend to such behaviors at all. They simply "reprimanded" the child in some way. It is often difficult to recognize that such reprimands are forms of attention and may actually reinforce behavior.

Rewards were often described by the teachers as something given to the student in a pleasant way, and punishments or reprimands in an unpleasant way. This described the *teacher's feeling* but not necessarily the way her behavior affected the student's behavior. For example, the teacher may say she punishes Charles by shouting at him when he gets out of his seat and runs around the room. If Charles does not get much attention for sitting and working, he may well increase his running around day after day to receive such "unpleasant" attention. In this situation the teacher's reprimands are not punishing in the technical sense, but are reinforcing. Actually, *the teacher should judge the effects of her behavior by the effect it has on the student*. If Charles runs around less and less and after a few days does not run around at all, the reprimand can be said to be punishing. But if he continues to run around day after day and perhaps even does it more often than before, the reprimand is reinforcing. In this example, immediate effects may conceal the real effect. That is, Charles may come and sit as soon as the teacher shouts at him and this might lead the teacher to think that the reprimand had worked. However, if she has to use the reprimand day after day and just as often on succeeding days it has clearly not been effective as a punisher.

There is another circumstance in special education which tends to conceal such behavioral effects. Classroom experience is not always mandatory and children who do not perform well in the classroom may simply be taken out of school until they seem "ready" for school. The conditions that lead to a child being expelled may be similar to those described above. If a teacher reprimands a child day after day for misbehaving, chances are good that this child will not survive in the school program. He will remain out until he is "ready" for school. The teacher has solved a problem (the student is no longer misbehaving in her class), but the solution is questionable. This kind of situation can often be avoided if one tries systematically to change behavior.

But reinforcement may also be mishandled. A teacher may indicate that she used reinforcement in the form of praise or candy whenever Jimmy paid attention to her lesson, but that he still would not pay attention very often or for very long: "Reinforcement just doesn't work with Jimmy." What this means is that the kind of praise or candy Jimmy received was not reinforcing. Some other kinds of reinforcers would have to be sought for Jimmy—and they *do* exist. Failure to find effective reinforcers for a given child reflect teacher impatience, discouragement, or perhaps lack of effort. Oftentimes, ingenuity is required. An M & M just isn't adequate for all children.

TECHNIQUES FOR CHANGING CLASSROOM BEHAVIOR

Systematic methods for changing behavior are lacking in most classrooms, and this reflects inadequacies in teacher education. Obviously teachers cannot be expected to use techniques to which they have not been exposed. Typically an education student is required to spend a good deal of time studying philosophies of education. It may be beneficial to have a philosophy in mind when working in the classroom, but this is where many education programs stop. The teacher is armed with knowledge of subject matter and/or educational philosophy but few if any *teaching techniques*. In the Faribault program it was clear that the teachers knew their material. Still, they just could not seem to "get through to some students." After discussing the behavioral principles and recognizing the importance of behavioral consequences, we began dealing with specific classroom problems. To no one's surprise, our first task was to eliminate a series of disruptive kinds of behavior so the student could attend to the classroom activities.

ELIMINATING DISRUPTIVE BEHAVIORS

One student would routinely get up and move about the classroom swearing and making noise. This happened daily, and sometimes two or three times in a period. The teacher usually tried to calm him down and cajole him into participating in the classroom activity. Occasionally he behaved so poorly that she had to have him taken back to his home building. The student's behavior disrupted the class and distressed the teacher since she felt that he could learn a great deal if he did not have that behavior problem. The teacher and consultant discussed this student's behavior and decided that he might be getting attention for behaving in such a manner. The teacher agreed to ignore the disruptive behavior completely and attend to the student only when he was behaving appropriately. She did this effectively, but the results were not as great as anticipated. Subsequently, a program was initiated that dealt directly with the vocal outbursts of this student. The teacher carried a small timer that operated like a kitchen timer.* She would set the timer for a short interval (two to five minutes) and whenever the timer finished the student would earn a point. After acquiring a specified number of points he could exchange them for access to some activity, usually listening to taped music. Whenever the student swore or shouted inappropriately, the teacher would reset the timer, thus delaying the availability of a point. This procedure was reasonably effective in decreasing vocal outbursts and the teacher planned to use it to train the student to stay in his seat. That is, the timer would run as long as the student remained in his seat and leaving his seat would result in the timer being reset.

Two observations concerning this procedure are in order. First, the teacher commented (and subsequently other teachers have agreed) that learning to ignore certain behaviors is very difficult, because in the past those same behaviors attracted most of her attention. Second, the degree of success with the timer game is directly related to the consistency of the teacher. When the teacher remembers to reset the timer immediately following outbursts and when it has timed out, the procedure is effective in a relatively short time. To the extent that she periodically forgets

---

* See M. Wolfe et al. (1970) for a complete description of the "timer game."

to reset the timer, one can expect the student to show little or no change.

Another case involved a student that was observed to learn very quickly at times, but would typically sit with his head down on his desk, stare into space, twirl around the room, or whine. Much of this student's behavior appeared autistic, although he had not received that diagnosis. His behavior was discussed and the teacher decided to use various kinds of reinforcement whenever the student attempted some work. Initially cereal was used, and after a few weeks a token system was initiated whereby the student could earn tokens just as he had earned cereal. He could exchange the tokens for access to activities, such as playing a game, or being read to for a few minutes. The effects of this procedure were seen within a week or so, and by the end of three weeks the student was participating in classroom activities almost 100 per cent of the time. The student acquired many new skills, and the "autistic-like behaviors" were rarely observed in the classroom. They still continued to occur, however, in his home building. This latter point is quite relevant. It demonstrates clearly that generalization from one situation to another does not occur "automatically," as some would believe. The fact that this child behaved one way in one situation and another way in a different situation indicates that he had formed a discrimination. That is, the classroom environment was a cue that study behaviors would be reinforced, and the building environment was a cue that other kinds of behavior would be reinforced.

Another technique for eliminating disruptive behavior is to remove the student from the reinforcing situation for a short time. This is called time out from reinforcement. The technique has been shown to be very effective in some situations, but it was not employed in the classrooms at Faribault for the following reasons. (1) There were no isolated areas available. Students could have been sent to a part of the Principal's Office, but this would only transfer responsibility for the student to someone else. It was also felt that the student might get to interact with adults in this area, which would tend to make the time out reinforcing rather than punishing. (2) Many students would resist going to a time out area and the teachers would be unable to physically get them there. If they did manage to do so, the commotion would often be more disruptive than the initial student behavior.

Let me stress that these reasons are specific to the situation at hand. The time out procedure per se is very effective when it can be used appropriately (Bostow and Bailey, 1969).

STRENGTHENING ACADEMIC BEHAVIORS

In the preceding examples disruptive behaviors were reduced by the teacher's ignoring them and by reinforcing incompatible behaviors such as studying. Of equal importance is the application of these methods to the development of academic behaviors. While discussion of disruptive and academic behaviors is separated here, one must frequently deal with both simultaneously in the classroom. A child that is not attending to the instructional situation has little chance of developing academic skills, whereas the likelihood of learning increases with attending. A large part of our effort to improve academic behavior was based on this premise.

A basic example of this relationship involved the consultant in a direct way. Upon entering the classroom, the consultant was usually greeted by the students with numerous shouts and gestures. These are characteristic in a large institution: "What's your name?," "What's he doing here?," "I had scouts last night." Most of the students would stop working whenever the consultant or anyone else entered the classroom. It is not uncommon for adults to interact with young retardates, especially when the child initiates the interaction. There are those who feel that this sort of interaction should be allowed to continue in order to increase the social skills of the students. On the other hand, these students had stopped engaging in appropriate study behavior, and there are certainly more appropriate times for such socializing. This problem was discussed with the teacher and we concluded that interacting with adults in the classroom was probably a reinforcing situation for the students, and if the person entering the room responded to the students' outbursts, his response would only strengthen the outbursts. To prevent this, both the teacher and consultant ignored those students that stopped studying when the consultant entered, and they interacted briefly with those who continued working. The form of this interaction was usually praise for working. Those that had been distracted were given attention shortly after they resumed working. In effect, none of the students were shortchanged on interacting with the consultant or teacher. This interaction was arranged, however, to reinforce appropriate study behavior rather than inappropriate behavior. The technique was effective in strengthening study behavior and resulted in the posting of a note outside each classroom (Figure 7-1). Feedback from the teachers suggested that this notice was very effective in reducing disruptions.

There were many classroom activities in which the teacher could work on the attentional behavior of her students. For instance, group activities related to reading, language development, or time-telling were often conducted with the students seated around the teacher. The teacher would arrange some materials and then call on a student to respond to these materials. Those paying attention responded appropriately whereas those not at-

---

ATTENTION

Visitors and/or Personnel

When entering this classroom please DO NOT interact with the students (ignore them) unless such interaction is initiated BY THE TEACHER.

Figure 7-1. A notice posted outside each classroom to reduce disruptions.

tending could seldom respond at all. Since the students' responses in this situation were likely to be a one-to-one interaction with the teacher, and since this was likely to be reinforcing, only those students paying attention were called on. This is the opposite of what often happens. Teachers frequently call on those *not* paying attention in order to encourage them to attend to the activity. However, if the ensuing interaction is reinforcing, the teacher has inadvertently reinforced "not attending." If the student wants attention, he can get it by not paying attention to the teacher. In our program the opportunity to respond to the teacher was reinforcing, and the amount of attending to the instructional situation increased greatly.

The same basic procedure was found effective for maintaining work behaviors while the students were at individual desks. The teacher moved around the room interacting briefly with those engaged in appropriate work behavior and ignoring those not working. It is critical to note that when a non-worker or non-attender began doing what he was supposed to do, the teacher did not ignore him for what he *had been* doing but rather reinforced him shortly after he engaged in appropriate behavior.

The degree of change that can be effected under the right conditions is clearly shown in the following example. The teacher concentrated her efforts on a student that had been extremely disruptive in the past. The frequency of his disruptions was decreased to a reasonable level, and emphasis was then placed on acquiring academic behaviors. The data shown in Figure 7-2 represent the change in behavior over five consecutive class periods and performance on a post-test (R) seven months later. The student was instructed in five academic areas and received tokens intermittently for correct performance in each of these areas. He received praise following each correct response. As soon as he earned five tokens he would exchange them for a short study break to do one of three things: (1) play with a teddy bear; (2) play with a picture of Batman; (3) have a piece of candy. Instruction resumed immediately after the reinforcement activity. The

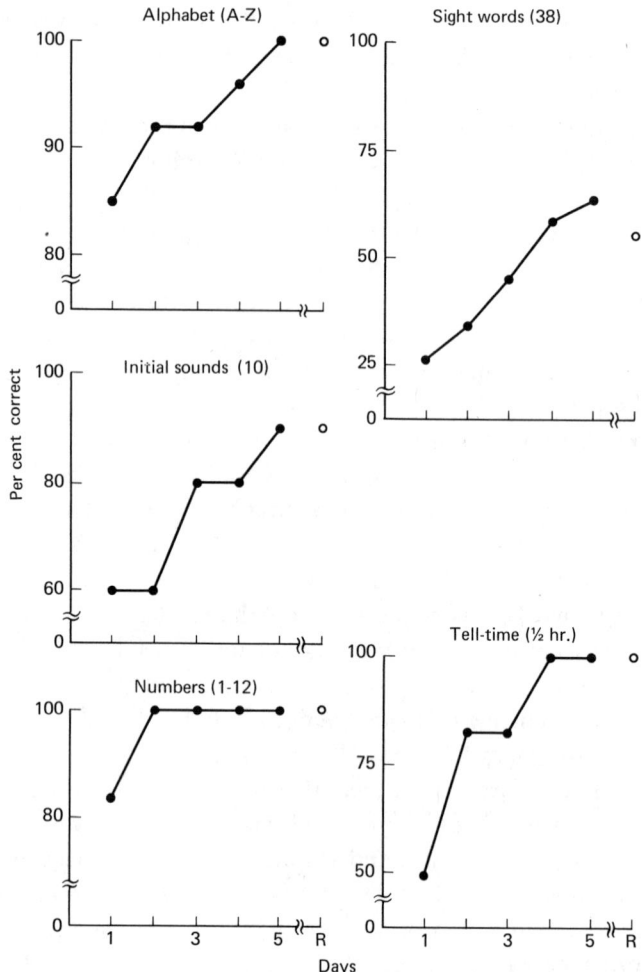

Figure 7-2. A student's performance in five academic areas. Each graph shows the acquisition of behavior over five consecutive class periods and the performance on a post-test (R) seven months later.

number of tokens earned during a class session (average length: one hour) varied between eleven and sixteen. Thus, the student was receiving two to three tokens per academic activity.

The first graph in Figure 7-2 shows acquisition of naming the letters of the alphabet. Each letter was presented on a flash-card. Correct identification of letters increased from 85 to 100 per cent over the five days. Recognition of sight vocabulary words (e.g. black, apple, cat, house, elephant, flower, kitchen) printed on flashcards showed a large gain. Initially, the student responded correctly to ten of the thirty-eight cards (26 per cent), and by the fifth day he read twenty-four of them correctly (63 per cent). There were ten possible beginning sounds such as b, f, d, and h printed on flash-cards. The student correctly pronounced 60 per cent of these on the first day and got 90 per cent correct on the fifth day. The naming of number symbols (1 through 12) increased from 83 to 100 per cent correct. Finally, the student learned to tell time to the nearest half hour. Initially he knew half of the twenty-four possible hand positions, and by the fourth day he identified all positions correctly.

The post-test, administered seven months after the week of training, indicated that the student had retained all information in four of the five areas. The only decrease was on the sight vocabulary words, and this reflects the lack of opportunity to use certain responses. The teacher introduced a different word list after the initial week of training and thus the student had no further contact with many of the words he had learned. The post-test results prompted the teacher to arrange opportunities for the students to continue using acquired skills.

The significance of this example is made clear by the teacher's comment attached to her report: "I think this shows a good indication of the rate at which these children can achieve under the right circumstances."

Another case dealt with the use of phrases and sentences in response to a question. One child typically responded to a question with one or two words, and when asked to imitate a longer phrase or sentence repeated, only the last word or part. The easiest solution was to diagnose a poor "auditory memory" and let it go at that. Instead a program was employed whereby the student was reinforced for imitating. He was given a sentence and was instructed to imitate the last word. Next the child was given the last two words to imitate, and when he responded correctly, he was given the last three, and so on until he was saying the whole sentence. This procedure was effective in developing the desired behavior in a week, and the behavior generalized to other situations. That is, the child responded with phrases or sentences to situations other than those in which he had been trained. Over subsequent weeks the teacher paid less and less attention to whether or not the student used complete sentences, and eventually the student reverted to his old ways. The teacher noticed the recurrence of this problem and realized she had stopped reinforcing the desired behavior. She subsequently initiated a program with her whole class very much like the one described earlier in the chapter (Wheeler and Sulzer, 1970). The students were shown a simple picture and asked to describe it in a complete sentence. Initially the teacher used prompts for the students to imitate. She gradually stopped using prompts and conducted the activity in the form of a game. The first student to describe the picture in a complete sentence received that picture for the duration of the activity. Initial results from this procedure were very encouraging and the program is being continued.

Still another case concerning speech involved a student that had a very adequate speech repertoire but whose rate of speaking was sufficiently high that he was often misunderstood. This student met with a speech therapist for a short time each day, and it appeared that the student enjoyed these sessions. The teacher therefore arranged for his trip to the speech therapist to be contingent on speaking slowly and clearly in the classroom. She structured a situation about one minute before each speech therapy session in which the student could respond verbally. He was prompted by the teacher to speak slowly, and if he did he was given a pass to go to speech therapy. If he spoke rapidly, he missed speech therapy that day. This never happened. The teacher gradually increased the length of time that the student had to speak slowly and clearly, and subsequently used such alternative reinforcers as a library pass.

These examples indicate the degree to which student behaviors can be changed when the teacher plans contingencies to change them. The learning that occurred was not accidental but resulted from reinforcement of specific desired behaviors. As indicated, teacher attention was usually the most effective reinforcer, and earning tokens which were exchanged for access to some activity was also effective.

The importance of reinforcement was shown in the example concerning speaking in complete sentences. When the teacher paid less and less attention to the manner in which the student spoke, he gradually stopped using complete sentences. When she reinstated the training program, his performance again improved.

PROGRAMMED INSTRUCTION

The use of programmed instructional material was not stressed in these classrooms, primarily because there were few programs available in the institution. Those that were available generally proved effective, supporting findings by McCarthy and Scheerenberger (1966). These authors reviewed studies comparing programmed instructions with traditional instruction in the areas of work recognition, spelling, time-telling, and reading, and found that programmed instruction was typically superior to traditional instruction in terms of rate of acquisition and retention. The reviewers concluded that some of the more salient features of programmed instruction are: "It requires a complete and detailed plan of what is to be taught, it systematically follows sound learning principles (e.g. small steps, immediate reinforcement), and, unlike most traditional education materials, is considered ready for use only after it has been field tested." An additional advantage of programmed instructional materials is that the teacher is not the focus of the learning situation and can circulate among the students, giving help where needed and reinforcing those behaviors she would like to strengthen.

Where commercial programs are not available, traditional materials can often be presented in a programmed manner. There seem to be three critical steps in programming non-programmed materials. First, one must determine that the materials to be used will teach what they are intended to teach. For instance, when teaching children to discriminate colors, the colors must all be presented on the same shape or form. If this is not done, the child may learn to discriminate shapes rather than colors. Second, the materials should be presented in small steps. One should train identification of a single color at a time rather than five or six. One might select a color that the child knows and have him name the color several times. Then add a new color and train him to name it, perhaps using imitation. Each color must be presented separately a few times to be sure he discriminates between them. Then another color can be added and so on. If the materials have been arranged in sequential steps, the point at which the student should begin can be determined. For instance, in learning to print, a student that can already trace well might skip the first part of the lesson, whereas one that cannot trace would have to start at the beginning. The final point is that correct responses should be reinforced *immediately*.

In systematic instruction of this sort, the student should progress through the material with few errors. If the child begins making errors at some point, the program can be altered accordingly. That is, steps can be added to the sequence, or the student can be moved back a few steps, or perhaps some steps can be removed. The point is that with a well-structured teaching program the teacher is aware of learning problems as they occur, not weeks or months later when the errors have been learned well.

ARRANGEMENT OF THE CLASSROOM

In the course of observing various classrooms at Faribault several features were noted that seemed to facilitate the over-all educational operation. These features are incorporated in the arrange-

THE SPECIAL EDUCATION CLASSROOM

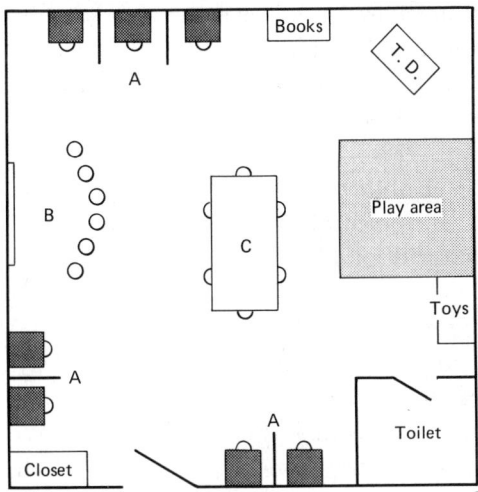

Figure 7-3. The diagram of a classroom which features three distinct study areas (A, B, and C) and a play area. Students learn behavior appropriate to each area when reinforced consistently for those behaviors.

ment shown in Figure 7-3. This sample classroom has three distinct work areas and a distinct play area. Each of the three study areas provided for a different kind of student-teacher interaction. The individual study desks (A) set the occasion for the student to work alone, and he had only periodic contact with the teacher. The teacher circulated among the students giving fairly immediate reinforcement to those behaving in an appropriate manner, and she worked one to one for brief periods of time. The arrangement of chairs around the chalk board (B) provided a situation in which the students and teacher were likely to interact a great deal. The teacher was close to all the students, could usually observe them all at the same time, and again selectively reinforced those behaviors she wanted to increase. Activities such as time-telling, reciting, responding to flash-cards, imitating, and "paying attention" were dealt with in this situation. The third work area (C) was arranged for group activities and was also used to initiate programs that were carried out at the individual desks.

Again, the teacher could supervise the entire activity and readily reinforce appropriate behaviors. The play area should be clearly designated in the classroom. An effective way to mark off this area is with a piece of carpet which serves to reduce noise as well as indicate the boundary.

The distinctiveness of each of these four areas is important with respect to developing stimulus control (discussed in Chapter 2). In general, this means that if the student is reinforced for behavior appropriate to each of these areas, he will learn to display these behaviors in the right situation. Some educators may find this notion bothersome, and yet we all learn to behave in this way. We learn that it is all right to "have fun" in some situations while in others we must be more serious and attend to our work. We learn to express our political views in some situations while in others it may be risky. In these examples some part of our environment signals what kinds of behavior are likely to be reinforced or what kinds are likely to be punished (keep in mind that people are part of one's environment). Thus, it seems reasonable to train the student to play and rough-house in the play area rather than in a study area. Similarly, group setting should be a signal to attend to the teacher, but attending to the teacher would be inappropriate when the child is in his individual work area. This kind of discrimination can and should be trained in the retarded, and it is surprisingly easy when appropriate behaviors are reinforced consistently.

CURRICULUM MODIFICATIONS

I have discussed ways to develop and change academic behaviors, but a recurrent problem is specifying what skills should be taught. In other words, what are the immediate goals of the educational process? Our goals, like those of most education programs, lacked specificity. Some of the stated goals included such things as "preparation for independent living," "becoming a good citizen," "job preparation," or "getting along with others." These goals were

THE SPECIAL EDUCATION CLASSROOM

sufficiently vague that it was usually impossible to specify just how to reach them or to determine when they had been reached. It also meant that the students and teachers waited for a very long time before having the satisfaction of achieving a goal.

Table 7-1. A sample of behavioral objectives selected from two functional levels. This sample is intended to show the general form of the objectives and does not indicate the teaching sequence or the complete repertoire of a class of behaviors.

Level 1

A. Self-care

   1. Toileting
      a. closes door
      b. goes alone
      c. flushes toilet
      d. re-dresses completely before leaving the toilet room

   2. Hygiene
      a. wipes messy hands on appropriate material
      b. does not pick nose

B. Social behavior

   1. Does not engage in physical contact (hugging, holding hand, etc.) unless given an explicit cue to do so
   2. Does not interrupt the interaction of others (vocal or tactile)
   3. Does not display tantrum behaviors
   4. Will work or play alone for at least five minutes in the absence of supervision or when instructed to do so
   5. Can work at an assigned task at least twenty minutes

C. Perceptual-motor (gross)

   1. Walk in an appropriate gait (heel/toe; legs bend; body upright; arms swing moderately) staying within a one-foot path
   2. Can step over a small object (shoe box) in path
   3. Can throw a tennis ball with one hand (any manner) to a three-foot diameter target on a wall
   4. Can pull an object (chair) toward self using a rope (any manner)

D. Perceptual-motor (fine)

   1. Can hold a crayon properly
   2. Can trace a one-eighth inch thick line without deviating more than one-eighth inch on either side (straight and curved line)
   3. Can draw a straight line using a ruler
   4. Can tear paper straight using a ruler
   5. Can assemble a ten-piece puzzle

E. Sense training and orientation

   1. Can point to appropriate body part when given a verbal prompt
   2. Can place an object in, on, under, behind, next to, beside, in front of, or between some other objects
   3. Can identify (name) gross sounds (music, hammer, bell, bird, truck)

F. Expressive language

   1. Can imitate phonic sounds
   2. Can imitate own name and teacher's name
   3. Imitates the names of objects in immeditae environment
   4. Can name two objects just described in a short story or film

G. Reading

   1. Can read all words on the Level I sight vocabulary list
   2. Can match printed words to objects in immediate environment

H. Numbers

   1. Can identify number symbols 0 through 10
   2. Can count at least ten objects
      a. touching objects
      b. not touching objects

Level II

A. Self-care
1. Can put on and remove clothing correctly, and without damaging it
2. Dresses appropriate to weather conditions 90 per cent of the time
3. Can tie a bow knot in shoe lace with shoe on foot

B. Social behavior
1. Can work at a task for at least thirty minutes without interruption
2. Will work or play alone for fifteen minutes in the absence of supervision
3. Answers telephone saying "hello" and giving first and last name
4. Can deliver a written message promptly (without being distracted to a nearby designated location or person)
5. Note: the student should have direct *structured* experience in the community no less than once a week
   a. does not initiate conversation with strangers passed on the sidewalk
   b. responds correctly to pedestrian rules (specify rules)
   c. does not yell or holler in a store
   d. can purchase a small item (gum) in a drugstore without assistance

C. Perceptual-motor
1. Can copy all capital and small letters of the alphabet
2. Can reproduce (write) each letter of the alphabet from an auditory prompt
3. Can print first and last name without a visual prompt
4. Can tie a double knot with clothes line
5. Prints from left to right, and top to bottom of page

D. Expressive language
1. Can identify and correctly pronounce the names of objects in the classroom
2. Can identify (name) action in a simple picture
3. Can describe four facts immediately following a short story or film
4. Can describe a self-experience in a complete sentence

E. Reading
1. Can read all words on the Level II sight vocabulary list
2. Can name initial phonetic sounds presented visually
3. Can read experience charts and a pre-primer with retention of one fact

F. Numbers
1. Can recite number sequence 0 thru 30
2. Can count at least thirty objects without a structured termination
   a. touching objects
   b. without touching objects
3. Can add and subtract using ten objects
4. Can identify and name standard coins

A curriculum was established that gave the teachers guidelines to follow and stated clearly what the students were to learn. Short-term goals were specified and every effort was made to eliminate undefined concepts. The result was a list of clearly specified behavioral objectives. The initial set of objectives (some of which are shown in Table 7-1) gave the teachers some clear target behaviors. Again, the emphasis was on specifying some short-term goals for the teachers. In so doing, some of the objectives were selected arbitrarily. The exact relevance of the specified student behavior to some later performance was not always clear. For instance, one objective was that the student should learn to color a simple picture staying within 90 per cent of the boundary. It may turn out that this skill is irrelevant to subsequent perceptual motor skills and thus could be dropped as an objective. This sort of refinement is carried out on a continuous basis so that the objectives continue to function for the teacher and the student.

The objectives covered a broad range of behaviors, such as self-care skills, social behaviors, and academic behaviors. Emphasis was placed on perceptual motor development, since these behaviors are often needed to acquire later skills, and on language development, because the lack of this class of behavior gives the retardate many problems in the greater community.

The behavioral objectives aided the teachers by providing them with a set of specified, observable behaviors to train. These behaviors were for the most part easily measured and thus there was little ambiguity as to when an objective was reached. What remains to be done, and is now underway, is to specify exactly the steps necessary to meet each objective. This involves listing each step in the teaching sequence and the type of materials best suited to teach that step. If the instructional plan is specified in sufficient detail, a fine analysis of instruction is possible. Learning problems can be spotted immediately, permitting determination of the exact part of the teaching plan requiring modification. Clearly this means the materials and students must be evaluated on a continuous basis, not once or twice a year. Perhaps the designers of instructional materials and methods have always had this sort of thing in mind. One can hope.

Some factors related to effective programming

A number of procedures and techniques for making the classroom environment one which maximizes the likelihood of learning have been discussed. Teachers that have seen or had first-hand experience with behavior modification have typically been impressed by its effectiveness and have continued to use it. Others have shrugged it off as a new gimmick, and some have found it ineffective. The programs in the Faribault classrooms have on occasion been ineffective, and I would like to discuss some of the factors that contribute to this problem.

1. Even though the reinforcement of desired behaviors was stressed, it was sometimes used too infrequently in the classrooms. The teachers reinforced some kinds of desirable behaviors but not others. It seemed that some behaviors should just "naturally" occur. I would suggest that we ask ourselves, "What is the immediate payoff for the student in doing this work or in learning this material?" There are usually long-range payoffs, but these are known to us—not the student. When it turns out that there are no immediate payoffs, then some artificial ones should be incorporated to mediate the delay of the long-range payoffs. This is essentially what token systems and the like are for. Johnny continues to work hard in his pre-reading workbook not because he wants to be a proofreader, but because he earns tokens for doing so. Susan follows the teacher's directions because she is praised for doing so, not because she wants to be a good citizen some day. The effect of the immediate payoff is to strengthen the behavior to the point where the student can make contact with the longer-range payoffs.

2. The need for consistency in reinforcing and ignoring student behaviors has been emphasized throughout this chapter and I will try not to belabor the point here. It is the case though that where behavior modification programs have not been effective, it is usually because of teacher inconsistency.

There is an even greater problem when the inconsistency is across environments. Certain behaviors may be reinforced in one situation and those same behaviors may be ignored or punished in another situation. If this statement sounds familiar, it is because it was used earlier to describe how certain parts of the classroom come to control the students' behavior. The student learns to behave one way here, a different way there. But we now

THE SPECIAL EDUCATION CLASSROOM

need to ask, "Are there behaviors that we want to occur in the same way under various situations?" Clearly the answer is "yes," and the way this is achieved is to make reinforcement consistent across those various situations.

The clearest examples of the need for consistency center around speech. A student may learn to pronounce words clearly in the classroom or with the speech therapist, but the rest of his environment ignores his speech or reinforces poor speech. The resident may make a grunt or groan and then immediately receive what he was requesting. Similarly, residents learn to speak in complete sentences under some conditions, but in most other situations they get what they want by mumbling a word or gesturing. Time-telling is only needed in the classroom. In most other situations

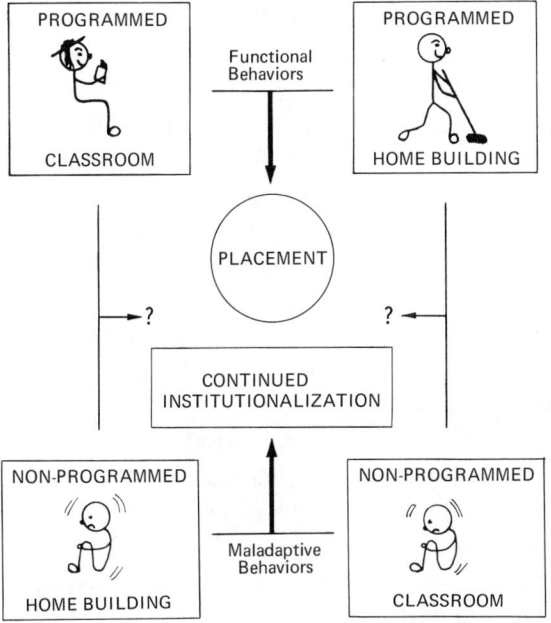

Figure 7-4. A diagram showing the probable consequence of consistency between home building and classroom environments.

someone will tell the resident when to do this or that. Earlier in this chapter a case was described in which many of a student's autistic-like behaviors were extinguished in the classroom but still occurred at a high frequency back in his home building. The inappropriate behaviors were not reinforced in the classroom but *were* reinforced in other situations. To restate the problem in general terms, learning that occurs in one situation may be interfered with or reversed by events in another situation. To the extent that we can reduce this inconsistency we can facilitate the development of functional behaviors in the retardate.

The probable consequences of consistency between classroom and home building are shown in Figure 7-4. The term "programmed" implies the use of behavioral consequences to develop specific behaviors. "Non-programmed" implies the lack of such planned contingencies. When both environments are programmed, there is a high probability of developing functional behaviors and subsequent placement in the community. When neither environment is programmed, there is a high probability of developing maladaptive behaviors which lead to continued institutionalization. The outcome of combined programmed and non-programmed environments is questionable. This situation would most likely lead to continued institutionalization because of the inconsistency, but it could conceivably lead to placement.

Any program designed for institutionalized residents must consider their total environment. As indicated, failure to do so may result in the development and maintenance of maladaptive behaviors which interfere with achieving the goals of that program. Additionally, "real world" situations must be established in the institution to prepare the residents for interacting appropriately in the greater community. This can be done in structured situations like those described above in which planned contingencies are used to modify behavior. It requires an institutional philosophy geared toward changing behavior rather than toward custodial care.

3. A factor related to environmental consistency is the periodic

use of drugs to change or control behavior. When a resident becomes over-active and hard to manage, he is made manageable with a drug. The drug may have no therapeutic value, but it slows him down to the point where he is no longer troublesome for the staff and other residents. This becomes a problem, however, when one wishes to engage the resident in some specific activity (e.g. a learning activity in the classroom). A student may normally attend to learning situations and be reinforced by the teacher for doing so. Then under the drug condition he becomes very inattentive and perhaps even drowsy. These behaviors are incompatible with attending and learning, and they put the student out of touch with potential reinforcers. He is no longer behaving in ways that the teacher can reinforce. This example is not hypothetical. Such occurrences are all too frequent and are troublesome for teachers because they cannot be sure what caused the student's behavior to change. Was it something they did in the classroom, or some outside factor?

One alternative is to replace this kind of drug use with procedures that alter behavior by changing the environment. Linda McConahey presents evidence in Chapter 6 favoring this approach. In the event that drugs are used to change behavior it would seem reasonable for those people who work with the resident to be made aware of the drug schedule. Better yet, they should be part of the process that decides whether or not a drug is used.

4. The expectancies of a teacher can have a startling effect on the performance of her students. Teacher expectancy is evident in every classroom, and often to the benefit of the student. When a student masters one unit of a lesson, the teacher gives him the next unit, *expecting* that he will perform well on it too. If the teacher did not expect this, the student might never progress beyond the first unit. In this instance the teacher's expectancy is firmly based on the fact that the student has performed well on the first unit. Teacher expectancy can be a problem when it is established with inadequate information. For instance, if the

teacher gives the second unit without knowing how the student performed on the first unit, or on the mistaken assumption that the student did well on the first unit, she may inadvertently initiate a problem. Expectancies are often based on hearsay, observations by others that may or may not be correct, or theories that are questionable and untested. These expectancies are apt to impede student progress. In a study of teacher expectancy Rosenthal and Jacobson (1968) randomly selected 20 per cent of an elementary school class and instructed the teachers that these children were of outstanding ability and would perform well. (Since the selection was random, it is likely that some of these children were actually average and below average). After eight months of school the I.Q.'s of all the children were retested. The students whom the teachers thought would do well did just that, and others showed little or no gain. The teachers were clearly not aware they were treating some students differently because of expectations, but this is what happened.

There are many instances of questionable teacher expectancy in the special education classroom. The following teacher comments reflect such unfortunate expectancies: "Jimmy is brain damaged," "Susan is a mongaloid and you know what that means," "Walter's learning ability is severely limited because he has such a short attention span," "Karen has a poor auditory memory," "Randy just isn't motivated to learn." Whether or not these comments are true (more often, they are not), their effect is to inhibit efforts at solving the behavioral problem. It is as though the problem is solved by giving a name to it, or providing a cause for it. In fact, the cause is *at best* a first step toward the solution.

Likewise, the problem of inappropriate teacher expectancies is seldom corrected by simply pointing the problem out to the teacher. This might be comparable to telling the disruptive student that he is disruptive. There is, however, a possible solution. The methods for changing behavior described in this chapter emphasize the *momentary behavior of the student*. The teacher deals with specific observable behaviors. General theories and clinical diagnoses become less important when dealing with moment-to-moment changes in behavior and this seems to result in fewer inappropriate expectancies. Applying methods to train Karen to speak in complete sentences is incompatible with just saying she has a poor "auditory memory." Likewise, training a student to attend to a learning situation for longer and longer periods of time is incompatible with saying he cannot learn because of a short attention span. The decrease in inappropriate expectancies may be viewed as a side effect of systematic teaching. It is clearly a beneficial side effect.

5. A more distantly related problem is that of long-range goals. The use of specified behavioral objectives was indicated in an earlier section to be of value to the teachers and students. The objectives made clear what would be taught and allowed for rather precise determination of when the objective was met. However, the fact that long-range goals are not always clear or realistic leaves the behavioral objectives subject to question. We can specify that Larry will learn to read and write, and we can specify the sequence that should be most effective in helping Larry to learn. What we often cannot specify is if or how Larry will use these skills. Will he remain in the institution? Will he be placed on a job? Will he go to a public school?

There is no simple answer to these questions. In fact, the likelihood of any of these outcomes is greatly influenced by national standards. If unemployment is high, few residents will be placed on jobs. Likewise, the retarded will not be readily accepted into over-crowded school districts. In view of this general flux it is probably best to arrange a sequential curriculum based on the resident: (1) remaining in the institution; (2) living in the institution while working or learning in the community; (3) living semi-independently; (4) living independently. This sequence should provide that all residents have the skills to maintain themselves within the institution. Those that could advance through later parts of the curriculum could do so with the hope (on our part) of eventual placement. Additionally, emphasis should be placed on training residents to train other residents—a concept that deserves much more consideration than is currently given it.

References

Baer, D. M., R. F. Peterson, and J. A. Sherman. The development of imitation by reinforcing behavioral similarity to a model. *Journal of the Experimental Analysis of Behavior*, 1967, 10, 405-16.

Baer, D. M., and J. A. Sherman. Reinforcement control of generalized imitation in young children. *Journal of Experimental Child Psychology*, 1964, 1, 37-49.

Bijou, S. W., and D. M. Baer. *Child Development: Readings in Experimental Analysis.* New York: Appleton-Century-Crofts, 1967.

Bostow, D., and J. Baily. Modification of severe disruptive and aggressive behavior using brief time-out and reinforcement procedures. *Journal of Applied Behavior Analysis*, 1969, 2, 31-37.

Bricker, W. A., and D. D. Bricker. A program of language training for the severely language handicapped child. *Exceptional Children*, 1970, 37, 101-11.

Craig, H. B., and A. L. Holland. Reinforcement of visual attending in classrooms for deaf children. *Journal of Applied Behavior Analysis*, 1970, 3, 97-109.

Guess, D. A functional analysis of receptive language and productive speech: acquisition of the plural morpheme. *Journal of Applied Behavior Analysis*, 1969, 2, 55-64.

Homme, L., P. deBaca, J. Devine, R. Steinhorst, and E. Rickert. Use of the Premack principle in controlling the behavior of nursery school children. *Journal of the Experimental Analysis of Behavior*, 1963, 6, 544.

Madsen, C. H., Jr., and C. K. Madsen. *Teaching/Discipline: Behavioral Principles Toward a Positive Approach.* Boston: Allyn & Bacon, Inc., 1970.

Mager, R. F. *Preparing Instructional Objectives.* Palo Alto, Calif.: Fearon Publishers, 1962.

McCarthy, J. J., and R. C. Scheerenberger. A decade of research on the education of the mentally retarded: a selected review. *Mental Retardation Abstracts*, 1966, 3, 481-501.

Meacham, M. L., and A. E. Wiesen. *Changing Classroom Behavior: A Manual for Precision Teaching.* Scranton, Penn.: International Textbook Co., 1969.

Rosenthal, R., and L. Jacobson. Teachers' expectancies as determinants of pupils' I.Q. gains. In R. G. Kuhlen (Ed.), *Studies in Educational Psychology*. Waltham, Mass.: Blaisdell Publishing Co., 1968.

Schutte, R. C., and B. L. Hopkins. The effects of teacher attention on following instructions in a kindergarten class. *Journal of Applied Behavior Analysis*, 1970, 3, 117-22.

Ulrich, R., T. Stachnik, T. and J. Mabry. *Control of Human Behavior*. Vol. II. Glenview, Ill.: Scott Foresman & Co., 1970.

Wheeler, A. J., and B. Sulzer. Operant training and generalization of a verbal response form in a speech-deficient child. *Journal of Applied Behavior Analysis*, 1970, 3, 139-47.

Wolfe, M., E. Hanley, L. King, J. Lachowicz, and D. Giles. The timer game: a VI contingency for the management of out-of-seat behavior. *Exceptional Children*, 1970, 37, 113-17.

Zimmerman, E., J. Zimmerman, and C. Russell. Differential effects of token reinforcement on instruction-following behavior in retarded students instructed as a group. *Journal of Applied Behavior Analysis*, 1969, 2, 101-12.

8
Behavior modification in occupational therapy

OCCUPATIONAL THERAPY DEPARTMENT*
FARIBAULT STATE HOSPITAL

Introduction

The purpose of this chapter is to describe the application of behavior modification principles to occupational therapy, illustrated by programs at Faribault State Hospital. Occupational therapy encompasses many areas of patient treatment. The American Occupational Therapy Association (1969) sums up the scope of this profession as "the art and science of directing man's response to selected activity to promote and maintain health, to prevent disability, to evaluate behavior and to treat or train patients with physical or psychosocial dysfunction." Occupational therapy, as applied specifically to an institutional setting, concerns itself with pathological processes as they interfere with normal living experiences. Priority of treatment is based on the needs of the residents and the philosophy of the institution.

Treatment emphasis should be on prerequisites for activities of daily living, cognitive skills, pre-vocational skills, and emotional maturity. In his role as a clinical practitioner, the occupational therapist applies the scientific method in evaluation, treatment,

* Occupational Therapy Department Staff, Faribault State Hospital: S. Kinsella, C. Berg, K. Smith, P. Scudder, A. Westling, L. Fellner, B. Nelson, J. Woodman, and M. Ahern.

and consultative services. As a consultant, the occupational therapist acts in concert with other disciplines to analyze the problem, make recommendations, and communicate these to the first-line supervisor to assist in the formulation of a plan of care or treatment.

In a state hospital for the retarded, the occuaptional therapist deals not only with the learning disabilities of the mentally retarded child or adult but with residents having physical handicaps, behavior problems, sensory deficits, or a combination of these. These considerations, coupled with the residents' wide range of abilities, require flexibility in designing occupational therapy programs. There is a wealth of excellent material available describing the application of occupational therapy techniques in the areas of physical dysfunction, perceptual-motor evaluation and training, activities of daily living, and diversional therapy. However, most of this material takes for granted that the patient worked with is able to follow instructions, that he can be instructed verbally or in gestures, that there is only one major handicap being treated, or, if others are present, that they are minor and easily handled. The latter assumption is understandable, since the importance of the occupational therapist's role in the treatment of the institutionalized multiply handicapped has only recently been realized. However, this is small consolation when the therapist is faced with a severely retarded child who is bent like a pretzel with spasticity and contractures, and who vomits voluntarily whenever he remotely suspects that therapy is about to be initiated. Consequently, much occupational therapy theory must be supplemented or tempered with additional treatment procedures facilitating training of the mentally retarded and/or multiply handicapped resident. One such procedure is the structured behavior modification program.

Behavior modification is not unfamiliar to occupational therapists. Although the formal concepts may be relatively new, the basic principle of reinforcing desired behavior has been used extensively and is recognized as an important consideration in treatment. Willard and Spackman (1963, p. 65) refer to the use of behavior therapy with psychiatric patients as "symptomatic therapy": "In symptomatic therapy the occupational therapist helps the patient to . . . alter, control or modify his behavior in order to allow him to function in society. . . ."

In her book, *Physical Disability—A Psychological Approach*, Beatrice A. Wright (1960, p. 339) defines this concept as it relates to handling the physically disabled child in therapy. She calls it simple "motivation":

. . . rewards and punishments can serve as powerful motivators of learning. They can do so in at least two ways. First, they can provide important information to the person as to what constitutes correct and incorrect responses. If the subject is reprimanded every time he makes a wrong move, and praised every time he makes the right response, then he may be able to correct his behavior and learn accordingly. . . . Secondly, rewards and punishments can serve to mobilize a person's energy and attention toward the learning task.

A systematic, structured application of this principle to the treatment of the institutionalized retarded is a new concept, however, and one which has proven to be of considerable value.

An occupational therapy program may use behavior modification simply to motivate a resident toward a particular task, or, if need be, to shape a resident's total behavior repertoire. The way in which behavior modification principles are applied within the therapy session is contingent upon several considerations, the most important being: (1) the type and degree of disability present; (2) the amount of time the therapist is able to spend with the resident; and (3) the amount of follow-through possible by ward personnel and other rehabilitation disciplines. The importance of these considerations and their effect on the occupational therapist's role in a behavior modification program will become more clear in the following section, which explains in detail a few of the occupational therapy programs at Faribault State Hospital that are making use of these techniques.

Illustrative programs

THE IRIS HOSPITAL IMPROVEMENT PROGRAM

In July of 1969 Faribault State Hospital received a Hospital Improvement Program grant to study techniques of training for severely and profoundly retarded adults (see Chapter 5). Because of this special assistance, the Iris Building program maintains an almost ideal resident-staff ratio and adequate building facilities. A certified occupational therapy assistant was hired with grant funds so that full-time occupational therapy consultation and programming would be available.

Twelve to fifteen severely and profoundly retarded women (ages ranging from twenty to forty-four at present) are included in the program at any one time. Programming is begun when the residents are awakened in the morning and is continued through bedtime. In order to facilitate effective training the residents are divided into two smaller groups according to their levels of ability. Each resident is thus assured the individual attention and assistance required in working with the severely and profoundly retarded.

The objectives of the Iris program are threefold: (1) Improvement in self-care skills is essential if a custodial care situation is to be avoided. (2) Since many of the Iris residents exhibit maladaptive behavior which may interfere with their ability to learn, the control of this behavior must be considered if training is to be effective. Few special programs are set up for the elimination of behavior problems, but general therapeutic techniques which are incorporated into the residents' daily routine are effective in decreasing the frequency of these inappropriate responses. (3) The development of self-care skills and other complex behaviors is based on growth in the areas of gross and fine motor coordination, perceptual skills, and adaptive behavior. Therefore, a variety of crafts, games, toys, and special activities are included in the residents' program as a means of increasing development in these areas.

Involvement of occupational therapy in the Iris program is ideal, since the therapist "belongs" to this building and is therefore able to spend eight hours a day, five days a week with her residents. Because building staff members work cooperatively in caring for and training their residents, the therapist's role is often indistinguishable from those of the other Iris employees. There are, of course, times when special professional knowledge and skills should be forcefully asserted. Thus, the occupational therapist communicates with her building supervisor and consultant psychologists regarding the application of behavior modification techniques in the development of specific resident programs concerned with aspects of treatment as well as training. She also consults with, assists, and provides in-service training for the psychiatric technicians who are responsible for carrying out the program. She receives direction in the area of occupational therapy techniques and application from the occupational therapy department when appropriate, and informs the department of her work through quarterly reports, weekly conferences, and occupational therapy staff meetings. Since all Iris personnel are encouraged to be consistent in their approach to the residents, the occupational therapist's use of behavior modification is identical to that of the other building staff.

The entire Iris program is based on the principles of behavior modification. Self-care skills are taught in a simple step-by-step process, with each successive step being reinforced as it is accomplished. For example, to teach toothbrushing the following procedure would be used: (1) Tell the resident to pick up the toothbrush. Demonstrate or assist him if necessary. Reinforce the resident for the appropriate response. (2) Tell the resident to pick up the tube of toothpaste. Demonstrate or assist him if necessary. Reinforce the appropriate response. (3) Tell the resident to remove the cap. Demonstrate or assist him if necessary. Reinforce the appropriate response. (4) Tell the resident to squeeze the tube. Demonstrate or assist him if necessary. Reinforce the appropriate response. (5) Tell the resident to put the toothpaste on the brush.

Demonstrate or assist him if necessary. Reinforce the appropriate response. (6) Tell the resident to put the toothbrush in his mouth. Demonstrate or assist him if necessary. Reinforce the appropriate response. (7) Tell the resident to move the brush up and down against his teeth. Demonstrate or assist him if necessary. Reinforce the appropriate response. (8) Tell the resident to take a drink of water. Reinforce the appropriate response. (9) Tell the resident to put the cap on the tube of toothpaste. Demonstrate or assist him if necessary. Reinforce the appropriate response. (10) Tell the resident to rinse the brush. Demonstrate or assist him if necessary. Reinforce the appropriate response.

Coordination and perceptual and social skills are approached in the same way, and desirable behavior is reinforced on occurrence. Before the resident can be expected to progress in skill development, undesirable behavior must be sufficiently decreased to enable the resident to interact with her environment appropriately. In the Iris program extinction has been most effective in reducing inappropriate behavior. The effectiveness of the extinction procedure (which in this case consists of ignoring specified behavior) suggests that many of the residents' maladaptive behaviors were attention-getting devices, that is, in the past those residents who were misbehaving often received more reinforcement through staff attention than those who were behaving appropriately. Regardless of the diagnosed degree of retardation or level of development, little time was required for residents to learn that attention was contingent upon maladaptive behavior. The use of the extinction procedure simply reversed the situation in that the residents now received attention for adaptive behaviors, and maladaptive behaviors were ignored. If ignoring these inappropriate responses was not effective, time out from reinforcement through brief (i.e. five-minute) removal from the existing reinforcing situation was used. Incompatible behavior was reinforced by rewarding the resident when she was not behaving inappropriately and by providing her with a socially acceptable substitute such as a toy, game, craft, or other activity which was particularly pleasant and meaningful to her.

While decreasing the frequency of undesirable behavior, the Iris staff members simultaneously shape desirable behavior. In doing this they follow written programs breaking the activities into basic steps. The residents are taught one step at a time, receiving reinforcement for each step completed. The first step is always nearest the goal, then additional steps are added onto the sequence to precede those already trained. In order for such a training program to be effective, appropriate sequences must be followed consistently by all staff. Residents initially may be able to concentrate only for short periods and may become easily confused and frustrated if this sequential approach is not used. However, as skill development increases in motor coordination, perception, and social behavior, program sequencing can be modified and reinforcement may be withheld until the entire task has been completed.

The residents' daily performance is recorded on specially constructed graphs so that all Iris personnel will be informed of any changes in the residents' behavior. The occupational therapist also notes resident performance in progress reports written every quarter. These serve to give the therapist, the occupational therapy department, and the other building staff an over-all view of the residents' progress in the program. It also promotes interchange of ideas and procedures among members of the occupational therapy staff and may facilitate introduction of new programs and permit others to avoid problems.

The Iris program staff has found that immediate reinforcement is needed to increase the frequency of desirable behavior. The staff begins by using social reinforcers (e.g. "very good" or body contact) and a candy reinforcer. As the resident's performance improves, social reinforcement alone is frequently sufficient to maintain the behavior. Delayed reinforcement in the form of tokens exchangeable for goods or privileges is introduced only after the resident has learned the value of the token.

The application of behavior modification principles within the Iris program is intensive, consistent, and thorough. This type of program is necessary because of the initial deficit of many adaptive behaviors. The program has been made possible by sufficient funding to maintain the number and quality of personnel, the services of two psychologists, and one full-time occuaptional therapist who assists in instructing staff, planning programs, and evaluating performance. However, the absence of such enviable conditions by no means precludes developing an effective behavior modification-occupational therapy program.

THE POPPY BUILDING BEHAVIOR MODIFICATION PROGRAM

Poppy building houses forty-eight women from twenty to sixty-six years in age. Levels of retardation range from moderate to profound, and all residents exhibit behavior problems. Since there is an adequate number of resident care personnel, the Poppy women are included in a half-day training program, with the South ward scheduled in the morning and the North ward in the afternoon. The residents are divided into six groups averaging eight per group for training. The groups include residents of varying intellectual abilities and degrees of emotional problems. Emphasis in the Poppy program is on self-care skills and development of adaptive social behavior (see Chapter 6).

Since the occupational therapy department, like other departments at Faribault, is a victim of inadequate staffing, the services of a certified occupational therapy assistant are available to the Poppy program for only two hours a day, five days a week. Due to time limitations and the number of residents treated, this therapy program is considerably less intensive than the Iris program. In therapy sessions, the occupational therapist supplements the building's training by following the same methods used by the Iris staff. Most of the Poppy residents exhibit severe behavior disorders interfering with their ability to understand, communicate, and conduct daily activities. As a consequence, specific occupational therapy treatment programs have proven to be of limited benefit. The therapist has therefore begun her program by defining one initial goal for the entire resident population: to decrease the frequency of the residents' inappropriate behavior and increase the frequency of acceptable responses, thereby enabling the residents to become more receptive to an intensive treatment program. Once this has been accomplished, the therapist will evaluate the residents' abilities and outline more specific treatment goals.

From Monday through Wednesday the therapist sees Poppy residents in small groups. The three groups on the North ward are scheduled for occupational therapy on consecutive mornings, one group daily. The Poppy South residents are similarly programmed in afternoons. Attendance at this program is strictly voluntary, with each resident "paying" the therapist two tokens to attend. The residents have the opportunity to walk from the building area to the main occupational therapy clinic and choose their own project from about five samples on display. The activities range from simple drawing and painting to moderately complex craft projects. Each project has a purchase price in tokens which is determined by its popularity and complexity. If the resident does not have sufficient tokens to purchase the project of her choice, she must settle for a less expensive activity. The residents are reinforced with tokens for appropriate behavior and good performance throughout the therapy session, so a resident may acquire enough tokens to buy a more expensive project as a second activity. On Thursday the therapist participates along with the Recreation Department in large-group programs. The entire North ward is included in the morning and the South ward in the afternoon session. Participation in these programs is also voluntary, and the residents who wish to attend are charged two tokens. Again, they are reinforced throughout the session for appropriate behavior and good performance. Several of the Poppy residents have been referred to occupational therapy for special programs. These are residents who do not or cannot participate in the group sessions because of severe behavior problems or limited attention span. The two hours on Friday are reserved for individual sessions with these residents, and the occupational therapist works with them in a small room provided within the building area. She discusses her treatment plans for these residents with the consultant psychologist, building staff, and her supervisor. The objective is to improve the residents' functioning in a group setting so that they may derive more benefit from the building program and the recreation and occupational therapy sessions.

In the application of specific behavior modification techniques, the occupational therapist approaches each resident individually, using whatever methods of reinforcement and punishment are most effective. All residents respond to and receive social reinforcement and tokens for appropriate performance. However, other individual reinforcers are also used. For instance, one resident enjoys walking around the table, so if she performs well for a certain length of time she is reinforced socially, given a token, and allowed to walk around the table. Another resident finds going to the toilet extremely reinforcing. When she behaves appropriately, she is complimented, rewarded with a token, and sent to the bathroom for a few minutes. In this way, the residents are not only learning appropriate behavior but are also becoming more aware of the value of a token, since they begin to associate the giving of a token with an activity which they personally enjoy. In order to decrease the frequency of undesirable behavior, the therapist prefers ignoring this behavior (i.e. the extinction procedure) while reinforcing the resident for appropriate responses. When more drastic measures are needed, the therapist may use isolation from the group—removing the resident to a corner and/or moving her to another table by herself. Since there is no area in the clinic which can be closed off, time out can be implemented only by briefly walking away from the resident. However, some of the residents enjoy isolation from the group, and if these women misbehave and do not respond to verbal instructions, they are sent back to the building with minimal physical or social contact.

Since the occupational therapist spends little time in the building, special effort must be made to confer informally with the building staff about the residents, their performance on the ward, and their progress in therapy. The therapist also keeps a daily record of the groups' performance, noting the projects each resident completed, the number of tokens paid, and the number of tokens received. Any specific problems or progress exhibited by the residents is recorded, and a copy of this form is submitted to the building staff when the residents return from therapy. Formal progress reports are written only for the residents seen individually on a referral basis.

The function of occupational therapy in the Poppy building program has been supplementary rather than intensive. The therapy session provides an opportunity to develop necessary behaviors but also serves as a break from the residents' weekly routine and is *in itself a reinforcer*. Besides providing carry-over of behavior modification techniques from a training program to an activity setting, the therapy sessions decrease the residents' inappropriate responses, provide a sense of accomplishment, and increase the frequency of desirable behavior. The occupational therapist can accomplish these goals only if there is good cooperation and communication, for if all staff involved with the residents are not working in the same direction toward the same purpose, any program—no matter how well organized—will suffer.

OCCUPATIONAL THERAPY IN DAKOTA BUILDING

Dakota Building houses severely and profoundly retarded men ranging from eighteen to sixty years of age. Most of the men exhibit some type of behavior problem. The psychiatric technicians have each been assigned a group of from eight to ten residents (see Chapter 4) and are responsible for training these men in self-care and social behavior. Each technician is provided with a room adjacent to the ward (formerly used for seclusion) which is equipped with tables and chairs, educational toys, paper and crayons, and related materials. The residents are programmed for eight hours a day, five days a week.

Because of insufficient occupational therapy staff, the occupational therapy department is only able to provide Dakota Building with minimal consultant services. The therapist spends one hour, four days a week with the technicians, rotating on a weekly basis from one group to another. While working with the Dakota technicians, the occupational therapist usually works on a one-to-one basis, concentrating on special problems with which the technician would like assistance. Occasionally the therapist will bring a simple activity involving papercraft, coloring, or painting in which the entire group can participate. Because the therapist spends so little time in the Dakota program, it is difficult to establish an effective relationship with the residents. In many cases the therapist is able to evaluate the resident and use various techniques and media which may enable him to perform in the desired manner. If during the week in the training area certain techniques are found to be beneficial to the resident, the therapist will recommend that these be incorporated into his daily program.

The occupational therapist uses educational toys, simple games, and recreational activities as well as elementary crafts. The therapist may bring these from the occupational therapy department or use what is provided by the building. Few of the Dakota residents engage in cooperative play with one another, although cooperative activity is reinforced when it occurs. For the most part, the residents perform their tasks independently with minimal group interaction. The occupational therapist is careful that the resident is told precisely what is expected of him and how to go about accomplishing it. In order to assure maximum success for the resident and minimal frustration, the therapist breaks a complex task into simple steps, demonstrating to the resident sequentially what is to be done. When the resident's response is not correct, the therapist immediately responds with a firm "no" and demonstrates the task again. The therapist may resort to a less complex task if the resident persists in responding incorrectly or becomes so frustrated that the experience is no longer reinforcing.

As a consultant in Dakota Building, the occupational therapist follows through with the program set up by the daily group leader. Methods used vary with the technician and the individuals in his group. Delayed reinforcement and more sophisticated methods of rewarding behavior are gradually introduced as a resident progresses. The therapist must also be careful to consult with the group leader in order to determine the task level on which the resident with whom she is working is able to perform. Otherwise the therapist may unwittingly ask the resident to complete a task which will lead to regression.

The limited involvement of occupational therapy in the Dakota Building program confines it to supportive rather than creative use of behavior modification principles. The main role of the occupational therapist is to suggest activities appropriate for the residents and to assist the psychiatric technicians in breaking down these activities into steps. Through the use of these activities, the technicians assist their residents in gross and fine motor skills, social behavior, and basic learning skills. Even with limited involvement, the occupational therapist can contribute much to the total program if the building staff is aware of their abilities, realistic in their expectations, and willing to follow through with any suggestions she may recommend.

Program considerations

Although the principles of behavior modification are simple, their application can become enormously complex. In establishing a program using reinforcement techniques, the occupational therapist should ask herself the following questions:

1. Are you reinforcing appropriate behavior as well as attempting to eliminate inappropriate responses? If the residents' behaviors are primarily maladaptive, are you attempting to simultaneously reinforce adaptive behaviors? Simply eliminating inappropriate behavior without also reinforcing the resident for responding appropriately is as useless as purely custodial care.

2. Are you realistic in your expectations? The resident should

only be asked to develop behavior patterns for which he is physically and behaviorally ready.

3. Are you applying your personal standards of achievement to the residents' performance? The ability of each individual resident must be considered and performance goals graded accordingly.

4. Are you expecting too little from your residents? All retarded individuals can learn or be trained. If your residents are not progressing, review and be prepared to change your program.

5. Are you making a point of rewarding those who are performing or are you giving more attention and encouragement to those who are not attempting to achieve? Social reinforcement is a strong motivator. If you consistently give more attention to those who are not performing in order to encourage their participation, you will usually find that the residents who are good achievers will cease to work in order to obtain more attention and that those who are being reinforced for not progressing will not progress.

6. Are you sacrificing quantity for quality? The effectiveness of the program will be limited by attempting to treat more residents than you can realistically handle.

7. Is your program well organized and well planned? The program should be tailored to the individual residents within the group. It is important to remember that what is reinforcing to one individual may be considered punishment by another. Conversely, what is punishment for one may be a strong reinforcer for another. The range of reinforcers should not be limited by your personal views as to what should or should not be a reinforcer. If it is, progress will be severely impaired.

What happens if . . . ?

The application of behavior modification techniques to an occupational therapy program is not without its frustrating moments as the therapist is often confronted with unusual situations which must be dealt with immediately. The following section deals with "what happens if" questions found to be most troublesome and some of the ways which have proved effective in dealing with these difficulties.

What happens if . . .

1. There is no time out room in the area? If time out is going to be used, there must be a specific area in the clinic provided for this. If there is not a time out room available but it is considered necessary to use the procedure, the therapist should isolate the resident from the group by moving his chair away from the rest of the residents (for example, into a corner) or, if possible, by sending him back to the ward. Of course, this approach only will be effective if the resident finds the group situation reinforcing and dislikes being isolated.

2. The resident disrobes? If this occurs in the resident's building, the resident should be totally ignored. If it takes place in occupational therapy, there are three possible ways of handling the situation:

    a. If the resident can dress himself, eliminate all unnecessary verbal and physical communication with him and tell him to get dressed. Ignore him until he does this and begin reinforcing him again only after he is completely clothed.

    b. Take the resident and his clothing to the time out area with as little verbal and physical contact as possible. Remove him only after he is completely clothed. If time out is to be used, however, one must be sure that this is not reinforcing for the resident, i.e. that he would rather stay with the group than be isolated from it.

    c. If the resident refuses to dress himself, he can be placed in time out for a few minutes with minimal verbal or physical contact. After this time the resident can be assisted in dressing, again with minimal communication from the therapist. If the resident does not attempt to disrobe, he may be taken out of the time out area and returned to the group. If the resident begins to disrobe, the therapist should again leave the time out area and repeat the above process until the resident remains clothed. Every effort should be made to ensure the reinforcing effectiveness of the group situation or else the resident's "choice" will be the minimal attention received in seclusion.

3. The residents refuse to work? If the resident enjoys being in the activity area, remove him from it with minimal verbal and physical interaction. If he does not enjoy being in this area, his program should be re-evaluated. If the program itself is not reinforcing for the resident, one can hardly expect his behavior to improve.

4. The resident does not have sufficient tokens to attend the occupational therapy session? The resident should not be allowed to attend. However, if the resident's behavior has been appropriate during the time the therapist is getting the group together and preparing to leave the building, the therapist may reinforce the resident with sufficient tokens for attendance. The therapist must be careful to reinforce adaptive behavior, however, and not just be "soft-hearted."

5. The resident misbehaves? If possible, it is best to ignore the behavior and withhold any physical or verbal contact with the resident until his behavior becomes appropriate. If, however, the resident is disrupting the group, use of the time out procedure or returning him to the ward can be used.

6. The resident is self-injurious? Ignore the behavior if the abuse is not so severe that it is an actual threat to the resident's physical health. During this time the therapist should make sure that there is a substitute activity (one which is a favorite of the resident) within his reach, so that he has a choice of either being self-injurious or working on a favorite

purposeful activity. When the resident ceases self-injurious behavior, he should be reinforced with attention from the therapist.
7. The resident interferes with another's work? If this is done for attention, the resident should be removed from the group and placed at a table by himself. If he continues to interfere, he should be removed from the activity area and placed in time out or sent back to the ward. If the resident interferes with another's activity because he wishes to work with that particular toy or craft, the therapist should place him in a brief time out, then provide him with the same activity or one which is similar.
8. The resident interrupts verbally? If the resident is able to understand, he should be told to wait until the therapist has finished what she is doing. If the resident is unable to understand this, he should be ignored until his interruptions cease.
9. The resident is aggressive to others? If a resident is observed to engage in aggressive behavior, he should be removed from the activity area with minimal contact from the therapist. When there are two residents actively fighting, the therapist must be sure that the resident she is punishing is the one who started the fight. Defending oneself against attack is not inappropriate behavior. If a resident has physically abused another person but was not observed doing this, the incident is best ignored.
10. The program has to be discontinued? If a behavior modification program is temporarily discontinued, the therapist may expect to see some regression in the residents' performance. Because of this, the level of tasks used by the therapist and the demands she makes on the residents must be lowered in complexity and more frequent reinforcement must be given when the program is reinstated.
11. The resident grabs food? Several different approaches are used to modify this behavior:

a. Place a resident at a table by himself so he does not have the opportunity to grab food.
b. When a resident takes food away from another resident, remove his meal temporarily. As soon as the behavior returns to normal, return the food.
c. Remove the resident from the dining room the first time he tries to grab food. Within an hour of the meal, the resident should be given the nutritional equivalent of the missed meal (for example, Sustigen).

12. The resident is incontinent? Again, several different approaches can be used with this problem:
    a. If the resident is being "deliberately" incontinent in order to get attention, the best way to handle the situaation is to ignore it. However, in some instances this is hardly a practical solution.
    b. If it is not possible to ignore the situation completely, the therapist should withhold verbal and physical contact with the resident while cleaning up with as little fuss as possible. The schedule of reinforcement can then be re-established and the resident should remain in the activity area until the session is over.
    c. If the resident finds going to the toilet reinforcing and is deliberately incontinent in hopes of being sent to this area, the therapist can use toileting as a reinforcer.

    When the resident is incontinent, one of the above procedures can be followed with one difference. After the incident is over and the schedule of reinforcement has been resumed, the therapist may use the toilet as a reward along with the usual type of reinforcement. That is, if the resident resumes his work and behaves appropriately, the therapist may tell him he is a good boy, give him a token and allow him to go to the toilet for a few minutes.

13. The resident "hangs" on the therapist (i.e. physically pesters)? The therapist should ignore the behavior and break

physical contact with the resident using as little verbal or non-verbal communication as possible. This should be repeated until the resident is no longer exhibiting this behavior, at which time he should be rewarded with attention from the therapist.

14. There are visitors in the area? In a strict behavior modification program, visitors who do not understand the nature of the techniques used can be devastating. If it is possible, visitors should be given a short explanation of behavior modification principles and asked to refrain from interacting with the residents. In areas where there are often unscheduled tours and the therapist is unable to speak to the observers beforehand, a sign can be posted on the door. In some areas of Faribault State Hospital signs read as follows: "Attention: Visitors and/or personnel when entering this room, please ignore the residents unless interaction is initiated by the therapist."

15. The resident enjoys time out? If a resident finds isolation from the group reinforcing, it should be used to reinforce appropriate behavior since it is not serving as an effective suppressing consequence. The therapist can try other techniques such as an extinction procedure or temporary loss of privileges. The therapist can review the resident's specific likes and dislikes and base the reinforcement program on these.

16. The technicians and occupational therapy consultants have difficulty communicating? This problem can occur for various reasons and is usually the fault of both parties. The therapist should be sure that the building staff knows the therapist's program and how it relates to the building's use of behavior modification. The therapist must make an effort to get to know building staff members so that they will feel free to communicate their observations and opinions, which can be extremely valuable. Staff in some buildings may resent the behavior modification program and anyone who at-

tempts to use these techniques with their residents. If in-service training in this area fails to make the staff more cooperative, the therapist should try to remain open-minded and friendly and not become defensive. In time staff members may begin to accept the program and the therapist when they realize that the therapist's primary concern, like theirs, is the welfare of the residents, and that the therapist is willing to assist them in any way possible.

17. The technicians fail to carry out their portion of the program? If this is done because the building staff is not certain how to use these techniques, the therapist can suggest to the building supervisor that in-service training sessions be held and encourage the technicians to request such training. If, however, the building staff simply dislikes carrying out the program, this becomes an administrative problem and the appropriate administrative staff should be informed.

18. The resident does not learn? Each resident, no matter how physically, intellectually, or psychologically impaired he appears to be, has the capability of learning. For some, the potential may be quite limited, but it is still there. If the resident is not learning, it is very likely that the program is at fault. Therefore, the resident's program should be evaluated and changed so that it better suits the individual's needs *and* abilities.

19. The program is not effective? Change it.

20. The staff is not reinforced? In any type of program, it is necessary for the staff to receive reinforcement for their efforts in order for them to feel that their work is worthwhile. This usually comes from obvious improvement in the residents and the comments of other staff as they notice this improvement. If the staff is not receiving reinforcement, the program is probably not effective and should therefore be evaluated and revised.

21. There are difficulties in scheduling? If the therapist finds

that the residents are being scheduled for other activities during their occupational therapy time, the therapist should bring this to the attention of the building supervisor and request a meeting with the building staff to discuss this difficulty. Changing program time to one more suitable for the building or posting the occupational therapy schedule may solve the problem. On occasion, simply reminding the staff of occupational therapy's schedule is sufficient. The building staff has many duties to perform. If the occupational therapist makes an effort to keep a regular schedule which has been explained to and approved by the technicians on the ward, difficulties such as this can usually be avoided.

22. There are objections to the program? Better communication of the program will usually take care of most objections as people are more likely to accept what they understand. If after the program is adequately explained there are still complaints, the therapist must be careful to consider these objectively. Others may have valid objections and constructive suggestions which may improve rather than disrupt her program.

23. The resident's parents interfere? If the resident's parents object to the use of behavior modification in their child's treatment program, every effort should be made to acquaint them with this technique and its benefits. The social worker should meet the resident's parents and explain to them the objectives of the program and the methods being used to attain them. If such a meeting is ineffective, and the parents continue to interfere, at Faribault they are informed by the administration that their child will remain in this program if he remains at the hospital. Although this is the procedure followed at Faribault State Hospital, each institution has its own administrative philosophy and the same solution may not be applicable in all situations.

24. The reinforcement used is not effective? It is rare that a resident will not respond to reinforcers such as food, social

praise, activities, or groups, but there are a few to whom such things appear to be meaningless. In these instances the therapist must evaluate the individual and discover what is reinforcing for him specifically. There are no residents for whom reinforcers cannot be found. The *only* limitations are the resourcefulness of the staff.

25. The activities used are not effective? The therapist can experiment with various activities until she finds something to which the resident will respond. If there are no activities which are reinforcing for the resident, the therapist may treat this as a desired behavior instead of a reward, and reinforce the resident for short periods of work by allowing him to do something he does enjoy, such as walking around the room, sitting, going to the toilet, or being isolated from the group in the time out area.

In conclusion

The occupational therapy department at Faribault State Hospital considers behavior modification to be a highly useful and effective tool in the treatment of mentally retarded and disturbed residents. It affords an avenue for development of basic and necessary skills which have been extremely difficult to develop in the severely regressed resident through application of other treatment techniques. This approach has been especially effective in developing such abilities as learning the value of objects, taking part in activities and personal relationships, developing preferences, being aware of others and cooperating within a group setting, and learning to control one's own behavior without external assistance.

However, the application of behavior modification techniques in an occupational therapy program is not as simple as it may appear. Teamwork and good communication between occupational therapy and building staff is mandatory and without it success cannot be expected. A treatment program making use of this approach must be well structured and consistent, and must provide for a maximum generalization from the occupational therapy clinic to the ward area. Applying behavior modification principles is not always the easiest way of handling a situation. The therapist is often forced to ignore behavior to which she would normally react strongly. But if she thoroughly understands the principles behind behavior modification and applies them consistently, she will soon be convinced of their value by the improvements to be seen in her residents.

References

American Occupational Therapy Association Newsletter, February 1969.
Willard, H. S., and C. S. Spackman. *Occupational Therapy.* 3rd ed. Philadelphia: J. B. Lippencott Co., 1963.
Wright, B. A. *Physical Disability—A Psychological Approach.* New York: Harper and Row, 1960.

9
Behavior modification in therapeutic recreation

JOHN RAW AND ERIC ERRICKSON

Only recently have concerted efforts been made to develop educational and recreational training programs for severely and profoundly retarded institutionalized persons. In the past, the primary emphasis has been on custodial care. For example, in 1956 the 3300 residents at the Faribault State Hospital, Minnesota, were cared for by 652 employees. With such a limited staff, it is obvious that only a minimal program could be offered—one emphasizing the provisions of food, clothing, shelter, and good medical treatment. Wolfensberger (1960) suggests that this kind of over-crowding was the result of over-emphasis on a medical approach to mental retardation. Once mental retardation is defined as a medical entity having no cure, the resulting program for the individual thus afflicted becomes custodial.

Other conceptions of mental retardation have also impeded the development of treatment and training programs. Vail (1966) and Goffman (1961) point out the subnormal expectancies for people in institutional settings. Wolfensberger also indicates that the retardate is viewed as a potential menace—assaultive, destructive, lacking direction or constructive purpose, and therefore requiring supervision in his environment. An alternate view portrays the retardate as a holy innocent, not responsible for his behavior. His retardation and handicaps are acts of God; he should be treated with pity.

Each of these points of view generates obstacles to the establishment of recreational and other programs designed to promote maximum achievement. A more hopeful view of the retarded person emphasizes the learning capabilities that he possesses and recognizes the possibilities for growth and development. Acceptance of this view of retardation encourages the establishment of a variety of treatment and training programs.

Since 1960 there has been an increasing emphasis on a behavioral model in the approach to the treatment and training of severely and profoundly retarded individuals. Early experimentation in psychiatric hospitals led to the development of training programs which emphasized a behavioral approach. This same approach was then applied to mentally retarded individuals. Perhaps the foremost advantage of the behavioral model is its positive emphasis on reinforcement for appropriate behavior using the techniques of shaping and training.

Social and recreational skills

The development of several levels of play behavior seems important for the mentally retarded. Gesell (1946) describes three sequential stages of the play behavior that is necessary in the development of social interaction skills—individual play, parallel play, and cooperative play. Particular emphasis in institutions for the retarded has been placed on the development of programs which feature cooperative play. Indeed, *Recreation for the Mentally Retarded* (Gesell, 1964) discusses cooperative play activities almost exclusively. However, many retardates need to be taught individual and parallel play skills before advancing to cooperative activities. Techniques which will teach cooperative activities to severely and profoundly retarded youngsters need to be developed, and Larsen and Bricker (1968) give suggestions for approaching this task of teaching play behavior.

The retardate needs to develop behaviors which allow him to reinforce others. His laughter and smile make him a more pleasant companion. In the small training groups at Faribault State Hospital, the residents who made little progress were those who gave little social reinforcement to the staff trainers.

When the basic self-help, language, social, and motor skills have been established, behavioral therapy techniques can be extended to teaching vocational and recreational activities. However, it should be obvious that the recreational therapist need not sit in abeyance awaiting the results of others before initiating programs. In fact, many skills learned in recreational situations can facilitate the ongoing training programs in other areas. Self-help, motor, communication, social, and recreational skills differ in some respect but have common elements as well. While learning skills in other areas facilitates acquisition of recreational abilities, training in recreational skills also facilitates training of self-help and other necessary skills. Therefore, recreational therapists should make every effort to integrate their training programs with those being conducted by other staff members.

Behavior modification and its role in recreation

The recreational therapist has in the past been bound, as have individuals in other disciplines (e.g. occupational therapists, speech therapists, and psychologists), by the absence of adequate techniques for training the retarded. One obstacle arose with some therapeutic recreators who felt that their role was to provide opportunities for recreation solely for those mildly retarded individuals who already had mastered most of the necessary skills. Their attitude entailed an emphasis on "recreation" rather than "therapeutics." On the other hand, many recreational therapists were stifled by those who felt that no therapeutic techniques could be effective with the retarded. However, the behavioral changes in self-help and other skills brought about through application of the techniques of behavior modification in patients previously thought to be untrainable provided the opportunity for recreational therapists to become part of a widened treatment program. The potential for the use of techniques which are genuinely therapeutic has brought at least some in the area of therapeutic recreation forward in a concerted effort to replace the superficial utilization of recreational activities with intensive treatment programs. For those in the area who have not yet taken this course we hope that we can, to some degree, suggest a direction for the establishment and implementation of recreation programs truly oriented toward a therapeutic approach.

The main goals of a recreation program in a therapeutic treatment setting in most cases are development of social abilities, peer interaction, and general appropriateness of interaction within groups of which the resident might be a part. The possible functions recreation therapy may serve where behavior modification is applied in other training areas fall in the following general categories: (1) as a reinforcer; (2) as supplemental training for other activities; (3) as an integral part of existing programs; (4) as a replacement for other activities when the residents have acquired sufficient skill in other areas and more time is available. These four functions are not mutually exclusive. For example, recreation therapy may be scheduled as a reinforcing activity itself and yet be a supplemental or integral part of other programs. The recreation therapist might take a group of residents to a gymnasium or park and train them how to throw and catch a ball, thereby providing activities which may be reinforcing for the residents. Additionally, the recreation therapist may include other training (naming colors, describing objects) to supplement the recreational period. The recreation period then becomes an integral and continuous part of ongoing training programs developing social, motor, and other skills.

Ideally, recreation therapy programs utilizing behavior modification techniques should serve all these functions. Success will, of course, depend in part on the cooperation the recreational therapist receives from staff dealing with other areas. However, in the absence of cooperation or an institutional behavior modification program, the recreational therapist can establish his own programs. Progress will not be as rapid but nevertheless is possible.

1. Recreation therapy as a reinforcer alone, with little relation to other programs and little structure of its own, is not an uncommon situation. This is, in part, the responsibility of the recreational therapist. When the recreation therapist does not actively take part in discussion and development of behavior modification programs with other staff, he may find his role reduced to one of providing unstructured "fun time." Under these circumstances, the recreation therapist may perceive that the residents do not even find "recreation" very reinforcing, and progress will be limited. However, if the time allotted for recreation is, in fact, a reinforcer (and it usually is) for residents, then it is the recreation therapist's responsibility to establish effective programs to strengthen existing behaviors and develop new behaviors. In turn, these programs are likely to make therapeutic recreation period more reinforcing for more residents.

2. When a recreation program has been appropriately developed, it takes on a supplemental role as an adjunct to other therapeutic regimens, either behavioral or medical. For example, activities involving gross motor coordination are essential to other activities involving fine motor coordination. Many of these gross motor activities may be effectively trained by recreation therapists. Of course, such training is also essential to the training of recreational skills which involve fine motor coordination. In terms of health problems, it should be obvious that the sedentary existence of residents in many institutions is itself contributing to physical deterioration. Suitable recreational therapy has obvious implications for the restoration of the physical well-being of the residents and therefore supplements the efforts of physicians to maintain the residents' health.

3. To the greatest degree possible recreational therapy should

be an integral part of ongoing behavior therapy programs in other areas. Success in maintaining integrated programs which emphasize the development of those elements of behavior which are common denominators for many activities requires: (1) a careful analysis of the behaviors, thereby enabling clear definition of the training techniques to be used by the staff members involved in different phases; and (2) cooperation and regular progress discussion and reports by all staff involved.

4. As training progresses and residents develop self-help and other skills, the time necessary for training and completion of the activities is reduced. Recreational therapy can then play a progressively greater role in the development of complex learning situations due to the residents' greater skills and increased time available. The more complex tasks and recreation therapy itself replace the training of skills which have become standard components of the residents' behavior repertoire. Naturally the replacement function is one which develops primarily as the overall program goals are achieved.

Within the framework of both behavior modification and therapeutic recreation, the general areas to deal with must first be determined. The decision will be based in part on the residents for whom the program is being established and the possible attainable goals.

The general plans must be made specific. Determine for each resident the goals or terminal behaviors to be achieved; the specific items, events, or behaviors which are reinforcing; the antecedent and consequent conditions for behaviors which exist or are to be developed. It is also necessary to determine what information is to be recorded and to develop a simple but accurate and objective recording method. Further, a clear daily and weekly schedule should be developed which, through promoting consistency for the residents, will facilitate training of specific activities.

Two miscellaneous but important considerations may help in constructing the schedule. One is that reinforcement is not only the dispensing of candy and verbal approval, such as "very good." The sequence of tasks or activities can also be scheduled so that less reinforcing activities are followed by more reinforcing activities. The other consideration is that programs can become tiring for the programmer. Therefore, within the confines of a schedule appropriate for the residents, the sequence of activities can be arranged so that those which are less reinforcing are followed by those which are more reinforcing for the recreational therapist.

Identification of existing maladaptive behaviors, their antecedents and consequences, requires direct observation, preferably in several different settings. To clarify this, consider the following example. It has been reported that one of the residents who is to be included in a program soils his clothing. To ascertain the extent of the problem and to perhaps avoid such occurrences during therapeutic recreation periods, the following steps are carried out:

1. Ten- to fifteen-minute periods during the day are specified during which the resident will be observed (this is referred to as "time sampling observation").

2. The periods include time on the ward, time in prescribed activities, and meal times.

3. The resident is observed during these periods and the events recorded include:
   a. where is the resident when the behavior occurs?
   b. when does it occur and for how long?
   c. what occurred just pior to the incident?
   d. what are the consequences of the behavior?

In your time sampling observations you note that the resident:
   a. is usually sitting in a chair on the ward when the behavior occurs and that it does not occur in other settings;
   b. the occurrences are usually in mid-morning;
   c. the resident has not been "directed" to toilet facilities since breakfast;
   d. the ward staff responds to these occurrences by immediately changing the resident's clothing.

Since this resident is to be included in the program, the therapist might discuss the problem with the staff and suggest that he be instructed to go to the toilet at regular intervals (with one toileting instruction coming just before the therapeutic recreation period). If the behavior occurs while the resident is attending the therapeutic recreation session, the consequence specified will be a time out from reinforcement. While this is a very simple example, the point is that, through brief observations using the time sampling procedure in advance of program onset, it may be possible to anticipate solutions to problems or avoid them entirely. Additionally, while observing the resident one may notice events or items which appear to be particularly reinforcing.

The evaluation of baseline rates of various behaviors (and therefore preliminary evaluation), as well as evaluation of progress during the program, can be carried out with the same materials. Development of a special scale may be preferable as long as it is based on objective criteria rather than subjective accounts such as "the resident enjoys the activity" or "this activity is very meaningful for the resident." Table 9-1 shows a possible list of behavioral objectives and the series of steps of the first phase in the development of cooperative behavior within a recreation therapy program. Initially it may be necessary to reinforce the resident's at-

Table 9-1. Individual activity (to participate in a simple activity or task to completion). Materials: five-piece puzzle, which has a specific sequence for correct completion.

1. One piece removed from puzzle; resident places piece in puzzle when instructed to do so. The instruction if "Put the piece in the puzzle."

2. Two pieces removed from puzzle but adjacent to correct position; resident instructed to place piece in puzzle. The instruction is given for each piece. Reinforce correct responses.

3. Two pieces removed from puzzle not adjacent to correct position; resident instructed only once to place pieces in puzzle. Reinforce correct responses.

4. Repeating steps two and three with three, four, and then five pieces removed. The instruction is changed to "Begin the Puzzle." Reinforce correct responses.

5. Puzzle frame is placed in front of resident with pieces in disarray next to it. The instruction is "Begin the puzzle." Reinforce correct responses.

Table 9-2. Cooperative activity with trainer. Materials: same as in Table 1.

1. The resident is given one puzzle piece and trainer sitting across from resident has one piece. Trainer places piece in puzzle; resident waits; resident is instructed to place piece in puzzle. The instruction is "Begin your turn *(name)*." Reinforce correct responses.
2. The resident is given two puzzle pieces; trainer has one puzzle piece. Resident is instructed to insert one piece. Resident waits while trainer inserts piece. Resident inserts next piece. The instruction is "Your turn *(name)*." Reinforce correct responses.
3. The resident is given three puzzle pieces; trainer has two pieces. Resident and trainer alternate inserting pieces. The instruction is "your turn *(name)*." Reinforce correct responses.
4. The resident is given all the pieces. The resident is to hand a piece to the trainer on instruction. The instruction "Give me a piece" is repeated twice. Then step three is repeated. Reinforce correct responses.
5. The resident is given all the pieces. The resident is to hand two pieces to the trainer when the instruction "Give me two pieces" is given. Then step three is repeated. Reinforce correct responses.

tempts to complete the task. This successive approximation technique might be used until the subject can respond by full completion of the task.

When the resident can satisfactorily complete the requirements of the first phase of training, the second phase is initiated. The

Table 9-3. Cooperative activity with another resident. Materials: same as in Tables 1 and 2. This procedure is used in evaluation only if the resident can carry out individual activity and cooperative activity with trainer. It is used in training when these two procedures have been learned by two residents.

1. The puzzle is placed between the two residents. One resident is given the box with pieces and the instruction "Give two pieces to *"(name)"* is given. The instruction "Your turn *"(name)"* is given alternately to each of the residents.
2. Step one is repeated but with the roles reversed.
3. The procedures of steps one and two are alternated but the instruction "Begin, your turn *"(name)"* is given only once at the beginning and the resident initiating the activity is also alternated.
4. The residents are given a very similar task and the procedure is carried on with the same instructions.
5. The parts of the similar task are given to one resident and no instructions are given. He is to dispense pieces to his "partner" and they should begin.

Note: When a number of residents have been trained with different partners, a longer task requiring more participants should be used.

initial cooperation phase consists of engaging in the task with the trainer (Table 9-2). When two residents learned to cooperate with the trainer, the final phase of the sequence involves training cooperation with each other.

In the initial evaluation procedure the sequence shown in Tables 9-1 through 9-3 should be carried out step by step until the resident no longer follows the instruction. This does not mean that the resident will go as far as his "level of ability." It simply means that under the existing conditions at the present time the resident will perform a certain number of steps. In approximating the training procedures as closely as possible in evaluation, one should reinforce the resident after each correct response during the evaluation.

This simple puzzle activity is used not only to illustrate a way to develop cooperative behaviors, but also to show that carefully delineated natural behavioral increments should be specified. The general format could be applied to many activities (for example, playing catch with a ball or training gross motor coordination on an obstacle course). If a step size too large for a particular resident is chosen, that portion of the activity can be broken down to smaller steps for him. Table 9-4 lists a general sequence which could be followed. This sequence is based on the principle of shaping, an important behavior modification principle (see Chapter 2). It can be applied at two levels. Within each activity it is applied to the sequential steps in training. Across activities and situations it is applied by including progressively more individuals and increasing the task complexity.

There are several advantages in using the sort of sequence described in Table 9-4. Following the initiation of the program, progress is systematically maintained by using conditions which are very much like "naturally" occurring development of ability, cooperative behavior, and peer interaction. The fact that the steps have been carefully defined, however, decreases the likelihood of failure and permits alteration of procedures when necessary. That is, since the sequence has been established and the results re-

BEHAVIOR MODIFICATION IN THERAPEUTIC RECREATION

Table 9-4. Schematic sequence for initiating and maintaining a behavior modification-therapeutic recreation program. After evaluation (indicates last level attained in preliminary evaluation), training begins for individual residents at their particular level. The initial stages of cooperative behaviors are developed between the recreational therapist (R.T.) and each resident individually—A, B, C, and D respectively. The next step of cooperative behavior is between two residents. Subsequent elaboration includes more residents and tasks which are similar to the initial training task. At step 2 of the first task several smaller steps are included to facilitate progress with resident D. Similarly, at step 2 of the second task additional steps are added for A.

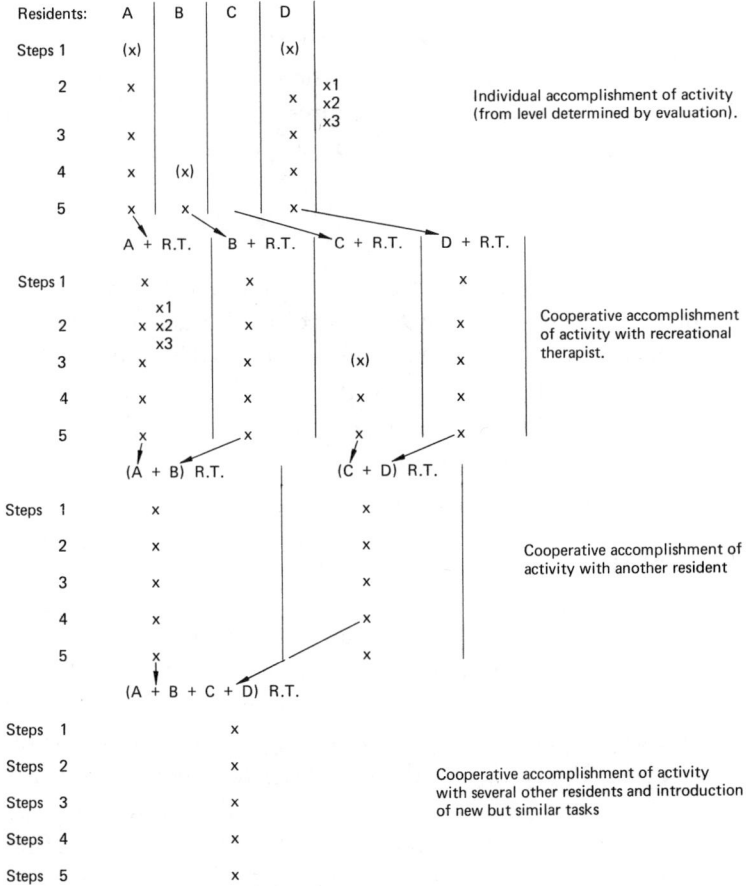

corded at each step, problems can be readily identified and solutions introduced. Finally, the recording of daily progress eliminates the need for subjective (and usually inaccurate) recall of the sequence of events. At any time, the recorded information provides a status report on progress. There is no need to gather shreds of information from different sources. It is all available in the material recorded daily.

Other considerations and supplements to the program

Since maladaptive behavior will occasionally occur, it is advisable to determine in advance the procedures that will be used to deal with it. Generally, a resident who is actively engaging in a constructive recreational activity, for which he is being reinforced, tends to exhibit little or no maladaptive behavior. Hence, one of the most effective ways of *preventing* maladaptive behavior is to adequately program activities to assure the residents' success. Occasionally, however, a resident may become distracted or in other ways disturbed, and then become unmanageable in the therapeutic setting. When this occurs, the most effective procedure is usually time out from reinforcement. That is, when the resident misbehaves during therapeutic recreation periods, brief termination of the reinforcing situation may be used to eliminate the behavior. In the case of one-to-one training this can be accomplished by simply turning away from the resident for thirty seconds, or standing and facing away from the resident. When the situation involves a group of residents, a brief (e.g. five-minute) dismissal from the group may be effective. Two things should be recalled in using the time out procedure: (1) as the term time out from reinforcement implies, it is essential that the existing situation is reinforcing for the resident; otherwise brief termination will have no effect (or may be reinforcing); and (2) the use of time outs longer than five to fifteen minutes is of little or no value. Ejecting the resident for longer periods may be reinforcing for the trainer, but it is not therapeutically useful. Nevertheless, the resident should not be permitted to re-enter the group if he has, during the time out period, begun engaging in another maladaptive behavior. The time out period should be extended if another maladaptive behavior occurs, but ideally the time out situation should be one which minimizes the opportunity to engage in new maladaptive behaviors. On the other hand, if he stops the maladaptive behavior as soon as the time out begins, it need only be of very brief duration (e.g. one to three minutes).

The progressive introduction of social and other reinforcers which maintain behavior in less artificial environments is an important transition. Early in training, candy and other tangible reinforcers may be essential to the establishment and maintenance of the desired behaviors. However, by repeated pairing of such phrases as "very good" or "that's right" or a pat on the back with the tangible reinforcers, these events will become reinforcers. Moreover, the development of the residents' verbal repertoires may possibly produce a situation in which they will supply verbal reinforcers to each other. While progress in this direction should be a goal, absence of such progress should not be considered failure. There is no reason why candy and other tangible reinforcers should not be used if they are effective in maintaining behavior. While resistance to this idea is common, the fact remains that many of our own behaviors are maintained by tangible reinforcers, and a resident is only human.

It was mentioned earlier that more complex activities should be introduced. Establishing a general direction and outline of the activities which will be used, based on common behavioral elements which provide a natural progression, is necessary. It will ensure smooth transition from activities of one level of complexity to activities of a successively greater complexity.

Conclusion

The preceding discussion is not unlike those found in other chapters. The role of the recreational therapist should be similar to that of any other specialist in the area of mental retardation. Development of skills in a particular domain should be the primary concern. The principles of behavior modification have often proven effective in achieving the goals of skills in recreational activities, cooperation, and peer interaction. The question at this point for those working in the area of therapeutic recreation is: "Is ours to be a profession which promotes unstructured, fun-time activities with only high-level patients or a progressive discipline which utilizes all available procedures in developing the skills and behavior of the mentally retarded?"

References

Gesell, A. L. *The Child from Five to Ten.* New York: Harper & Brothers, 1946.

———. *Recreation for the Mentally Retarded.* Atlanta: Southern Regional Education Board, 1964.

Girardeau, F., and J. Spradlin. Token rewards in a cottage program. *Mental Retardation,* 1964, *2,* 245-51.

Goffman, E. *Asylums.* Chicago: Aldine Publishing Co., 1961.

Gorton, C. E., and J. H. Hollis. Redesigning a cottage unit for better programming and research for the severely retarded. *Mental Retardation,* 1965, *3,* 16-21.

Larsen, L. A., and W. A. Bricker. A manual for parents and teachers of severely and moderately retarded children. *IMRID Papers and Reports,* 1968, 5 (22), J. F. Kennedy Center for Research on Education and Human Development, Nashville, Tennessee.

Vail, D. J. *Dehumanization and the Institutional Career.* Springfield, Ill.: C. C. Thomas, 1966.

Wolfensberger, W. Schizophrenia in mental retardates: three hypotheses. *Amer. J. ment. Defic.,* 1960, *64,* 704-6.

10
Guidance for the parents of retarded children

ROGER JOHNSON

Background

Any program for the retarded can be implemented more successfully by first securing the support of parents or relatives. Prior family approval will minimize administrative problems that almost always arise when a facility decides to change their care, training, or education of someone else's child. Furthermore, parental involvement often results in parental financial support of the new program. Yet, most important of all, family support focuses attention on the fact that the facility is trying something new—perhaps improvement in the child's condition is not impossible! The treatment staff, the administration of the facility, and the relatives become bound together in the hopeful expectation that something good is about to happen.

A full knowledge of outpatient guidance for the parents of retarded children aids immensely in the implementation of any new treatment program—whether it be conducted in a private or public, residential or day-care facility. Knowledge of this kind best comes from understanding typical case histories of afflicted families, usual reactions and adjustments to the label of mental retardation, pertinent variables affecting parental attitudes, and clinical decisions based on specific diagnostic entities.

The parental dilemma

"He looks so different. Is . . . is he normal?" the new mother asks hesitatingly.

The nurse glances ever so discreetly, ever so sadly at the doctor. Firming his face the physician silently sits down at the bedside, lowers his eyes, and reaches for her hand.

"Is my child . . . ?"

"We'll have to have some laboratory studies before we can say exactly," the doctor interrupts. "I'll admit that your baby looks a bit different, but no two babies ever look the same, Mrs. Chance. No matter whether or not the child is normal, we don't want to start labeling him as inferior, now, do we?"

The strange composure of the doctor and the tenseness of the nurse fill the silence that follows. What the doctor says seems to make sense, but it's like a thin sheet of logic over an unknown abyss of feelings.

"Look how happy he is to see you, Mrs. Chance."

The mother glances with love and horror at the wide-set eyes, the tiny nose, the small chin, the low-set ears. When she examines the infant more closely, she will notice webbing between the toes and a cleft palate inside the mouth. But at this moment she is not inclined to examine her first newborn closely. In some respects, she may not want to see the baby at all.

Outside the room, tensely happy with anticipation, paces the young father. He jumps at the doctor entering the hallway.

"Is it a boy?"

"Yes, Jim, it's a boy."

The doctor's voice is slightly more reserved than usual; his smile is slightly more forced than usual. Already Jim detects that something is wrong, but he wants very badly to believe the child is all right—is normal.

"How much does he weigh?"

"I don't know yet, Jim, but he looks a little smaller than average."

Now it starts to register. The doctor is preoccupied; he is taking too long to answer questions he must have heard hundreds of times. The new father's face looks quizzical for a moment then bursts open again with excitement.

"Can I go in and see the two of them now?"

"Sit down a minute, Jim. Let me explain some things to you," says the doctor with eyes lowered while extending an arm toward two chairs. "There's something you must understand before you see your wife and newborn son for the first time . . ."

It will be a long time before Jim understands the situation. Parents must often find their way through a labyrinth of emotional conflict in accepting a mentally retarded newborn baby. The first difficulty is to accept what the doctor has just said.

"It can't be!" "How do you know?" "How can you be so sure so early?" These are the statements people usually make when all the expectations, love, hope, and planning that culminates in the birth of a child seem to be shattered by the words "mentally retarded." The simplest way to cope with a disaster like this is to convince yourself that it really hasn't happened. This temporarily comforts the stunned parents.

Perhaps it seems strange that intelligent people will actually disbelieve what the physician tells them about their own baby. It even seems more ridiculous when parents continue to deny what has become obvious to relatives and friends. But, it is common and normal—at least if it isn't carried too far.

These parents have suffered a great shock, and they must find some way to absorb it. So, they enter a stage of denial, which may last from a few minutes to years. No doubt it serves a useful purpose at first, when it spreads the force of sudden devastating disappointment over a period of time. However, as long as the parents cling to denial, they will not be able to realistically plan for a baby who is going to need at least as much planning as the normal child. Whatever good purpose denial temporarily serves, it will only isolate its users from the long-term solution to their emotional dilemma.

Our illustration indicates that retardation is not a problem confined to the individual with a low I.Q. At first "the problem" is essentially a parental or family problem. It is essential to know what parents typically go through when programming for the mentally retarded.

Typical states of parental readjustment

Most parents traverse a typical pathway toward adjustment. When first told that the child is mentally retarded, parents often express denial quite vividly in such statements as "I don't believe it," "I won't believe it," etc.

If denial continues for months or years, it results in the parents marching from clinic to clinic, doctor-shopping for a different diagnosis. This is not only expensive in a financial sense, but expensive emotionally (for the parents, the baby, and all concerned). Time and again they will be disappointed; time and again they will get their expectations up; time and again they will mistrust and disbelieve the people who are honest with them. The resulting suspicion of those who are honest can render them susceptible to being victimized by faith healers and all sorts of quackery. Moreover, denial carried to this extent results in bad planning for the future of the child or in no planning at all.

After the mother and father face the fact that their child is mentally retarded, they seem to seek absolution in finding someone to blame for it. Perhaps this happens because we live in a blame-oriented society. Whatever the explanation, it is typical for parents to go through this phase. And, as with denial, the danger lies in becoming fixated with this type of adjustment.

Usually the first person who gets blamed is the obstetrician or family doctor who delivered the baby. Occasionally legal maneuvers toward compensation are initiated by parents. But the doctor who delivered the baby is almost never to blame, and even less frequently can malpractice be proven. If the parents conclude that it wasn't the delivery, they usually start searching through each other's family tree for a genetic cause. This can be devastating. The counselor who deals with parents of retarded children must anticipate this stage and guide the parents through it. It is easier to guide parents when the exact cause of the mental retardation is determined, but the counselor must convince the parents that finding someone to blame does not solve the problem and that blaming each other can only intensify their feelings of despair.

As the parents grope toward readjustment, the next obstacle is to admit that finding the cause is not going to make their child normal. But even after recognizing this, they are not necessarily ready to accept the prognosis.

Thus they enter a stage characterized by a fervent belief that they can find someone, some pill, or some treatment to make their child normal. Parents who were doctor-shopping during the stage of denial sometimes return to this behavior. But too often, having learned by this time that their chances of hearing what they want to hear from a physician are small, parents seek out other possibilities beyond the boundaries of legitimate medical practice. Fortunately, this research usually does not last long.

When this stage comes to an end, parents are left with the unavoidable fact that their child is retarded and is going to be retarded for the rest of his life. At this point many blame themselves and usually go through states of depression. Unfounded feelings of guilt are not only deleterious to the parents, but deprive the child of mothering that he especially needs. To speed parents through their depression, the counselor often has to directly point out that blaming themselves is not the most adequate adjustment.

Next the parents reach what is usually the final stage of adjustment, consisting of over-striving toward a socially appropriate ideal in order to crush the basic urge to do the opposite. Parents become over-protective and over-indulgent toward the retarded child in order to stamp out the unacceptable feeling that they do not want that defective offspring. Actually, this factor may have been operating from the beginning, but it usually emerges following the stage of depression. At first glance it may not sound harmful. After all, do extra portions of love and affection ever injure a child? Perhaps not, if it is simply love. But when the parents feel that they must give their child his way all the time, that the child should never be disciplined, and that he should be protected from all possible environmental difficulties, they are likely to ruin the learning opportunities a retarded child so badly needs. As has been said before, the retarded child needs chances to learn as much as anyone. The retarded child, as any other child, does best with a clear set of family rules and regulations. Over-protective and over-solicitous parents minimize the chances of a beneficial growth and development period.

Factors affecting parental guidance

These typical parental reactions are mediated by several social factors. There is evidence indicating that older parents in general do not adjust as well as younger parents to the news that their child is abnormal. There are several possible reasons for this. For example, older parents are more likely to have had normal children already. The normal children are probably more rewarding to the parents and this could result in rejection of the retarded child. It is also possible that inter-sibling difficulty could create more problems than when the retarded child is the firstborn. Alternatively, the adjustment may be exceedingly difficult for older parents who have long wanted a child and are faced with the problem of retardation in their first and possibly only child.

Introverted parents seem to react poorly and with bewilderment. They don't express their feelings as easily as more extroverted people, and consequently adjusting to the shock of a retarded newborn is more difficult.

For some reason professional parents in general seem to have a more difficult time adjusting. Perhaps it is that professional parents are more likely to express concern, seek help, worry over their own adequacy, and read about possible cures than non-professional people. It may be that non-professional people are simply not as aware of the possibilities for help and guidance. It takes more specific knowledge to work with these parents, but, when readjusted, they can be valuable allies to any program.

It also seems to be true that low-income parents have a difficult time adjusting. This group is, as a rule, suspicious of middle-class institutions. They don't talk easily to the professional people in community clinics, and they don't see mental retardation the way the middle class does. This may be because they don't place the emphasis on learning and succeeding intellectually that the middle class does. A good many of these families may well have a difficult time adjusting because middle-class professionals don't know how to talk to them. The typical, semi-sheltered middle-class professional person doesn't understand their values or the different view they may take of the education of an offspring.

Those who work with the parents of mentally retarded children should also be aware of the emotional background of the family. The family that was disturbed prior to the birth of the mentally retarded child usually does much worse than the stable family. In this situation it is often difficult to sort out the various problems. It is not hard to recognize husband-wife hostility, but this may have little to do with the birth of a mentally retarded child. The diagnosis may simply precipitate difficulties in a marginally adjusted, emotionally unresolved marriage.

Highly mobile families do not adjust as well to a mentally retarded child as families with well-established and continuing ties in their environment. What is cause here and what is effect is a matter for speculation. But in most cases it is reasonable to assume that constantly relocating their home adds an extra burden to parents and children.

Not surprisingly, when there is a single parent rather than two parents, the adjustment is more difficult. The parent who has lost or been separated from his mate usually has more than his share of problems to begin with. Naturally, this complicates adjustment to a retarded youngster. And, of course, there is always comfort in facing problems with someone.

Fanatical parents have an extremely difficult time adjusting. Whether they be health fanatics, religious fanatics, or money-making fanatics, their chances of a favorable adjustment to a mentally retarded child are very small. Often a therapist will have to continually remind the parents of the reality of their situation. That is, there are many instances where the therapist simply has to set up the rules and give advice.

IF THE CHILD REMAINS AT HOME

Whether or not the parents decide to keep a mentally retarded child in the home depends on a number of things, including their acceptance of the problem, the apparent severity of mental retardation, whether a workable schedule for attending to the child can be achieved, how effectively the parents have been assisted in establishing a plan to develop the child's abilities, and, though frequently ignored, monetary factors may be relevant. If the child remains at home, it is particularly important that the parents have assistance. Frequently clinics or special institutes are associated with or part of a university or college where consultants in behavior modification are available. The retarded child may be included in special programs, receive professional aid from the staff, or a list of suggested places where such aid may be obtained. Whether the parents wish to deal with a university-affiliated program or engage a recommended clinical behavior therapist in private practice is of course their choice. If the parents accept either of the above suggestions, they should remain in contact with groups such as the Association for Retarded Children (ARC). Those who are uncertain of the efficacy of behavior therapies or behavior modification techniques specifically or those who are unfamiliar with such techniques might be interested in specific examples of failure or success.

Examples of failure are readily found. Many parents keep a

mentally retarded child at home until "they can no longer handle the problems" and then place him in an institution. Allen was such a child. He remained at home until he was ten years old. The history in Allen's chart states the first behavior he engaged in when he learned to crawl was hitting his head against a wall. Subsequently he developed a number of other maladaptive behaviors. He hit his head with his hands and appeared to vomit at will. His parents' solution to the head-hitting problem was to restrain him in bed where he then received all his food and attention. When admitted to the hospital Allen engaged in the head-hitting and vomiting behaviors. The hospital's initial solution was to put a helmet on his head and tie the hand with which he hit his head inside his clothing. Allen's parents visited frequently and his vomiting increased after each visit. Prior to departure at 4:00 p.m. Allen would say that he wanted to go to bed. His parents were permitted to place him in bed because they wanted to do things for him. The problem was brought to the attention of behavior modification consultants who instated a program involving reinforcement for adaptive behaviors and non-reinforcement for maladaptive behaviors. Allen's vomiting behavior went from an average of five times per day to less than once a day within two weeks. His head-banging began to occur less frequently and he began to interact in more appropriate ways socially. Soon Allen will not require the helmet for "self-protection." The main point is that Allen's parents were not cruel and heartless people. They certainly did not want to have Allen restrained when he was at home. Indeed, since Allen was retarded his parents wanted to do everything possible for him. However, they had simply not had the guidance which may have helped them work with Allen and develop appropriate behaviors. It is unlikely that Allen would be in the hospital at the present time had his parents been provided with the information and help they needed.

Allen's case is to be contrasted with that of Greg, age eight, whose parents were determined to keep him at home. Greg had been in a special class in the public school, but because of periodic incontinence, hyperactivity, and occasional tantrums was dropped from the public school program. His parents were told that unless he received special intensive training before the following fall institutionalization would almost certainly be required. Fortunately for Greg, a community Day Activity Center was located near his home in a large city. The Center had a behavior modification consultant on its staff who helped Greg learn to help himself. Initially, emphasis was placed on reinforcing proper toileting. Before long, incidents of incontinence had become so uncommon as to no longer be considered a problem. By gradually requiring Greg to sit quietly and attend to a task progressively longer to receive reinforcement, his hyperactivity was brought under control. The special teacher found that the tantrums were markedly reduced and eventually eliminated if the tasks given Greg were within his ability range. When Greg was given tasks that were too difficult, he became increasingly agitated and finally "threw a tantrum." Most importantly, Greg's mother visited the Day Activity Center and learned to use behavior modification methods to train Greg at home. He had many areas of deficiency which made life difficult at home for Greg and his family. Training in buttoning buttons, tying shoelaces, and general help at home which had previously seemed impossible soon became feasible once Greg's mother understood the principles and their application.

IF THE CHILD IS PLACED IN AN INSTITUTION

When parents have adjusted to the problem of having a mentally retarded child, they may rationally choose to place the child in an institution. Many children are placed in institutions because the parents wish to escape the problem. Under some circumstances this may be an acceptable solution, since the parents' success in developing the child's abilities at home will be limited due to their failure to resolve their own problems. In arriving at a rational decision, a number of factors should be considered.

Most arguments for institutionalization of the retarded, with the exception of severity of medical problems related to retardation, are primarily based on social problems and not the efficacy of institutionalization as a course of action. Therefore, it should be stated again that all options—foster homes, special schools, and the like—should be considered before parents place a child in a larger state institution. If the parents feel they are incapable of dealing with a retarded child at home, they should carefully investigate the alternatives and not consider a state institution as the only choice.

Some of the factors which are relevant in arriving at a decision to institutionalize a child are:

1. *Severity.* There are in fact some genetic anomalies which create medical and behavioral problems which can seldom be handled adequately in most homes.

2. *Presence of other children.* While this is commonly used as "the reason" for placing a child in an institution, many parents with retarded children have found that the child does well at home with his normal siblings. In other instances in which the siblings' emotional status is jeopardized for other reasons, institutionalization may be the only recourse.

3. *Income.* Except in terms of costs of special private schools, mildly retarded children pose no greater financial burden than a normal child, though insufficient income is often used as a reason for institutionalization.

4. *Effects on relatives.* This is sometimes considered to be a valid reason for institutionalization while it may primarily be a rationalization. As a consideration for institutionalization it may primarily indicate the prevalence of the stigma attached to having a retarded child. Some families are faced with the dilemma of a geriatric grandparent plus a retarded child, or a severely ill parent plus a retarded child. Under such circumstances, institutionalization may be an acceptable alternative.

5. *Non-acceptance by the public schools.* This is a genuine problem, since many schools will not accept children who do not

perform adequately on standardized tests. Under such circumstances it may be best to investigate other options (for example, private schools).

Generally, institutionalization is an inadequate solution. Most retarded children can progress adequately if given the opportunity to do so. A retarded child will not become a professional or highly skilled worker in the usual sense, but given appropriate training can succeed in many areas which are useful and necessary in our society. Few, if any, useful tasks will be performed by the same individual after twenty or thirty years in most state institutions. The hospital systems of most states are poorly funded and not well equipped to train anyone for any task. A prime example of the unfortunate aspects of institutionalization is demonstrated by a thirteen-year-old boy. His parents had a number of difficulties and rather than seeking adoption or keeping him at home, they placed him in a large state hospital. After several years in the institution, the boy progressed well in the special school but engaged in a variety of maladaptive behaviors on the ward. The behavior modification consultant for the school and the hospital's program director stumbled on the child's abilities and were determined to discover why he had been institutionalized. The parents' difficulties were discovered and they were persuaded that the boy would do well if placed with another family. At present placement is being sought. The reason for the difficulty is that the child has been institutionalized, and while he is relatively bright, other families do not want a child with his history. Had someone caught the error before institutionalization, he would probably be doing well as a member of a family wishing to have another child. What will happen now is uncertain.

As suggested in the preceding example and as is known to individuals familiar with state hospitals, institutionalization is too often a way to hide, but not solve, the problems of the retarded.

Parents should contact the ARC and obtain as much information as possible about the home or institution which would best serve their child's needs. Having arrived at this solution based on institutional programs and anticipated child problems, the parents may wish to see their child frequently. Parents can influence the placement of their child within the institution and the extent to which he is involved in activities or training programs. They may have to face arguments from staff, social workers, nurses, or administrators, but they should not give up. They must recognize the limitations of resources for public institutions. However, it is equally important that they make an effort to improve conditions through organizations such as the ARC. They may wish to discuss with the administrator the possibility of establishing behavior modification programs if they do not exist in their child's institution. Most institutions have parent groups which meet regularly, and the parents should make an effort to obtain speakers who can discuss medical, genetic, or social problems of retardation. However, it is to their greatest advantage if they receive information about ways of dealing with behavioral problems through consultation with the staff supervising the behavior modification programs. Parents are often discouraged and frustrated when they see their child feeding, dressing, and otherwise caring for himself in the institution, only to discover that he will not engage in these behaviors when at home for a visit. Therefore, learning and applying the principles and techniques used in the institution's behavior modification programs can make home visits more enjoyable, educational, and worthwhile for the parents and the child.

An example of the difference between the behavior in an institution and that which might occur at home on a weekend visit is illustrated in the case of Buddy Y. Buddy was seven years old and often went home on weekends. One Friday he incurred a scratch on his leg while playing with other children. His mother arrived at 4:00 p.m. and took him home. A short time later she called and stated that Buddy could not walk and that he had a scratch on his leg. When asked what she had done, she said she had carried him from the car to his bed and fed him. Buddy remained in bed all weekend and "could not" walk. When returned to his building on Sunday afternoon, he immediately began walking. Had

Buddy's mother known how to deal with his maladaptive behavior, it is probable that many episodes of this nature could have been avoided. The positive aspect of this episode is that subsequently Buddy's parents learned how to handle such problems using positive reinforcement for adaptive behaviors and extinction (or ignoring) of maladaptive behaviors. Buddy's later visits home were substantially more pleasant for him and his parents.

The preceding suggestions and examples suggest some things a concerned and interested parent can do. However in most cases parents will not know where to begin or what to do if the counselor does not put forth the possibilities. Therefore, failure of the parents to take some of the desirable steps may not be their fault. It may be that the counselor did not take the time to make the options sufficiently clear. At other times it may be that the counselor was not able to adequately communicate the ideas to the parents. Again, it is important that the counselor consider those factors based on the social, ethnic, and economic status of the parents which are related to success in counseling. If the counselor feels that he cannot communicate with the parents, he should make every effort to find someone who can. Effective counseling should not involve pride to the extent that one is unable to recommend others who might be more successful in a given case!

Resources for parental counseling

The first step in finding a counselor should be to contact the ARC, which can provide a mailing list of potential counselors. Another possibility is the office of the state's Commissioner of Mental Health or Mental Retardation. In some states this may mean contacting the Department of Public Welfare while in others the County Health and Welfare Office may be appropriate. Most government agencies can also list several centers (public or private) where parental guidance can be obtained. Many parents are able to adjust and plan effectively with the help of periodic visits to their family doctor or pediatrician. Still others live in communities where Day Activity Centers, child psychiatric clinics, or child guidance clinics are handy. Perhaps there is a community mental health center nearby.

Should everyone who has a mentally retarded child seek guidance? Quite definitely, yes. It is not simply a matter of finding someone to help mother and father adjust; effective planning for the future of the child is also at stake. Parents are not anticipating the birth of a retarded child; hence, when it happens, they are unprepared. They don't know that agencies or facilities exist that can help in the growth and development of their child. Parents have many unanswered questions regarding the future. An evaluation (both medical and psychological) is mandatory. An exact medical diagnosis can occasionally help predict the child's development. Sometimes it can lead to genetic counseling, or, in rare instances, there may even be biochemical treatment available. As a child grows, periodic examinations can result in more accurate planning. Indeed, it is as important to know what the child can do as it is to know what he cannot do.

Guidance and counseling also give the parents an opportunity to share their anxieties with an objective third party. Once again, it is a matter of facing problems with someone instead of alone. Most parents will shop around for help in diagnosing and planning anyway. Hence, by contacting well-known professional organizations or public agencies they are better protected from charlatans, inappropriate advice, poor planning, or no planning at all.

IV
Implementing programs

11
Implementing behavior modification programs

JOHN GRABOWSKI AND TRAVIS THOMPSON

Introduction

Much of what has been written about behavior modification consists of reports of case studies, program descriptions, or analysis of critical variables in solving a single behavior problem. Very little has been written about the practical problems associated with implementing large-scale behavior modification programs in existing settings, with existing staff, and with limited resources. The purpose of this chapter is to provide a tentative analysis of some of the formal and informal contingencies prevailing in a large state institution as well as some suggestions for avoiding problems in implementing programs and solving them if they develop.

A state hospital consists of bricks, mortar, beds, and many thousands of over-stuffed file folders; but, more importantly, it is a very complex social system. Yet, if one is to have any success in implementing a therapeutic program within a state hospital, he must attempt to come to grips with the system. One soon discovers in working in a state institution that the behavior of patient-residents can be changed with perseverance. However, one discovers equally quickly that *implementation* of behavior modification programs conducted by state institution staff is very difficult. The problems of implementation are faced by staff in all areas—administrators, ward staff, special services staff, and consultants alike.

Those working in the field of behavior modification have grown up with the credo "the client is always right." Stated simply this means that the client's behavior (in this case, the staff's behavior) is always orderly, predictable, and, in principle, understandable if an experimental analysis is pursued to determine what it is that controls his behavior. Despite the complexities of the variables controlling the behavior of each member of the staff of a large state institution, including that of the consultants, one can begin to make strides in the direction of effective program implementation if he continually keeps one question in mind: "What are the factors which control the behavior of each of the members of the staff with whom I must interact, and in what way can I help him get what it is he wants within the system"? This question must be asked by all staff members in the system, including the program designer.

Typically, formulation of the goals of an institution tend to be governed by financial and political considerations essentially irrelevant to the problem at hand, i.e. helping the resident. A ward staff member may design an effective program for a resident and have all his efforts thwarted by an administrator's arbitrary ruling. Alternatively, a progressive administrator may find his efforts constantly frustrated by staff members who do not wish to see changes made in the system. The degree to which goals can be realized is often a function of three key factors: (1) financial resources; (2) administrative structure; and (3) ideas for effective therapeutic programs.

FINANCIAL RESOURCES

It is often said that no amount of money is enough in a large state hospital, suggesting that inefficiency, waste, and poor management are the prime factors responsible for the failure of many state hospitals to develop good programs. It is quite true that money will not do the job alone. If one has inadequate administrative structure and a deficit of good ideas, all of the money in the world will be of little value. However, financial resources are essential in that they make available the necessary staff, equipment, and environment in which to conduct therapeutic programs.

ADMINISTRATIVE STRUCTURE

The administrative structure provides the procedural framework for the implementation and maintenance of programs. In many respects it is the most important factor in any behavior modification program within a state institution. One way of looking at the administrative process is that it provides formalized procedures for job or task definition, and provides consequences for staff behavior. A good administrative structure indicates to whom each person is answerable, and specifies clearly the behaviors for which a person in a given position will be reinforced. Unfortunately, in many large systems the contingencies may be met and yet the reinforcers may not be forthcoming. On other occasions reinforcers are presented (e.g. increased pay, better hours, more facilities) with no relation to behavior. For example, an administrator who does very little administrating may receive salary increments while a hard-working ward staff member does not! Therefore, many of the difficulties lie not in the individuals working in the system but rather in the contingencies under which they must function.

IDEAS

In many respects state hospitals have long been devoid of the opportunity to implement new ideas. While ideas for change may be developed by hospital staff, implementation is hindered by a variety of problems, including, at times, one or another staff member (who may be found in almost any position) who is unwilling to assist in implementation. Occasionally this resistance is due solely to the historical problems discussed in Chapter 1. Whatever the source, it slows progress. The same applies to many private institutions for the retarded. Though the physical environment of private institutions may be colorful and clean, and though there may be a relatively favorable staff-to-resident ratio, many of the deficits and disturbed behaviors seen in state institutions occur there as well. This is because inadequate teaching procedures are generally used in both situations. The "blame" for the inadequacy of teaching procedures should not be considered to rest with those using them; rather the problem lies in the relatively recent development of behavior modification method which has not yet allowed for widespread implementation.

Requisites for establishing programs
ADMINISTRATIVE SUPPORT

Administrative support is essential to the successful initiation and maintenance of behavior modification programs. If they are to succeed, higher administrators must understand the general approach and their support must be something more than passive tolerance. There is little doubt that enthusiastic support from high-level administrators is the single most crucial factor in establishing a behavior modification program within an institution. Administrators have the potential resources for hiring consultants, obtaining or directing materials, delineating goals for staff, and (within limits) reinforcing staff members for their efforts. In the absence of such support even the most energetic and creative ward staff will find it difficult, if not impossible to achieve their goals.

Unfortunately, the many endemic problems within a large institution consume a great deal of the time and energy of administrative staff. Exceptional staff performance frequently goes unnoticed or may be punished by peers who are made to appear less effective. Optimally, administrators should re-evaluate the relative time and energy spent in "problem solving" as opposed to reinforcing staff and *avoiding the development* of problems. Too often we expect technician staff to reinforce patients and forget the fact that they too must be reinforced. Administrators sometimes find that their initial efforts to reinforce staff are rebuffed. Repeated attempts and flexibility in the types of reinforcers used will, however, eventually lead to acceptance.

Administrators can often serve their administrative functions best by supporting programs in ways that are effective reinforcers for outstanding staff performance. Unfortunately, administrators often feel they are forever on the giving end but never on the receiving end of the reinforcement relation. Within the hospital itself there is no one "higher" to reinforce them. In most state hospital systems reinforcement of the highest administrative staff is limited, and the central state organization which should be reinforcing the administrators' behavior communicates largely with edicts concerning problems. The maintaining contingencies are therefore not unlike those operating within the hospital itself.

Administrative interest and support may be manifested not only by direct communication through formal channels but indirectly as well. Periodic visits to buildings by administrators will perhaps initially generate some misgivings on the part of the staff. However, if it were made known that an administrator was going to stop in a building once a week, the misgivings could be attenuated. Eventually the staff might find the arrival of the high-level administrator reinforcing if genuine and knowledgeable interest was expressed during the visits. An unusual demonstration of interest in ascertaining the problems facing on-line staff and determination of their reinforcers was carried out by an administrator at Faribault State Hospital. He worked the 3:00 p.m. to 11:30 p.m. shift in a building as an on-line staff member for several weeks. While criticism could be directed at the validity of staff behavior patterns during this period compared to other periods, the behavioral changes due to his presence which probably occurred may have been maintained. He found the period enlightening and useful. It is probable that the experience promoted greater tolerance for administrators among the on-line staff as well. While not all administrators could successfully carry out this approach, it indicates that interest, concern, and desire for communication can be expressed in different ways. Administrative personnel at other than the highest levels are extremely important in the maintenance of behavior modification programs. Depending on the size of the hospital, there may be administrators responsible for several buildings. At Faribault State Hospital the intermediate administrative position is the unit director. Support by the unit director is essential to program success. A person in this position may be subject to substantial pressure from above and below. Coordination of programs and services for the buildings in a unit is the unit director's responsibility, as is the task of mobilizing resources made available by higher-level administrators. They not uncommonly bear the brunt of complaints from their staff about changes or implementation of new procedures. Too often they are attacked from all sides.

Within the structure described there are usually individuals directly responsible to the unit director for maintenance of building programs. The individual responsible for activities and subsequently behavior modification programs in a building may be a registered nurse or a staff member who through expertise or longevity achieved the position. Ideally the person responsible for management of a behavior modification program should be someone specially trained for this role.

The administrative "chain of command" traverses a path from the hospital administrator, program coordinator, and medical director (who may be of equivalent status in the structure) through unit directors or other intermediate levels to the building level. Support at each level is essential for optimal progress and each level may contribute or detract from programs in different ways. The types of contribution and/or hindrance fall roughly into two categories on a continuum. The high-level administrators provide primarily resource and organization support and are minimally involved in direct implementation of programs. Unit- and building-level administrators are primarily involved in implementation. Intermediate-level administrators are in a position to obtain resources and implement programs. High-level administrators can indicate support in their public statements, through continuing follow-ups, and through interactions with other staff. Intermediate- and building-level administrators are also effective in this role. Any administrator at any level who interacts with his staff at all levels implements and maintains programs more effectively. Any administrator, high-level or building-level, who sits in his office, apparently shielded from the problems and successes of others, will meet with many problems and few successes.

THE PROBLEM OF PARALLEL STRUCTURES

Any good administrative system should have clearly defined channels of authority, in which each person has one person to whom he is answerable concerning each type of activity and which ensure feedback and recognition for carrying out the specified duties, particularly those in excess of usual requirements. Whenever any system is devised involving parallel channels of authority, individuals within the system are encouraged to circumvent one of the channels of authority by means of the other. For example, if a consultant designs programs for the staff in a specific building and if, in addition, the institution has a full-time psychologist hired for similar purposes, the staff can avoid conducting the programs designed by the consultant by appealing to the institution's psychologist for reasons for not carrying out the programs.

Closely connected to the problem of parallel structure is lack of clear authority. Consultants who design programs or therapeutic procedures can *recommend* but have no direct authority to ensure that the programs are carried out. Similarly, many of the special service departments within an institution—such as the psychology department, the occupational therapy department, the recreation therapy department, etc.—may recommend procedures to the staff, but the staff is often free to ignore them. Concurrently, staff members of such departments in their "consultant" role are often unresponsive to ward staff requests and fail to recognize the limitations placed on ward staff. This is wasteful of everyone's time, and is a poor administrative arrangement. The interaction between limited financial resources and less than adequate administrative structure can be seen most strikingly when there are not enough funds to provide the necessary supervisory personnel to see that programs are carried out or to provide a vital communications link between ward staff and personnel of other areas. During periods when an on-line program supervisor has been located in buildings, we have typically found that programs proceed effectively with minimal plateaus. However, when financial resources have diminished, leading to removal of supervisory personnel from the buildings, programs have faltered and in some instances have virtually stopped.

STAFFING AND ADMINISTRATIVE STRUCTURE

It is important to recognize that there are two administrative structures within an institution. There is the official structure showing lines of authority. If the staff is pressed, various personnel, from department heads to psychiatric technicians, will follow the official administrative structure to the letter of the law. However, in day-to-day conduct of the institution's affairs, quite a different structure and set of controlling factors is in effect. This consists of the "hidden" staff structure, which is based on social pressures upon building staff and among departments within the institution. Many of the resistances, the negativism, and the problems associated with implementing programs grow out of this hidden structure. Personnel in all areas who were not included in early planning or development of ideas may occasionally resist changes of which they were not primary formulators. Building supervisors are not inclined to insist upon compliance with regulations and program procedures when confronted with threats of resignation or more subtle social threats by the staff. Jealousies aggravating staff members in different departments or in different buildings often control the degree to which staff and other buildings are willing to implement programs that they believe are for the patients' benefit. Rumors, eavesdropping, and after-work discussions over a glass of beer are primary sources of information about the hidden structure. Effective communication within the official structure helps to reduce the degree to which the hidden structure can undermine effective program development, but it remains difficult to overcome the problem. Perhaps the key issue in all of this is the absence of additional privileges and payoffs which should be forthcoming when behavior modification programs are implemented. Staff members at all levels are asking one another to engage in a wide range of new behaviors and are establishing new contingencies for each other with few or no additional reinforcers for implementing the major changes required at the onset of the program. Within the formal structure of an institution there are ample contingencies specifying that this or that must be done on demand, but reinforcement, one of the basic principles of behavior modification, is chronically ignored.

Introduction of consultants

The psychiatrist or psychologist who is introduced as a consultant for behavior modification programs is in a peculiar position with respect to the existing staff structure. The knowledge needed to produce results is assumed in the hiring, but the authority to insist on implementation is limited. Given limited authority, it is essential that the consultant make every effort to understand the existing system and in particular the staff hierarchy. The initial introduction of the consultant should be carried out through established channels. For example, the high-level administrator should discuss the matter with intermediate-level administrators who will be working with the consultant. A brief informal meeting is likely to attenuate complaints of surprise introduction of an outside "expert." A meeting of administrative personnel and the staff of buildings with whom the consultant will be working should be arranged and an indication of the administration's backing should be given. This procedure generates the appearance of a solid front, and avoids circumvention of the lines of authority by staff members opposed to the programs. Additionally, a memo to individuals responsible for various departments with whom the consultant might have contact will alleviate feelings that a given department is being ignored.

Failure to follow the proper channels of authority can be very damaging. In one instance, a unit director requested services of a behavior modification consultant at the behest of a building nurse. Due to limited available time, the usual path of making arrangements through the unit director was not followed. Instead, the consultant went to the building and observed the resident exhibiting the behavior problem. All went well, and the maladaptive vomiting and head-banging behavior of the resident were eliminated. The staff seemed interested in extending these methods to other cases and establishing a ward-wide program.

Error I. A lecture and discussion series was arranged through the building nurse who was asked to communicate this to the unit director—after all, it saved time.

Error II. A proposal for a ward-wide program was distributed to the hospital program coordinator, unit director, and building nurse, but insufficient time for evaluation was permitted.

Error III. Several staff members who were peripheral to the situation, but mildly interested, were not invited to assist in implementation of the program—time was of the essence.

Error IV. The problems of concomitant errors and insufficient time were exacerbated by a meeting reminiscent of the Romans' Colosseum entertainment. The consultant had unwittingly placed his head in the lion's mouth. In the name of "saving time," time itself had been wasted and other residents were not helped.

It is possible that the effort should not have been attempted at that time in that place. However, proper introduction by the administrative personnel and following channels of authority might have avoided the demise of the consultant's effectiveness in that unit.

CHANGING STAFF PERFORMANCE

As suggested earlier, the success of a behavior modification program is limited largely by the degree to which staff behavior can be changed. As indicated in the above example, the behavior of one group of staff members, the consultants, must change to coincide with the existing system, provided the alterations required do not render him totally ineffective. Similarly, staff behavior at all levels must change to accommodate new approaches to patient or resident care. Staff behavior is governed by numerous factors, only one of which relates to changes in the behavior of the residents with whom they work. Unfortunately, civil service personnel procedures make it very difficult to provide meaningful consequences for staff performance. Verbal encouragement from administrative superiors is often a weak reinforcer. Time away from work is difficult to arrange since regulations often require that all employees receive the same time off. Bonuses or other monetary consequences are generally impossible within the system. Essentially the only consequence the institution can provide is for inappropriate staff behavior or dereliction of duty, i.e. suspension or firing the employee.

There are several problems with this general framework. All staff—including administrators, ward staff, and other personnel—require feedback on their own performance. Feedback should be frequent and should emphasize positive reinforcement for effective performance. As indicated above, while feedback is possible, it is very difficult to provide frequent, meaningful positive reinforcement for effective staff performance. The few consequences that are available largely involve social recognition from other staff members at all levels. Such social consequences can backfire as well, however. When there is strong negative feeling among some staff, they will bring substantial pressure against other staff members receiving recognition for successfully establishing a new program. In some instances employees have stopped working on behavior modification programs rather than tolerate the pressure from some of their fellow staff members. Succumbing to pressure from other staff members is not limited to any one group. The pressures have been observed to affect ward staff, consultants, and administrators alike.

STAFF REINFORCEMENT

The reinforcers for various groups may differ. For occupational therapists behavioral change of residents may be a successful reinforcer. This should not be relied on as the only reinforcer. Attention from administrators, building staff, and others can be extremely important in maintaining behavior as well. Recognition for success is similarly a reinforcer for administrators, consultants, and building staff.

Staff groups who are often neglected early in program development are food service and maintenance personnel. The extent to which such staff groups are included may vary, but it is important to make them familiar with the programs and procedures. The assistance of food service staff can be relevant in training residents to engage in simple kitchen duties. The consultant in one building found it useful to include food service staff in building staff meetings, though in most buildings their attendance is not considered necessary. When a token system was implemented, the assistance of dining room and kitchen staff was essential. Their inclusion in planning meetings was important in over-all cooperation. In general, it is desirable to familiarize *all* staff with program goals and methods.

Failure to discuss programs with ward staff who are not directly involved with training can be a particularly damaging error. In one case teaching sessions were the responsibility of one group of specific staff members, while those staff members who were assigned to the locked ward were seldom involved in the program, and their assistance was not enrolled. Problems chronically plagued the programs. For example, residents' shoes were "lost" by the ward staff and hostile exchanges between ward and behavior modification staff were frequent. Subsequent inclusion of the ward staff in some aspects of the program substantially reduced the friction and resolved a number of related problems.

The behavioral change in one particular staff member was most notable. Mr. X, who was considered a good worker, chronically threatened to resign, would not cooperate, and generally created difficulties. The source of the difficulties was the perceived preferential treatment and status differential which developed between ward staff and behavior modification technicians. The behavior modification technicians had regular discussions with the consultants, received additional recognition, and were generally lauded for their fine work. Mr. X also worked hard, but received little recognition. It was decided to establish simple programs on the ward where Mr. X was responsible for the residents during the evening. A toileting procedure was outlined and it was explained to Mr. X that his assistance was necessary in the evening when all the residents were on the ward. He implemented the procedure immediately and became one of the most effective and helpful staff members in the building. While the dramatic change observed in the case of Mr. X is unusual, it clearly points to the problems which exclusion from the implementation of new procedures can produce. The example should also clarify the fact that at least some of the problems which arise are administrative (including consultants') errors unrelated to the efficacy of the procedures being implemented.

STAFF TRAINING

Staff training in behavior modification, like most other staff training, remains a poorly understood art. The objectives *should* be to enable the trained staff members to identify behavior problems, to design procedures to change resident behavior, and to effectively carry those procedures to fruition. However, in practice, the relation between these objectives and the training procedures employed is at best vague. Often many questions remain unanswered, and the program designer-implementer must proceed by a series of educated guesses. For example, is it necessary for the staff to learn technical vocabulary to carry out effective programs? Is it better to learn by modeling or by successive approximations? Should primary emphasis be placed on precision or on breadth of application?

Many different procedures have been used by consultants at Faribault State Hospital. Initial training emphasized lectures as a primary means of communicating information. It was soon obvious that this was one of the less effective modes of staff training. While the initial lecture series used to train staff in an early program consisted of five one-hour sessions, subsequent training included only four half-hour sessions. As the consultants' knowledge of the staff increased, the number and duration of lectures decreased and the application of the principles increased. The form of the lectures was varied depending on the number of participants and characteristics of the staff involved. Thus, with small groups the lectures were relatively informal discussions, while with larger groups a more formal structure was used. Every effort was made to relate examples which were relevant to the staff. Following each short lecture, materials were dispensed providing an example of a simple behavioral problem, and the staff members were asked to develop a program. Alternatively, a situation was described and the staff members were asked to write out the steps for a procedure to modify or develop the behavior. When the basic principles had been learned, each staff member was required to select one resident and increase the frequency of an adaptive behavior or decrease the frequency of a maladaptive behavior. The program coordinator noted at that time that one of the reinforcers for some of the staff members was successfully changing patient behavior. Establishing and maintaining a simple individual program served as a *practicuum* through which the staff gained experience in the use of procedures. Perhaps more importantly, many of the staff learned that the procedures were effective in their own hands. The most effective *practicuum* examples were often those related to decreasing the most annoying maladaptive behaviors. For example, if a staff member was able to develop a resident's self-toileting, dressing, or feeding behavior, the amount of unpleasant work was decreased. The staff member no longer found it necessary to clean the floor after soiling, help the resident dress, or feed him. More time was also available for working with the resident in other constructive activities.

In early training efforts films were not used extensively, but later they were incorporated into the lecture series. Sequences of actual behavior modification sessions carried out by other staff were later used to demonstrate principles and procedures. As the development of effective training procedures progressed, it was found that on-line staff members who had been involved in programs could be effective in training new staff members. These individuals were occasionally mildly harassed by their peers, but, as the role of instructor became accepted, these on-line staff members became effective teachers. While consultants have a certain aura of the "beneficient stranger," they also are indeed strangers and are not totally accepted by the staff.

After the staff has been trained in the general area of behavior modification and has experience in applying the principles, in-service training should be continued. In one procedure each staff member is asked to present recorded instances of a resident's behavior, the program used to increase or decrease its frequency, and the results of the program. This procedure often proves effective in maintaining staff interest and permits the staff and consultant to discuss approaches to alteration of behavior problems as they arise.

The administrative staff and consultants have found that two factors must be considered with respect to the effectiveness of a trained staff member. Some staff members become articulate in discussion about behavior modification and are adept at communicating the principles, procedures, and examples to others, but are not necessarily interested in carrying out the procedures with residents on a day-to-day basis. Individuals who are articulate in the vocabulary and principles of behavior modification can be used as effective instructors for new staff. Other staff members may not use the terms appropriately but nevertheless may be very effective in applying the principles to modifying behavior. Whenever possible, staff should be permitted to occupy a position (in function, with or without the title) in which they are most effective. For instance, Mrs. Z had many clerical and secretarial tasks which she carried out effectively; however, she was also adept at reinforcing residents for existing adaptive behaviors and establishing new behaviors. Therefore, whenever possible the unit director for whom she worked arranged for her to work with residents in special programs.

Ideally a program manager having administrative authority should be assigned to each building. An individual from almost any discipline can serve the program manager function if trained properly. Often the program manager would be a nurse, occupational therapist, recreation therapist, or a staff member without specialized training.

Another more general category of training which has not been explicitly planned at Faribault State Hospital involves familiarizing *all* staff with the general principles, methods, and goals of behavior modification. A number of problems confronting implementation of behavior modification programs at the hospital have been related to lack of familiarity with behavior modification as a treatment discipline. Requesting secretaries to type necessary materials met with difficulties on occasions. The business manager found the quantities of paper used to distribute copies of recording sheets and procedure to on-line staff excessive. Some on-line staff, middle management, and professionals did not understand the basis for writing procedures for teaching various activities. Several professional staff members considered it inappropriate that they should be asked to apply their discipline in a manner which they thought relegated them to the role of "technician."* A number of other problems of similar nature could have been avoided if *all* staff had been exposed to the principles of behavior modification and particularly the relevance of their role in ensuring program maintenance.

SOME RULES OF THUMB FOR CONSULTANTS

Over the years of the behavior modification programs at Faribault State Hospital, the consultants have arrived at some "rules of thumb" in implementing behavior modification programs. In this section these generalizations will be enumerated.

1. As a consultant, one must always keep in mind that he is an outsider intervening in established social structure. If a behavior modification program is to be accepted, it must be kept in mind that *it is the program of the institution, not of the consultant.* Thus, successes of a program are successes of the institution. On the other hand, the consultants must share with the institution in program failures. Should the consultant take credit for program successes and heap responsibility on the institution for program failures, he will effectively estrange himself from the institution and, as a consequence, seriously damage the program.

2. Accept the existing administrative structure, avoid the image of perennially complaining about the institution, and offer positive, tenable alternatives. Changes are best made gradually and by positive example, not by complaining.

3. Become thoroughly familiar with the institution, administrative, and staff structures. This means spending time with the administrators, department heads, nursing and physicians staff, as

---

* This particular problem was in part simply one of verbal behavior and the existing hierarchy. "Technician" is a position title for on-line staff at Faribault State Hospital. Unfortunately, some of the professional staff are not familiar with (among other things) the concept of technician as one who engages in practical application.

well as technicians, i.e. staff at every level of administrative authority throughout the institution.

4. Become familiar with the hidden structure of the institution. One of the best ways to come to a better understanding of the hidden structure is to spend time on the wards working alongside the staff, spending coffee breaks with them, or in other ways to interact with the staff in their day-to-day working environment. In this way the values, expectations, and the social pressures which are brought to bear on the staff members will become more apparent to the consultant.

5. Become sensitive to the "channels" within the institution, being wary of avoiding channels as a means of "accelerating" implementation of a program. *Avoiding key channels can have a disastrous effect.* In the name of accelerating implementation, a program may be set back or, for all practical purposes, stopped.

6. Be very careful to avoid threatening the administrative authority of others within the institution. As a relatively naïve outsider, it is very easy to unwittingly overlook the fact that "advising" someone how to do their job can easily be misinterpreted as assuming someone else's administrative authority.

7. Avoid bringing in outside experts or administrators to exert pressure within the institution. This will invariably be resented and backfire in the long run.

8. In initiating a program, require a written contract concerning the details of the program *in advance,* approved by all parties at all levels of administrative authority. If any of the parties involved fail to carry out their part of the bargain, and the program has not gone as anticipated, it is useful to have a written agreement indicating the responsibilities of all persons involved. In that way the precise locus of the program failure can be identified and the necessary steps to correct the problem can be taken.

9. "No data means no programs" is the motto of one of the consultants at Faribault. In general, the staff will not want to keep careful records of procedures and patient behavior, which are essential for maintaining effective programs. Therefore, any chart-

ing or recording which is required should be kept minimal, if it is to be done at all, and the staff should receive frequent feedback for their recording.

10. Don't expect the staff to generalize from one case under one set of circumstances to others under other circumstances. Whereas recognizing similarities in behavior problems from one situation to another may be second nature to an experienced consultant, such generalization on the part of the staff is uncommon. The staff will tend to see specific instances rather than general classes.

11. Initiate a building-wide program only after demonstrating success with one or two residents' problems. In general, the staff will be more receptive after they have seen the procedures work. After all, in most instances the staff has been given promises many times before, and why should they believe another "expert"?

12. Whenever possible, include staff in program decisions in modifying program changes.

13. Avoid rigidity. If a particular procedure is not effective in changing resident behavior, the procedure should be changed. It is not the resident who is at fault but the procedure or the way in which it is being implemented.

14. Give the staff frequent, summarized feedback on the data they have recorded. There is little in it for the staff to record data if no one takes time to go over the data and help them interpret it.

15. Respond to positive comments and useful suggestions by the staff and avoid responding to "baiting." Philosophical and purportedly humanistic arguments are often designed to irritate the consultant, other ward, or administrative staff rather than to help the residents or protect their rights. To become engaged in such arguments is to encourage cantankerousness by the staff rather than to encourage more effective behaviors, such as solving programming problems.

16. Ensure variability in the staff's day to avoid boredom. It is a mistake to schedule more than a few hours of continual resident training consecutively for the staff. Resident training requires tre-

mendous perseverance and it is unrealistic to expect anyone to persist in teaching for an extended period without changes in activity.

17. *Reinforce progress!* In working with the retarded, changes in resident behavior are very slow. It is essential to reinforce the staff frequently for small steps toward the goal of training the residents in self-care. As noted previously, this is difficult due to limitations of available reinforcers. Those reinforcers which can be used should be made frequently available.

18. Whenever things aren't going as one would like to have them go, ask yourself, "What is it that maintains the staff behavior, and in what way can that consequence be made available to them contingent on improving resident behavior?" If a consultant keeps this question in mind, he can be much more effective, and in the long run the residents are the ones who will benefit.

FROM THE VIEW OF WARD STAFF

Perhaps the overriding problem in acceptance and implementation of behavior modification programs for the ward staff is historical. The educational departments of many state hospitals for the retarded stress custodial and medical care. A majority of training time deals with proper cleaning procedures and bed making on the one hand, and dispensation of medications and bandaging wounds on the other. The custodial-medical approach to the retarded historically reflects the view of professional groups and society as whole (see Chapter 1). Therefore, the resistance to and/or disbelief in the usefulness of behavior modification techniques expressed by ward staff is a reflection of the training they have received. Additionally there exists the problem that other "new" techniques have been initiated in the past and have not been successful. Therefore, ward staff are perhaps understandably skeptical about another new technique for training the retarded.

Ward staff who received training in behavior modification have pointed out a number of problems in implementing behavior modification methods. First, much of the behavior modification approach appears contradictory to the traditional hospital training program. Next, some staff members point out that, while on paper the principles of behavior modification appear to be effective, implementing them in a ward situation might prove difficult. The foregoing observation is accompanied by the comment, "Show us." Behavior modification as a therapeutic discipline, despite the relative clarity of the procedures, remains to some extent an art. The aspects of art which must be conveyed are perhaps best achieved by demonstration and once learned are sharpened and maintained through practice. Therefore, the individuals expected to apply the principles of behavior modification and maintain programs were to a great extent justified in requesting more explicit training than is available in a lecture or a verbal example.

When the staff members had been trained, they were expected to begin using the principles of behavior modification to develop residents' adaptive behaviors and eliminate maladaptive behaviors. Staff members were then confronted with multiple problems, including those arising from the prevailing custodial-medical atmosphere and those due to administrator and consultant errors. Some staff members within buildings were not willing to apply behavior modification techniques. Apparently the contingencies under which they had previously worked were well established. Fortunately, most of the staff members were interested and willing to apply the newly learned techniques.

When the staff of the buildings which had been designated for the development of behavior modification programs had successfully established and maintained these programs, they were faced with another barrier. It could only have been disheartening for the behavior modification technicians to have achieved major alterations in residents' behaviors only to be confronted by statements by some administrative and medical personnel that nothing could change or had changed. Some individuals who were indirectly responsible for administrative aspects of program implementation were oblivious to or perhaps begrudged the success of the staff who were responsible for practical implementation.

Subjectively, and with occasional objective verification, it became clear that the controlling contingencies of the hospital could be changed and that the efforts of the ward staff were crucial in establishing change.

In conclusion

The problems confronting ward staff, consultants, and administrative staff are generated not by any one group. As indicated earlier, staff behavior in a state institution is under the sway of existing contingencies. Many of the contingencies (including formal and informal rules) in state hospitals have permitted or in some cases encouraged unproductive and even counterproductive behaviors. It is equally true that the contingencies can be changed. In the case of Faribault State Hospital, through the combined efforts of individuals in administrative positions, special services personnel, and, above all, ward staff, steps have been taken to make such changes. Some individuals have been unable to accept new programs because of long years spent working under outmoded contingencies. For the majority, however, the additional effort required to initiate and maintain major changes in orientation have proved well worthwhile.

Subject Index

academic and pre-academic behavior, 32, 33, 34, 84, 91, 109, 169
acquisition behavior, 24, 101–2
administration, 49, 50, 79, 100, 136, 270, 272–75
administrative structure, 271, 275–77, 285–86, 290
aggressive behavior, 86, 91–93, 110, 163, 169, 170, 182, 229
Anna State Hospital, 8, 70
anorexia, 8
Association for Retarded Children, 49, 258, 263, 264
attention, 12, 13, 31, 169
attention getting, 40
autisms, 7, 8, 12, 24, 36, 37, 38, 39, 40, 44, 133, 134, 190, 228, 259. *See also* specific autistic behaviors

backward chaining, 29, 31, 83, 116
bathing, 68, 69, 129
behavior modification, 8, 9, 17–18, 78
brain damage, 12, 208

chaining. *See* backward chaining
chlorpromazine, 152, 153, 159, 160, 161, 165, 166, 169
Clinical Global Impressions, 152, 161

Columbus State School, 70
community, 209. *See also* placement
consultants, 81, 125–26, 127, 136, 191–92, 224, 270, 275, 277–79, 285–88
contingency, 22
cooperative behavior, 173, 224, 246
curriculum, design, 209
custodial care, 6, 7, 21, 35, 66, 67, 78, 96, 100, 108, 288, 289

deficits incurred in institution, 7, 8, 21, 35–36, 78, 91, 263
destructive behavior, 92, 110
Detailed Behavior Evaluation, 151, 161
discharge, 71. *See also* placement
disruptive behavior, 53, 61, 62, 63, 64, 66, 86, 89, 90, 182, 183, 188, 189, 190, 191, 229. *See also* specific behaviors
Dixon State School, Illinois, 71
double blind, 153
dressing, 65, 85, 86, 88, 89, 109, 117, 162, 163
drugs, 78, 92, 93, 94, 97, 152, 153, 159, 160, 161, 165, 166, 169, 170, 182, 207

291

SUBJECT INDEX

electric shock, 44
etiology, 10
extinction, 35, 37, 38, 40, 44, 218, 230, 231

fading, 29, 33
food grabbing, 61, 62, 63, 64, 66, 86, 89, 90, 229
freedom, 13

generalization, 184
genetics, 254
geriatric patients, 12, 13
group: composition, 85, 142, 171, 216, 222; size, 103, 104, 105, 113, 114, 156, 239

hand washing, 31, 58, 60, 68, 129
head banging, 36, 37, 38, 39, 40, 44, 133, 134, 259
history of treatment, 5
hoarding, 163, 170
Hospital Improvement Project Grant, 99–100, 103
housekeeping behaviors, 110, 129, 156
hyperactive behavior, 12, 13, 25

IQ, 11, 12, 82, 108, 147, 171, 185, 208, 254
institutionalization, 209, 260-63. See also placement

lying on floor, 64, 170

maintenance behavior, 25, 112, 133
Massachusetts School for Idiotic and Feebleminded Youth, 4
menstrual cycle, 152
Mental Retardation Center, Colorado, 146
Minnesota Institute for the Defective, 4
misconceptions, retardation, 9, 10
multiple schedule, 159

nocturnal enuresis, 97
Nurses Observation Scale for Inpatient Evaluation, 152, 161

observation. See recording

Parsons State Hospital, Kansas, 9, 70, 104
Peabody Language Development, 183
Peabody Rebus Reading Program, 173
Perkins Institution, 4
placebo, 152, 153, 161, 165, 166
placement, 71, 78, 94, 116, 117, 209, 258, 259, 260–63
program design: alterations, 56, 60, 62, 63, 79, 80; by consultants, 81, 83, 115, 116, 126, 127; by staff, 83, 96, 126, 127; small steps, 21–22, 24, 29, 219, 246–47
program goals, 50, 80–81, 108–10
program manager, 284
programmed instruction, 197, 198
punishment, 43–44

quadraplegic, 12

recording, 86, 118–20, 128, 131–32, 140, 152, 161, 170, 175, 219, 242, 243, 244, 248, 286–87
reinforcement: accidental, 37; delay of, 23, 204, 219; frequency of, 24, 25; of incompatible behavior, 38, 39, 80, 88, 90, 92, 248; intermittent, 25; principles, 21, 22
reinforcers: examples of, 54, 84, 140, 193; idiosyncratic, 27; selection of, 233; staff attention, 22, 26, 27, 36, 37, 134–36, 187–88, 193
retardation classification, 10, 12, 17, 82, 83, 100
rocking, 163, 164, 170

School for Idiots, Imbeciles, and the Feebleminded, Faribault, 4
seclusion, 40, 81, 86, 92, 93, 148, 167, 172, 173, 174
self-care. See specific behaviors
self-feeding, 89, 90, 109, 117, 129, 162, 163
self-injurious behavior, 7, 8, 12, 24, 36, 37, 38, 39, 40, 44, 92, 94, 97, 133, 134, 190, 228, 259
shaping, 29, 30, 53, 54, 68, 71, 73, 83
shaving, 91, 173

SUBJECT INDEX

sleep patterns, 97
smearing, feces, 88, 130
special education, 86, 200, 203
special schools, 209, 259, 260. See also placement
speech, 30, 34, 86, 90, 91, 162, 163, 184, 185, 195–97, 205
staff: behavior change, 94–96; cooperation, 79, 122, 127; reinforcers, 85, 86, 87, 95, 96, 232, 271, 273, 279–80, 288; resistance, 80, 231, 232, 271–72, 279–80, 281, 287; training, 78, 85, 104, 113, 122–24, 145, 146, 149, 185–86, 232, 281–84, 288–89
staff-resident ratio, 50, 53, 56, 81–82, 99, 107, 108, 121–22, 216, 220
State Department of Public Welfare, Minnesota, 49
stimulus control, 34–35, 51–53, 89, 97, 98, 101, 170, 199–200, 204
string chewing, 130
successive approximations, 30, 244–45

time out, 40–43, 174, 182, 218, 227, 228, 229, 230, 231, 248; duration, 41, 42, 43, 248
timer, kitchen, 189–90
toileting, 39, 67, 68, 85, 87, 88, 109, 117, 129
tokens, 28, 69–75, 141, 155–58, 161, 164–65, 171, 183, 184, 193–94; exchange of, 70, 73, 74, 133, 140, 153, 154, 155, 157, 158; fines, 130–31, 143, 146, 176; review, 69–70, 139–41; stealing, 172
tooth brushing, 91, 155, 217–18
transfer, 78, 94, 116, 117. See also placement

untestable, 12

Vineland Social Maturity Scale, 104
visitors, 96, 231
vocalizations, bizarre, 90
vomiting, 259

Wild Boy of Aveyron, 4

Author Index

Abel, V., 142, 177
American Occupational Therapy Association Newsletter, 213, 235
Anders, T. R., 102, 137
Atthowe, J., 139, 176
Auxter, D., 70, 76
Ayllon, T., 8, 14, 45, 70, 76, 131, 139, 140, 141, 142, 176
Azrin, N. H., 8, 14, 45, 70, 76, 131, 139, 140, 141, 142, 176

Baer, D. M., 184, 210
Bailey, J., 182, 191, 210
Ball, T. S., 139, 146, 176
Barbuto, P. F., 104, 105, 137
Barr, M. W., 5, 14
Barret, B. H., 9, 14
Belmont, J. M., 102, 137
Bensberg, G., 45, 80, 98
Birnbrauer, J. A., 139, 176
Birnbrauer, J. S., 139, 147, 176
Blatt, B., 14
Boren, J. J., 159, 176
Bostow, D., 182, 191, 210
Braun, S. H., 105, 122, 136, 137, 138
Bricker, D. D., 184, 210
Bricker, W. A., 83, 98, 184, 210, 239, 250
Burchard, J. D., 139, 146, 176

Colwell, C. N., 105, 137
Cortazzo, A. D., 102, 105, 138
Curtiss-Wedge, F., 4, 14

Davis, W. E., 103, 105, 107, 137
deBaca, P., 182, 210
Devine, J., 182, 210
Diamond, L. S., 159, 177
Dimascio, A., 152, 177
Doll, E. A., 10, 14
Doris, J., 6, 15

Ellis, N. R., 9, 14, 102, 137

Fischer, J., 139, 177
Fitzhugh, K. B., 144, 177
Fitzhugh, L. C., 144, 177
Flournoy, R. L., 102, 104, 137
Fuller, P., 8, 14

Garlington, W. K., 139, 140, 142, 144, 177
Gesell, A. L., 238, 250
Giles, D., 189, 211
Girardeau, F. L., 9, 14, 70, 76
Goffman, E., 237, 250
Goldfarb, W., 6, 14, 15
Good, W. W., 159, 177
Gorton, C. E., 104, 105, 106, 137, 138

Gray, R., 80, 98
Gross, M., 159, 177
Guess, D. A., 184, 210

Haim, D., 159, 178
Hanley, E., 189, 211
Haskell, R. H., 4, 15
Haughton, E., 8, 14
Haywood, H. C., 102, 137
Heal, L. W., 102, 137
Heistad, G. T., 160, 177
Hitchman, I., 159, 177
Hollis, J. H., 104, 105, 106, 137
Holtzman, W. H., 159, 177
Homme, L., 182, 210
Hopkins, B. L., 182, 211
Hunt, J. G., 144, 177

Itard, J., 8, 14

Jacobson, L., 208, 211

Kanner, L. A., 3, 4, 5, 15
Kaplan, F., 14
Kastler, J., 80, 98
Kelleher, R. T., 139, 177
Kidder, J. D., 139, 176
Kimbrell, D. L., 104, 105, 137
King, L., 189, 211
Klaber, M. M., 7, 8, 10, 11, 15
Krasner, L., 139, 177

Lachowicz, J., 189, 211
Larsen, L. A., 83, 98, 239, 250
Lawler, J., 139, 147, 176
Lawrence, J., 159, 177
Lawson, R., 69, 70, 76
Leath, J. R., 102, 104, 137
Lent, J. R., 139, 141, 177
Levinsky, D., 140, 147, 178
Liberman, R. A., 139, 145, 177
Lindsley, O. R., 9, 14, 15, 80, 98, 101, 137, 149, 177
Lloyd, K. E., 139, 140, 142, 144, 177
Love, J. G., 104, 105, 137
Lucero, R. J., 49, 75
Luckey, R. E., 101, 105, 137

Mabry, J., 45
Marks, J. B., 159, 177

Mautner, H., 159, 177
McCarthy, J. J., 197, 210
Meacham, M. L., 45
Miller, L., 103, 105, 107, 137

Nawas, M. M., 105, 122, 136, 137, 138
Newell, P., 159, 177

Olson, G. W., 152, 159, 178
Otis, L. S., 160, 178
Overton, D. A., 159, 178

Perline, I. H., 140, 147, 178
Perry, R. M., 140, 146, 178
Peterson, D. B., 152, 159, 178
Peterson, R. F., 184, 210
Phillips, E. L., 140, 178
Pollack, S. L., 159, 178
Premack, D., 71, 76, 140, 178
Provence, S., 7, 15
Pryer, M., 9, 14

Reese, E., 85, 98
Reeves, W., 159, 177
Rickert, E., 182, 210
Roberts, C. L., 140, 146, 178
Robinson, H. B., 9, 15
Robinson, N. M., 9, 15
Roos, P., 80, 98, 103, 105, 107, 137
Rosenthal, R., 208, 211
Rothstein, C., 159, 178
Russell, C., 140, 141, 178, 183, 211

Sanders, C., 69, 70, 76
Sarason, S. B., 6, 15
Scheerenberger, R. C., 197, 210
Scherber, J., 49, 75
Schuster, C., 159, 178
Schutte, R. C., 182, 211
Shader, R., 152, 177
Sherman, J. A., 184, 210
Spackman, C. S., 215, 235
Spradlin, J., 139, 141, 177
Spradlin, J. E., 9, 14, 70, 76
Stachnik, T., 45
Steinhorst, R., 182, 210
Sterling, M., 159, 177
Stewart, J., 160, 178
Sulzer, B., 183, 196, 211

AUTHOR INDEX

Tague, C. E., 139, 176
Thompson, T., 159, 178
Thormalen, P. W., 7, 15
Tobias, J., 102, 105, 138
Torres, A. A., 160, 177
Tourlentes, T. T., 159, 178
Trainor, M., 103, 105, 107, 137

Ulrich, R., 45

Vail, D. J., 49, 75, 237, 250

Watson, L. S., 69, 70, 76, 105, 138
Wheeler, A. J., 183, 196, 211

Wiesen, A. E., 45
Willard, H. S., 215, 235
Winkler, R. C., 140, 142, 178
Wolfe, M. M., 139, 176, 189, 211
Wolfensberger, W., 237, 250
Woodcock, R., 173, 178
Wright, B. A., 215, 235

Zimmerman, E., 140, 141, 178, 183, 211
Zimmerman, J., 140, 141, 178, 183, 211
Zocchie, A., 159, 178